Reviews

"Prasanta Chakravarty's *The Creature: In Power and Pain* excavates the triangular foundation implicated in its title—the nexus of exposure and contingency that is sentient life—with a combination of breathtaking breadth and poetic precision. Picking up the implicit challenge of what was left unsaid by the humanistic presuppositions of Elaine Scarry's seminal *The Body in Pain*, in a series of variegated yet interlocking essays, Chakravarty compels us to confront the fundamental precarity that makes creaturely existence a realm, in equal measure, of agony and wonder."

—William Egginton

Decker Professor in the Humanities,
Director, Alexander Grass Humanities Institute,
Kreiger School of Arts and Sciences,
Johns Hopkins University

"By distinguishing pain from averse feeling and suffering, *The Creature* takes us headlong into the recent philosophical debates on the phenomenology of pain. To the afflicted creature, there is no *what-it-is likeness* of the pain experience. Humanities, be prepared to inhabit the medical world of pain asymbolia and chronic pain, where pain is no longer a symptom or sign but a disease that needs to be managed more than cured.

I started *The Creature* on a Good Friday and continued reading it over the Easter weekend. The book succeeded in invoking in me the holy shiver that must have gripped the crucified creature before the numb pain settled down to suffering. No regime of security or philosophical placebo can protect the wrecked mechanism of the creature caught between power and pain. Being stunned matter that cannot distinguish between mutual embrace and slaughter, the creature cannot be socialized through grief or compassion. The chapters in this volume explore our creaturely condition by delving into the works of some extraordinary thinkers, including Gabriel Tarde, Aniket Jaaware, Simone Weil, Oxana Timofeeva, Jibanananda Das and Ernst Bloch. This is a major work."

—Sanil V.

Professor of Philosophy,
Humanities and Social Sciences,
Indian Institute of Technology Delhi

"Philosophical gestures that tackle reality in its totality have become rare. All the more so when they attempt to grasp it in its most effective reality. This is what Prasanta Chakravarty dares to do by analyzing the relations of power and pain that form and deform what he calls creatures. These relations of power and pain make visible both the vulnerability and the resistance of creatures. Chakravarty follows this mechanics of power and pain in common experiences but also in extreme experiences, showing the moments when power and pain are reversed ... until we are confronted with the enigmatic possibility of a process of decreation."

—Thomas Berns
Professor of Philosophy and Ethics,
University of Brussels

"This is an ambitious, brave, intense and genre-defying study of the condition of creaturehood in its radical contingency: its fragility and its force, its desolation and its plenitude, its resilience and its precarity, its power and its pain. Expansive but in control of its tantalizing range, the book deftly straddles authors, texts, intellectual traditions and artefacts that stretch from Vico to Das, Unamuno to Kane, Tarkovsky to Bresson, to mine both the philosophical and the formal scope of creatureliness, and, finally, to reflect on its own undoings. A rare marriage of scholarship and minute attunement, rigour and imagination, textual and experiential, the book meets its subject on the threshold between affect, ethics and aesthetics. Its difficulty is no less than a challenge to dare to be fully human."

—Subha Mukherji
Reader in Early Modern Literature and Culture,
University of Cambridge

The Creature

The Creature

In Power and Pain

Prasanta Chakravarty

BLOOMSBURY
NEW DELHI • LONDON • OXFORD • NEW YORK • SYDNEY

BLOOMSBURY INDIA
Bloomsbury Publishing India Pvt. Ltd
Second Floor, LSC Building No. 4, DDA Complex, Pocket C – 6 & 7,
Vasant Kunj, New Delhi, 110070

BLOOMSBURY, BLOOMSBURY ACADEMIC INDIA and the Diana logo
are trademarks of Bloomsbury Publishing Plc

First published in India 2021
This edition published 2021

Bloomsbury Academic
An imprint of Bloomsbury Publishing Plc

ISBN: HB: 978-93-54351-16-7; eBook: 978-93-54351-32-7
2 4 6 8 10 9 7 5 3 1

Typeset in Manipal Technologies Limited
Printed and bound in India by Replika Press Pvt. Ltd.

“Opacity was a very important quality that I really wanted to grasp.”
~Déa Kulumbegashvili on her film, *Beginning*.

“One hears that a human stays not human
for twenty-four hours each day
Every hour or half he turns nonhuman
Then does it not behoove that for
Twenty-four hours a day
a nonhuman stays not inhuman
For a little while between he turns humane perhaps
With such hope do so many people keep sharing their sorrows
They ask questions; keep dispatching pleas of so many hues”
~Kumar Ambuj, *Condolence Meeting*

Contents

Introduction: The Omen of Nothing

A strong gale. Tiles blow off the roof and fall hither and thither. The tiles had no choice in being tiles or for being placed thus as tiles. But they bear the consequences of being tiles on a roof on a windy night. The moment of the fall is *a still*, an arrested conjuncture. But the effect is instantaneous, and lasting. Sometimes, tiles may have to bear the initial responsibility, which is what Simone Weil feels, when she compares such falling tiles with people who we designate as criminals. The impotence of penetrating the mysteries of our predicament is actual and technical; not real. The consequences of such predicament are material and far-reaching. To be placed in the world is irreducible. To be placed in the world is to be exposed to affliction. Apportioning responsibility or susceptibility to agents for contingent acts and happenings is a matter of debate.

Robert Bird, a scholar on Russian literature, film and modernism, and a universally loved man, died of colon cancer on 7 September 2020. In an essay published shortly after his death, Bird considers Andrei Tarkovsky's final months as the latter battled with lung/throat cancer.[1] Bird tells us that "Tarkovsky's enigmatic final words in his diary, dated 15 December 1986, provide a brutal verdict on his cruelly curtailed life: 'A camera negative, cut up for some reason in many random places'" (Bird, 2020). The central question that occupies Bird in the essay is whether there can be any meaningful relationship between Tarkovsky's ailment and his works. How does one account for such a pernicious and impersonal force? Bird systematically goes through Tarkovsky's own attempts to reconcile his works, thoughts and his ailment. One way to create meaning is to retrieve the works as redemptive sacrificial acts. As his condition deteriorated, for a brief period, Tarkovsky sought solace in heterodox methods, like anthroposophy: trying out untraditional, natural medicines and immersing in bucolic surroundings. He was disappointed though, and soon returned to chemotherapy. But "medicine teeters unsurely on the border between the body and its grave, *soma* and *sema*" (Bird, 2020).The sick body needs to be poisoned again with radiation. The other way of grappling with such an ailment is to work towards a clean conscience or memory, which will prepare oneself to die. But what use personal penitence for propitiating the 'misbegotten cosmos' that we inhabit? If Tarkovsky's body is being consumed by the prayers and protective spirits that he invokes, what faith and commonality? Cancer destroys the very faith in miracles. As he writes, Bird makes an important pronouncement: "Cancer is a disease without moral cause, but not without moral consequences" (Bird, 2020). The crucial thing is the environment of fear and anxiety that it fosters. And stigma, with no other external signification. It is an altogether different frame of living where power of a random force coheres inextricably with the numb pain of a new being within the canceral, and therefore, carceral environment.

This interruptive, anonymous force is the subject of the book, what Bird calls: *an omen of nothing*: "The contingency of these omens is something I hold onto. It drives home the fragile wonder of the world we share, as taut and fluid as the ocean. It is so different for each of us, yet it becomes a medium through which we share stories, images and words. Like the cinema. Like cancer. Like Tarkovsky?" (Bird, 2020). By recording his sensation in words in such a manner, Bird does something extraordinary. He looks directly at the moment of his reckoning. Eye to eye. He considers what the Spanish savant Miguel de Unamuno has described as "our moral destiny without flinching, to fasten our gaze upon the gaze of the Sphinx, for it is thus that the malevolence of its spell is discharmed" (Unamuno, 1921/2013).

Contingency is constant. It is the commonest thread that binds us all, something that we conceal from even our innermost core—skirt or camouflage—lest we break down and dissipate in highlighting our vulnerabilities. But are we ever a collected bundle of nerves and muscles (as Hume had experimented)? Contingency forces us to confront idle randomness in a serrated cosmos. Like grass and water, we begin to tremble and shake when confronted by calamity. Like fire, we rage and rummage for a cause where there are none to be found. Contingency is necessity; an opaque and inert force that goes on creating violence and vulnerability, a sealed-off vortex, where there is free play between power and pain. Nothing is transparent in that territory, nothing motivates acts and pronouncements. Force refuses to see us. All communication, all subjective exchanges are withheld and frozen. Buffeted, embodied traces of beings clutch onto a blank routine. That is all.

The mechanics between power and pain begets the creature.[2] Suffering ceases to make sense for the one who is afflicted with pain. Suffering does not have the formal elegance of pain.[3] Only the anonymous focal point of affliction brings forth a being that we call creature. The creature begins to interact with the world in a new manner. It eats, sleeps, takes a walk. Only the spatio-temporal dimensions of its existence alter irretrievably once the creature becomes aware of its journey on the knees—as a thrall and a journeyman nomad. As the hunted, it confronts the eternal indifference and mutedness of force. All identity is frozen. The world passes by such a being. The more it endures, the greater its perdurance into individuating itself as a creature.

It is an abiding conundrum, another act of contingency perhaps, that the one who endures agony also exerts it as a force over another body in equal measure—not as acts of vengeance or bad faith, but through deeds of forgetful randomness. The hunted turns into the hunter as the fresh prey emerge in the horizon. The impulse for this inversion has to directly do with the astute observation of Peter Wessel Zapffe in his seminal essay "The Last Messiah": "The craving for material goods (power) is not so much due to the direct pleasures of wealth, as none can be seated on more than one chair or eat himself more than sated. Rather, the value of a fortune to life consists in the *rich opportunities for anchoring and distraction offered to the owner*" (Zapffe, 1933, emphasis mine).[4] Simple preying is an exercise in distraction. Collective preying is a form of purchasing social indemnity. The latter soon develops into a gestalt, a manner of creating meaning in certain culture circles. When power/pain inserts itself within sequentiality and accident, each creature begins to disfigure and distort the other, as it were. Nay, each transgresses its own soul. This inherence of power and pain in the same being/collective is a running thread in the book. Sometimes, power is refinement, a certain disdainful style of operation. In such cases, it rises above mere consolidation of material goods or aggrandizement. A disinterested force, it simply reveals itself out of nowhere. Such power is magisterial, like the one described by Robert Bird: we can name it *force grande*. Regardless, power and pain are circular pursuits. Each feeds on the other. The arc is the distillation of a supernova that erupts within creatures. Creatures themselves are brought within the ring of such necessity and are reminded of their status by emerging circumstances propelled by force. Sometimes, the collective fury of such creaturely vulnerability turns combustible, inverts itself and converts the natural into the social. Pure dread reigns. On rare occasions the arc takes creatures to the shores of the marvellous and the miraculous. Such events are inflections. Those are moments of fragile and receding emergence (Fig. 1).

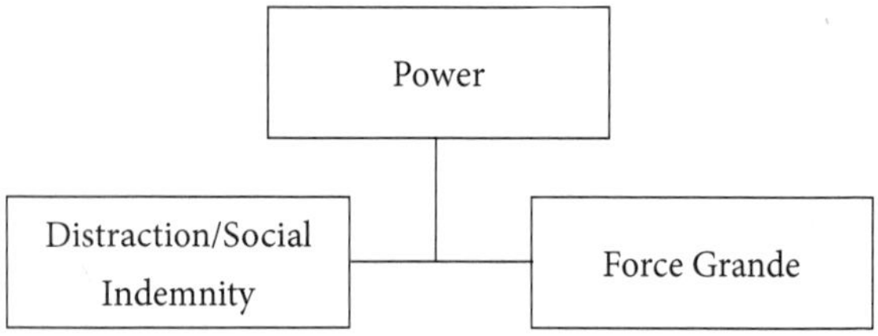

Fig. 1: Trajectories of Contingency

Between power and pain, in such rare moments of emergence, hovers a kind of aching generosity that comes from afar—surpassing love and submission, which are open to the demands of the capacious spirit. The distance between such love and all creation is infinite. But the expansiveness of the soul-force is totally and completely felt, and becomes tangible, for such generosity is always open to our desires, hopes and dejections. The stirrings can be felt in the marrow. But such a form of generosity is also blind and distant, giving yet erratic. Is grace powerful enough to abolish temporal horror? One can prolong security, but cannot avoid absolute wreckage. In the tentacles of the 'pure arbitrary', creatures have no holder to lean upon. The right to weep and curse ends in resignation and in the absurd. But resignation does not take away the material impact of force. The idea of absurd is far too abstract to confront catastrophe. Metaphysical or philosophical placebos are mere distractions to the creature. Within the regal realm of catastrophe, despair resides alongside awe. Only rarely does such a condition produce limitless generosity in the creature—one that has begun to trudge the abandoned pathway. The rootless and the nomad can feel the touch of such generosity. This is the 'second sight' for the creature.

The Anonymous Focal Point of Pain

Creatures are reminded time and again that they are but bones and skin. They are hounded, tracked down and nonchalantly abandoned, maimed or annihilated through clinical methods of relational sociability. Such nonchalance has much less to do with the primitive rituals of scapegoating or sacrifice, than with periodic rifts in little spaces, where, like scorpions and hamsters, creatures are unable to distinguish between mutual slaughter and mutual embrace. And yet, they needs must operate from within such caverns of relationality. That is the reason Gabriel Tarde says that *everything is social*; there is hardly anything natural with and within creaturely accommodations. Tarde's formulation is even better expressed by Maggie Nelson, when she says, "Everything is nice" (Nelson, 2011). This zone of sentient neutrality, one that runs athwart nature and the human, is where all identity is suspended. Nothing is revealed. All that remains is radical inarticulation. The one who is branded by affliction shall keep on only half his soul, as Weil had predicted.

Pain is the condition of confronting complete unknowability. Nights simply arrive. All movement is frozen. Creatures save nights of such inarticulation. The numbness is all too material. Soma, which faces the night, is not a living being, but the *live body.* The afflicted body is a conglomeration of limbs and sinews, "as moved by the joints" (Snell, 1953).[5] The creature in pain is an anatomical substance, something that can be peeled off in an instance. The skin is the finitude of the body; the body being but a chassis where pain inheres, finds a niche, a veritable harbouring station. Pain is the aperture in the limbs. When excruciating pain hits the body below, straight at the anchorages of limbs and at neuromuscular junctions, all voluntary muscles attain complete paralysis. Numbness, therefore, literally means complete loss of expression: evanescence of moan or grimace. Such neutrality belies all feelings and trauma which are mere personal reactions to distress. Affliction runs a wedge between the sensory and the affective part of pain, so that creatures have little window to wallow in suffering. This state extends involuntarily through emanating of sounds (arising out of the deep jaw)—actual and mechanical guttural sounds of the gutted; muffled sibilants rushing out in ghostly half-utterances. Unmingled babble. Mladen Dolar gives it the name of voice: "*it is what does not contribute to make sense*. It is the material element recalcitrant to meaning, and if we speak in order to say something, then the voice is precisely that which cannot be said" (Dolar, 2006).[6] Soon muscles retract again, as they go through protracted periods of non-reaction. A howl/scream is yet to be formed. Howling to creatures comes much later, only when sibilants are gathered adequately within the jaws do they move to the lungs, so that they can come out as yelps and howls. And since there is no addressee to the scream; there is none to appeal. The mechanical sound of pain emanates in ripples from the numbed animal much earlier and returns periodically to its bones for the rest of his living days. The shaken, paltry creature bides time. But relief in earthly existence is a chimera; arrival of grace even more so.

The afflicted is indeed *marked out* for corporeal mortification. Leslie Fiedler has correctly diagnosed that "Extreme affliction … is a nail, whose point is applied at the very center of the soul, whose head is all necessity spreading throughout space and time" (Fiedler, 1951).[7] All forces come together in order to create a kind of a condition that can only be described as *ecstatic stasis*. The question of joy or salvation in suffering is alien to the focal point of emanating pain. It is not a matter of practice and self-penance. It is impossible to cultivate pain. That would be a self-regarding mode of extracting pleasure out of suffering, integrating the self back into the sociable as a mitigating domain of seeming normalcy. To protest suffering, as opposed to acknowledging suffering, is beset with another problem, one that has been eloquently explained by Susan Sontag in *Regarding the Pain of Others*. Suffering, which is often accessible, can be commoditized or shared through exchanges of feeling or experience. This form of suffering as witnessing is of recent vintage in human imagination. In an era of shock, such witnessing comes with image-making and the diffusion of such images. Suffering has gradually been culturally acclimatized as an assault on the sensibility of the viewer, and as such, has become a thing to be celebrated. Sontag alerts us that such a culture essentially relies on a "system of maximal reproduction and diffusion of images" (Sontag, 2003). Such a phenomenon has taken an altogether different dimension in the age of ultra-familiarity of agony, where ruin is channelled through information outlets, images, memes and graphics. Consequently, there is often a surfeit of understanding on the part of the viewer, which inevitably involves misreadings, misrememberings and an ideological use of pain. Pain is often turned into suffering by a skillful mediation of iconography.

But pain cannot be bound by suffering. It is a different beast. There is no purifying balm to the garbled sounds of affliction that arise out of the ribs of the creature and yet is suppressed in and through half-tones and distractions. To bring the social to bear upon the afflicted is one way to shroud pain. This is how collectives turn *responsible* in charting out the sociable. This is done by ritualizing pain through counter processes that vainly try to submerge the half-uttered sibilants and howls of the creature into an anaesthetic stupor: as effected by keening or chanting (communal ways of channelling pain within the accessible dimensions of suffering) or collective sloganeering or picketing (sociopolitical methods), for instance. To philosophize is the other route to distract creatures off the mechanical power of pain and an attempt to remove us from the blinding force of corporeal contingency by producing coherency. For instance, attempts to hunt for a causal series of psychosocial elements in order to explain misfortune and/or impermanence. But misfortune is also not pain. Misfortune is an eventual condition that gives precedence to determinism for creaturely affliction. Its explanatory power is likely to lead to resignation or stoicism, states that buffer and shield us from the source and power of afflictive pain.

In the realm of existential transitoriness, the movement of pain from the focal point to the peripheries and back is a constant, circling process. At its epicentre, pain is the name of a reversible process that acts between the tangible and the touchable, a process testifying to what Merleau-Ponty has famously said about one hand touching the other.[8] The epicentre of pain is at once subjective and objective (the body subject), limbs and soul intertwined in and through a certain chiasm. The physical guttural centre of affliction is not chunks of sensory flesh, but striations of tissues that take a strange colour as the storm hits the creature. The body turns attentive. Horizons of senses gape open and a new modulation within the striations of the limbs begins to take shape—slowly but steadily. This is the *protuberant flesh* of the pain, a crystallization that palpitates and envelops the creature, henceforth, in the living nerves and marrow. The physical form turns utterly uncanny. What comes first—the gestures and guttural sounds of pain or the immaterial pain within? There is the twining. David Abram sums up such a frame and state quite accurately: "Yet 'I' do not deploy these powers like a commander piloting a ship, for I am, in my depths, indistinguishable from them, as my sadness is indistinguishable from a certain heaviness of my bodily limbs, or as my delight is only artificially separable from the widening of my eyes, from the bounce in my step and the heightened sensitivity of my skin" (Abram, 1996).[9]

Pain is eccentric. The uncanny epicentre of pain metamorphoses. It travels from the focal point to the nooks and crannies of the creature, embedding itself silently among diurnal duties and habits that the creature must go through. Emanating from the nerve centre, pain reverberates across the cosmos and engulfs an entire ecosystem. The process often starts with a stoic denial of pain. The movement, therefore, begins from a stage of indifference to or dissociation from pain. This is the condition of *pain asymbolia*. The afflicted creature is lobotomized to the level of routinizing pain into daily work and play. This is the neutral purgatory of persistence, the very obverse that characterizes wound and unpleasantness. Indeed, pain has nothing to do with any ersatz sensation of it. Just as Richard Foreman has said: "We use language not to destroy but to undercut pinings of *there*" (Foreman, 2013). The *there* asserts itself without trying to absorb pain. Therefore, the movement of pain is characterized by dissociation from feeling rather than the summoning of it. In the words of Nikola Grahek, "The case of pain asymbolia is the most convincing evidence that pain without any appropriate pain behavior is possible" (Grahek, 2001).[10] Such a condition can only materialize when affliction spreads evenly from the somatic to every other matter that the creature interacts with, but without calling forth any sensory or affective subjective placebo or prosthetic system in order to mitigate the sensory aspects of suffering. There is no *what-is-it likeness* experience for the afflicted. Therefore, there is also no objective quotient of pain—to be extracted and clearly presented. The force spreads. Its necessary arrival is almost a premonition—like an elderly woman in Nuri Bilge Ceylan's film *The Small Town* (*Kasaba*) says: "This pain is like the weather forecast" (Ceylan, 1997). This stage and condition of asymbolia clearly shows that creaturely vulnerability is about being in pain without feeling pain, so that it cannot be described or articulated. It is an abyssal secret, an intolerable proximity. The waves of pain are 'bunched together' and then they 'spread out' in a Doppler-like effect. Each wave falls over the next. The shrillness approaches and recedes, ebbs and flows. Pain is the very condition of existence, a potential that lurks all the time among creaturely transactions (Fig. 2).

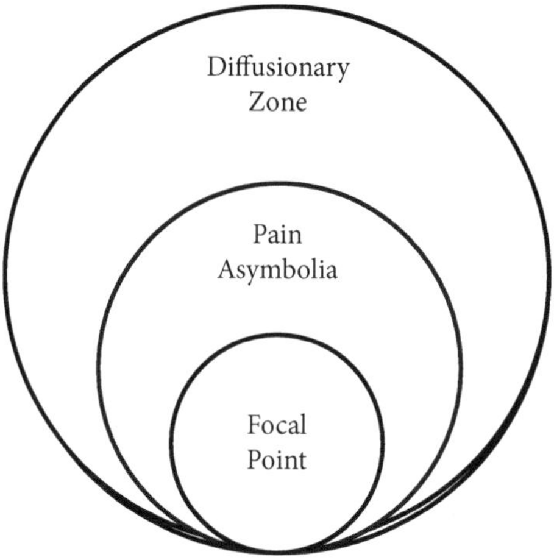

Fig. 2: The Ambience of Pain

But asymbolia is not an aneasthetic state of numbness.[11] Rather, it is more the manner in which the event of pain takes the shape of the world. In this volume, such a state is best described by Oxana Timofeeva's usage of the term *toska*—a condition of unbearable pressure which interrupts the flow of living itself. In Max Scheler's words, such pain becomes a kind of a presentiment—"like a heavy breath, or seems like an obscure glimmering that surrounds" the world (Scheler, 1954).[12] As the world immerses in the inevitability of the condition of neutral sorrow emanating from affliction, creatures can see the focal point of pain and *fortuna* more vividly. The traffic between the actual catastrophic events of humiliation and the condition of destitution form a complementary arc that ascertains each other. The element of the event is felt by the creature as it also begins to note the alteration in the world's make up: "Grief seems to pour out from the event into unlimited space" (Scheler, 1954). Such a form of flow is not to do with any elegiac condition. Quite the inverse. In this context, Robert Zaretsky has reminded us of Simone Weil's illustration of two women holding identical letters announcing the demise of their sons. The first one glances at it and faints. Till the dying day, her facial and bodily expressions shall never be the same again. The second woman cannot read, and hence, is unmoved. Zaretsky tells us that Weil's point is not about the reaction that brute sensation elicits from us. The first woman behaves in a way as if the pain were in the letter itself. It jumped out of it, as it were, and hit her like a rock. Pain is given to one's sight: "It is as if the impact of the meaning is objective, not subjective, and comes not from the women's inner world, but from the physical world outside of her. It is as real, in short, as a punch to one's head from another's fists. Yet, we also know that the letter's meaning, and the visceral force it carried, depends upon this particular woman. One need not be illiterate to dodge the blow of this particular meaning; one need only not be the mother of this dead son" (Zaretsky, 2021).

To those who are in the throes of such *poor life,* the arc marks very early on an essential truth about the workings of powerful force: that it is at once completely unpredictable and yet totally inevitable and necessitated as a recurrent and contingent phenomenon that must define the creature. Only rarely, from within such neutrality, may appear a certain degree of diligence and generosity. But the generosity that may arrive, if it does at all, will have to first let pass all common creatures through a mutual purgatory—little caverns of intimacy. Sharon Cameron is profoundly aware of the steep price of such a common predicament: "To be competent to speak of pain is to speak of pain that isn't yours. This requires experiencing pain that is yours. Pain experienced *as if* it were your own," she says (Cameron, 2000). And yet creatures cannot be absorbed in the experience of pain, unlike beings. They *know pain.* Creatures pass through the common condition of pain.

The common condition of pain indeed was most rigorously studied by Elaine Scarry almost four decades ago, in a work that is still unsurpassed in the sheer reach and depth of her concerns—ranging from bodily perceptions of pain, mediated through the figural/fictional, taking into account the issues of doubt and belief and a sharp realization that the collective perception of pain depends often on 'making pain real' and on the power to 'describe pain'. The present work differs precisely on the premise of the ethical nature of the common condition that informs Scarry, which is based on an *a priori* idea of human sentience, and not on creaturely affliction. Scarry's profound humanism not only shines forth in the very choice of the two case studies that frames her path-breaking work, namely torture and war, but also in the philosophical dualism over which pain operates, in her view. In the framework, the certainty of one's bodily pain can only be communicated to others through the bridge of sentience. The pain of the vulnerable is thus transferred to create and appreciate an ethical climate of human suffering. Scarry's work on pain has, therefore, been rightly commended "for its thickly affective atmosphere of intelligent compassion, of tender regard for the vulnerable human being, and also for a committed moral optimism" (Harpham, 2001). Pain and beauty in Scarry ultimately hinge on a morally beneficent momentum—"seeing the pain and wishing it gone" (Scarry, 1985).

A creaturely foray into power and pain cannot afford the luxury of compassion. It is impossible to differentiate sentience in a world that is blind and throbbing with contingency. Creatures are stunned matter, unable to project and reciprocate pain to others. Creatures *are*. Projection and sharing of pain can only happen when it is converted into grief, hurt or suffering, which can then be used to make the external world sentient. The imaginative, the mythical, the epiphanic and the generous are concerns that make a large part of the present work, but it keeps away from the humanistic hope that sorrow can be made otherwise. If at all, one must look for freedom within the more esoteric and difficult zone of opacity and radical non-communicability. The question of relief is not relevant to the creaturely predicament. The world is animated as such, of which the condition of pain is a given.

That the condition of painfulness has little to do with sensitivity, privacy, self-intimation or with any representation of pain is most vividly and systematically charted in Aniket Jaaware's work on touch and destitution, the subject of the fourth chapter in the book. Jaaware addresses the problem of not knowing where to go with our creaturely sense of fallenness, humiliation and abandonment. He brings down all reflectivity to touching and not touching—which characterizes the condition of untouchability and destitution associated with it. The idea of touching is worked out through metaphors and figures of speech rather than for seeking any internal consistency in any subjective experience of pain. To Jaaware, any idea of freedom must consider and confront directly our thrown condition—which is immediate, material and tactile. Freedom from ontological pain also means, according to Jaaware, to get rid of 'segmented sociability' and think in terms of difference and plurality among destitute creatures *as such*. The specificity of destitution, in this case the ontological condition of touchability, is the most important aspect for delineating humiliation and loss in Jaaware.[13] The ripple effect of pain that suffuses like mist, in order to create a certain ambience and texture of life and one that is at the same time absolutely material and tangible in its felt impact, is also the subject of two other chapters in the volume: one deals with a creative biography of Jibanananda Das (Chapter Three) and the other which accepts Simon Critchley's invitation to reconsider constitutive violence and rage in tragedies and look for an outside, vis-à-vis the *polis* (Chapter Nine). We shall return to the tragic in greater detail soon. Suffice it to say here that both the chapters consider the implications of 'social cut' in all its bareness and reach. The three modes of the creaturely—the *plastic*, the *forlorn* and the *elsewhere* are attempts to construct an independent mini-tapestry as creatures face, confront and follow the vehemence of affliction and take its force and gift to culmination points through imaginative and figurative means.

Though affliction has nothing to do with the mere sensory or with the reparative-affective, it must be emphasized that negotiating the complex terrain of painfulness is not to indulge in *pain eliminativism*. Theories of pain eliminativism, based on cognitive complexities, could quickly lead to a kind of reductive sub-personal and functional analysis of pain and its transmission, completely skirting the power of the phenomenological depth of the condition of lurking affliction that besets creatures. The cognition of painfulness is the mode and matter of limbs and sinews—a domain of distilled voice. The neutral power of affliction is far from congenital dissociation from pain. It is never 'life-alien' and geometric in nature.[14] Rather, any distancing from subjective sentimentalism of suffering is an act of entering the province of painfulness as a constitutive condition of living. Pain is not an assemblage or a device. It is a terrible gift, a rare lucidity, a violation of measure. Like coughing and hiccups, pure babble returns within the general condition of affliction. Creatures unveil themselves to the world and to themselves only through infinite affliction. The eruption of brutish uncanniness is very well described by Julia Kristeva as a loathsome zone, which assails the being with an uneasy estrangement about its selfhood: "Not me. Not that. But not nothing, either. A 'something' that I do not recognize as a thing" (Kristeva, 1982).

The Stunned Giants and the Recurring Flood

Any conception of power that relates to the creaturely must begin with an understanding of deep time.[15] The absolute experience that the bipedal man meets, as it changes its horizon of grasping and gazing, is a tremendous transformation in creaturely perception. The world rushes in, generating a situation when the creature now has to face bouts of threat and force. A new world has to be hewed out of the prehistoric. In *Work on Myth*, Hans Blumenberg has to say this:

> Whatever may have been the appearance of the prehuman creature that was induced, by an enforced or accidental change in the environment it inhabited, to avail itself of the sensory advantage of raising itself upright into a bipedal posture and to stabilize that advantage in spite of all of its internal disadvantages in the functioning of organs—that creature had, in any case, left the protection of a more hidden form of life, and one, in order to expose itself to the risks of a widened horizon of its perception, which were also those of its perceivability. (Blumenberg, 1985)[16]

To understand the nature of the first man, and thereby to historicize the creative creature, also constitutes the profound philological project of Giambattista Vico. The first man, Vico deduced, operated mutely and then poetically—or metaphorically, through myths and fables. At first, there was flood and fire, which giant creatures had to encounter as terrifying forces unleashed upon them by the gods. The myth of Jove turned simultaneously poetic and real as the bipedal creature heard rumblings of fire and thunder in the horizon. Man became aware of his place between the sky and earth.[17] This was the moment of *radical exposure* for man as a creature. Fear and confrontation with the cosmological led to the emanation of grumbling and passionate expressions from the giants. Is this philological home, the earth, where humans examine history from the point of view of the maker, or is it that with Vico, we must always return to the earth as the empty space that creatures inhabit, a space where *poiesis* and praxis collide?[18] Making is action. And history takes a fabulous turn. Vico's humans are *wandering ferals,* deeply attentive to the voices and gestures of the earth, of the body and of the awe inspiring and unpredictable firmament.

The logic of terror and myth is about the hidden and the esoteric, that lie strewn all around us, guided by some wondrous and excruciating force—the terribly sublime, red-hot molten magma of contingency. The age of gods and the age of heroes reserved the wherewithal to confront terror in a wholly original fashion, which eludes the age of the humans.[19] But civilization is hardly a linear and a finished process, whereby we might reach the final world of legality and sociability, in order to rest forever. Civil life eludes creatures and the 'cut' lurks with all its vehemence within the imitative hive of creatures. The hives and caverns of the creaturely are run by auspices and oracles, not by rules of the nations and governments. The heroic and the godly stay dormant underneath the civilizational veneer as reflux. From time to time, the power of their crushing force stuns creatures. The *recorsi*, especially the reflux of the force of the tragic-heroic, is the most radical challenge to all things that mark the liberal variants of sensitized non-living.

The first component, therefore, in destitute creatures waiting for the divine wrath (*timor dei* of Vico—fear of God) to arrive as the clap of the thunder is the felt hermeneutical power of the myth in actual terms. This is the *fons et erigo*. Divine wrath is split into the very material concerns of philosophy and anthropology when all corporeal vulnerabilities, the very condition of painfulness, confront recurring and contingent forms of palpable terror. The immanent power of raw terror is purely mechanistic in the sense that it is fabulous. It is for this reason that "the first language for Vico is monosyllabic and develops a process of signification based on visual and acoustic elements; it is not the expression of human subjectivity, freedom or action and takes place as an event deeply implicated with nature and the body, as a combination of voices, gestures, bodily expressions" (Lollini, 2011).[20] Creatures confront power foremost in and through the conjectures of the sky and the earth. The force and power of terror emanating from the circuits of the world reaches the bone marrow. Nights turn luminous with spears and shrapnel. And creatures gawk. Like rabbits, they seek burrows and bunkers, where there are none.

Gregoire Chamayou has traced the tension between the finitude of the body and the wrath of the contingent force by foregrounding the relationship between the hunter and the hunted. The second chapter of the book addresses this concern. Chamayou tries to give us a diachronic ontogeny of manhunting. Beneath this tracing, there is also a core existential query: "What happens in your head if you are hunted? What happens in your head—if you hunt other human subjects?" (Chamayou, 2012). What is the nature of the subjectivity in such states of consciousness? Indeed, the game of hunting is outside the purview of conventional warfare. Hunting does not claim moral justness. The neutrality of hounding a prey means "to be able to kill without being able to be killed; to be able to see without being seen" (Chamayou, 2012). The hounded creature is a harvest to be consumed or excluded. The power gradient is placed at the forefront of such a relationship. From the side of the hounded, the most important features are to acknowledge attrition and strategization. But as the prey begins to wonder about its status, a remarkable inversion begins to set in, the mark of a Vichian reflux: the reflection of the violator in the violated. With hunting, which is the inversion of reverence, "the real humans disappear and in their stead appear duplicates of themselves ... accompanied by an alteration, by an occultation of reality and an inversion of the relationship between cause and effect" (Godelier, 1999).[21] Is there no escape from the coupling that takes place between the hunter and the hounded, the power gradient shifting from one side to the other until it reverses its tilt?[22]

The encounter of the creature with the unknown, the acknowledgement of its abjectness and the power of its adaptability to resurrect is also at the heart of Gabriel Tarde's sociology—where the vicissitudes of sociability confront the contingent and calamitous 'cut'. How can the contingent force be also inevitable, he asks? Or are there only molecular facts that collide with each other, differentiate and diffuse and lead to a gradual equilibrium until that equilibrium destroys itself to those molecules? The first chapter of the book delves into a sociological experiment, an arche-Vichian moment: through the processes of a fortunate event, a fictional construct, Tarde takes us back to a state of bereft abjectness and geological calamity. It is also a journey into the poetic and the mythical. The fabulous force of the power/pain resides in the cusp of the miraculous and the mimetic.

Indeed, Gabriel Tarde shows us the mirror: that the underside of civility is pure calamity. And therefore, to confront calamity and seek recovery is a social act, brought about by re-enacting some form of necessary fiction among the members of the cavern, which we prefer to call society. The new social emerges as and when contingency strikes. Creatures can only turn properly social if they pay heed to the conjunctions of history. Time gets realigned into meaningful eras with periodic alignment or conjunctions of planets and with creatures working within those planets.[23] Creatures rediscover the force of the tectonic shifts within their lives and inner constitution when such conjunctions take place. Peculiar and bold changes begin to shape relationships between creatures and the world and between creatures themselves. These realignments starkly begin to bring out and foreground the coupling of power and pain anew.

The periodic recurrence of tumult is a zero-sum enterprise that could actually deepen democracy, but could also lead to the complete topsy-turvy of all settled variations in modes of the existing governance. This insight is one of the central lessons of Niccolò Machiavelli's oeuvre, dealt in Chapter Five. The game of cat and mouse is most powerfully and mercilessly played between the aristocracy and the plebeians so that new cycles of order can be created—which are the originary moments of history. Such processes must pass through a purgatorial route. The plebs must constantly foment tumult and needle the *grandi* in order to create an independent zone of power emanating from their precarious condition. From the side of the *grandi*, the imperative is to maintain the esoteric and secret ways to govern—to deploy *force grande*. But since human appetites are always greater than their power to secure the fruits of their desire, there are spillovers and excesses, which give rise to the condition of painfulness and a climate shrouded with absolute millennial uncertainty. The disbalance leads to enmity and war, eventually leading unto annihilation of large swathes of creatures.[24] But only destruction can lay the grounds for foundation. Therefore, in Machiavelli, constituent power arrives as the ongoing mutation as creatures wish to intervene and make a mark in history. Mutation "establishes the logic of time on an ontological horizon of dense, multidirectional, and changing materiality" (Negri, 1999). Time turns polyvalent. Mutation means whatever is fatal and natural turns into history. And such a mutation is given direction by the political actors through a combination of judgement/prudence and arms. The subject intervenes in action as will and concentration.

The Vichian formulation finds a definite and definitive imprimatur in Simone Weil's evolving thoughts about force and pain. Force is characterized by equity in Weil—its scythe falls on each and every creature. This is the justice that the *actual* provides us with. Power begins with a terrible force and maintains a fluid state of rupture. Force is essential for attesting the *agonal* spirit of a community and its exigent power is always tragic. God is absent in *The Iliad*. It is only pervaded by force and misery. Creation is abandonment, Weil believes.

The twining of the condition of painfulness and power is an inextricable necessity in Weil, and necessity at once frees and enchains all creatures.[25] That we must shorten the space of our subjective indulgences in order to get a clear, unclouded sense of the *actual* is Weil's singular wager. This gradual process of waning of the subject's judgement and selfhood she names as *decreation*. The decreated condition of the creature is the most acutely and materially creaturely. Decreation is a process and happens to those who have directly felt and mediated the coupling of force and affliction, but *sans* sentimentalizing the relationship through any altruism. Decreation is pure and non-interior particularity that the creature might encounter in its worldliness. But it is simultaneously a process that the gods must also have to go through. What is present of God is his absence. The significant question is whether Weilian *decreation* is a meditative method of practicing Stoic *attached-detachment* or is it a deeper and singular immersion into the material condition of painfulness?

Within this structure, to minimize and negotiate the contingent forces is a constant hope and wish of the Vichian mind—from Xenophon to Machiavelli, from Spinoza through Tarde to Weil. But any attempt to get rid of contingency means recognizing the obligation to face the full brunt of its menacing force directly. *Fortuna* is the name of the unforeseeable and the unprogrammable, which is historically determined. Hence, 'injustice of things' must be met nonchalantly. The hounded can only wait relentlessly for the contingent force to arrive and go through its terrible power. The power of force helps generate *virtu* and fortitude in the destitute. By taking head-on the delirious core of destitution, the creature expresses, emerges and transfigures all perspectival relationality. By at once baring force and pain, Weil wishes to bring forth the hidden, or what Roberto Esposito calls the *impolitical*, seeking "the torn heart beating from within extreme discord" (Esposito, 2015). But is there a remainder to the zero-sum theme, inaugurated by the hunter and the hunted? Can the hope of transfiguration exorcise the neutrality of affliction? Is there any other possibility outside of the dichotomy of *agone* and *will-to-power*?

Grace No Deliverance, Rhythm No Closure

No deliverance is sought by Weil. No 'poietic secularization' of the arche coupling of pain and power—of force that bloodies skin and flesh. Creatures beset by power can only seek reduction of being. Therefore, she pronounces "We are nothing but creatures. But to consent to be nothing but that is like consenting to be nothing. Without our knowing it, this being which God has given us is non-being. If we desire non-being, we have it, and all we have to do is to be aware of the fact. . . . To teach us that we are non-beings, God made himself non-being" (*First and Last Notebooks*, 217–218). Is this our non-being, the gift of dereliction, a way of being caressed by divinity? Since speculative philosophy is neither able to allay affliction, nor can it stave off the absurd and bare power of force, what possibilities of freedom from the twining of pain and power? Does embracing decreation give the creature some closure or alter its state of creatureliness? (Fig. 3)

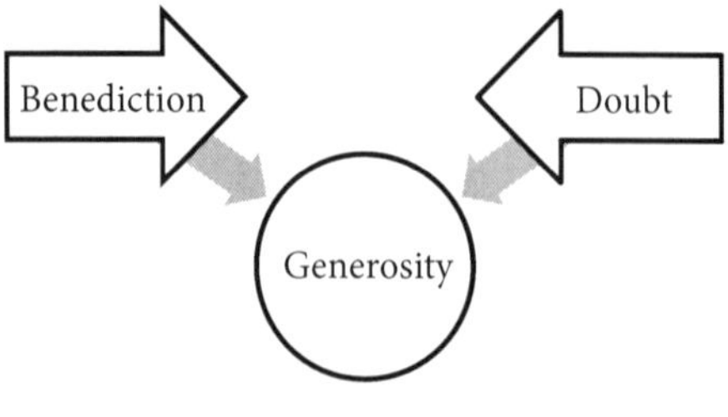

Fig. 3: Modalities of Second Sight (A)

Earlier, we had referred to the 'second sight' of the creature—forged out of love and abdication. Chapter Eight takes us to Lev Shestov, the Russian savant and visionary, who does not give heed to palliatives, is blessed with such a sight. Instead, he gets headlong into divine providence in his later works as the only way to gain freedom, if at all. This is not a cobbled pathway. Moral ideals, nature, or refuge in tradition bring us no respite from relentless force. The whole creature becomes Shestov's object of enquiry, and his method: to get rid of psychological determinism (the anxieties of guilt, condemnation and/or death) and shuffling untidiness of the being. His journey is towards a state of ontological faith, which is not moral action. Fideism is not a matter of moral righteousness. Shestov holds on to the nodal point of pain resolutely without taking resort of any abstraction. He confronts the condition of accident. Was he able to uproot pain, as he wished to?

Shestov lets pass the tragic secrets of life through the sieve of faith in the particular work that we read in this volume, but his interest is wider: total abdication in order to be free: "And we have to abdicate.... We have to understand the full horror of the situation described by Nietzsche through the mouth of an insane man, hidden beneath Heine's humor, experienced by Dante behind his door, the horror that gave rise to the tragedies of Shakespeare and the novels and sermons of Count Tolstoy."[26] He cherishes the fact that Chekhov was able to create 'out of nothing'. Chekhov, like Shestov after him, is the frequenter of the minimal domain of translucence. Art, like faith, is a domain of mystery and ecstasy, not truth. And here the greatest challenge that Shestov takes on is the salvific notion of *ataraxia* in philosophy. To indulge in *ataraxia* is to evade affliction, through a process of reflection. *Ataraxia* embraces rigour in order to bypass lucidity. On this point, he is remarkably close to Weil's thinking.[27] It is only that he calls forth for submission instead of *decreation*.

The freedom for the spirit is an infinite waiting; not to be hastened. It is a journey over the accidents of neutral despair and faith 'an idle stroke'. It is in the context that Shestov calls the mystic *dukhoborec* (spirit-wrestler). Mystery cannot be solved, but the miserable vagabond and the idiot travels along with it, not knowing where he is going. He is an initiate. This expectation of the miracle is a vent to freedom, which may well be misplaced. 'Whence come evil?' is such a question to which there are no answers. None to this one either: 'Why does that which *is* in no way correspond to that which we wish would be?' These are not appropriate questions to the theory of knowledge. Regardless, the spirit-wrestler goes on in his quest without chasing explanation. He believes that miraculous transformations are impossible and, therefore, are a possibility, howsoever dim and receding the prospects might be. Is it in silence that Shestov sought freedom? As Howard Barker has noted, "Like the colour black, there are colours within silence" (Barker, 1989), though Shestov's quest is hardly about silent humility and meek resignation. His is a joust with God. And the plea, torrentially eloquent. The pivotal question is: if creatures submit to providence, as Shestov asks them to do, do they refrain from looking directly at the actualities of pain? Is it eventually a kind of transference of inevitability to the majesty of God?

This idea of the riddle—one that resides quizzically between quest and silence, is the singular motif that runs through many works of Raymond Geuss, the subject of Chapter Six. The celebration of puzzlement is at the heart of his works. Following Joseph Joubert, the French 'man of letters' who writes in his notebook that "Clearness is so eminently one of the characteristics of truth, that it often even passes for truth itself" (Nelson, 2009), we must realize that much in our wondrous and baffling life must remain crystal clear, and therefore unexplained. One can observe and experience the creaturely gift of terrible pain and imagine the moments of magic. This he calls *invitation*—to look at, observe or consider something. Such an invitation refrains from indulging in concepts and *lines of argument*. An invitation makes no claims or demands. Geuss's quest is far more sceptical and speculative when compared to the fideism that Shestov submits himself to, and yet between the two of them, we see a real tussle to address affliction and its effects and along with them, an urge to seek an independent space from which living can be lucidly looked at. One acquiesces, the other bids us welcome. But welcoming the little-understood wonders of the world also means a kind of acquiescence to pain, for as Unamuno writes, "in the depths of the abyss, the despair of the heart and of the will and skepticism of reason must meet face to face and embrace like brothers" (Unamuno, 1921/2013). This is the most intimately loving and tragic embrace of all, played out within living itself.

The invitational nature of Geuss's quest is completely passionate and serious about life and about the extinction of it—riddles that must remain unexplained. Much like Shestov, in his own way, Geuss wishes to abandon all abstraction, so that he can enter the rough and tumble of living—the realm of the creaturely. In Geuss, therefore, will and intelligence, matter and reflection cohere in deference to the coupling of pain and power—the terrible and playful nature of hovering uncertainty and its awaiting scythe. That is the reason Geuss celebrates playfulness, in games and proverbs.[28] Proverbs often come in sets of two, sometimes diametrically opposite in their wisdom and context: "That a proverb aptly catches something about that (some) aspect in no way implies that it exhausts all that can rightly be said" (Geuss, 2020). Such is living, contradictory and equally valid. Geuss affirms positively what Unamuno had pronounced much earlier, that "the vital sense has to do with living," not abstraction (Unamuno, 1921/2013). At the heart of Geuss's sensibility is a metaphysics of rootlessness and drift. Possibilities often have priority over fixed reality, but the radical uncertainty, propelled by force, imbued within such possibilities make them more *actual* in their very fictiveness. Hence, Geuss calls forth Artaud in order to define the real in terms of the actual: "That is 'real' which imposes itself so uncomfortably on my body that I cannot ignore it and also wish to swat it away.... Pain is not the only condition in which something is pressed out of the body, so that a physical negation becomes real and concrete. Shitting is also a process of negation: I do not wish to retain this matter any longer. [Therefore] obviously there exists some 'thing' other than me: I want to extrude it" (Geuss, 2020). Geuss acknowledges affliction and yet he reserves a residual hope for remedy arising out of such delirious condition. Geuss is the philosopher of affirmation who is aware of the unexplained and unexplainable secrets of life. Living, indeed, is participating in such a terrible beatitude.

In Chapter Seven, Oxana Timofeeva precisely sends us such an invitation, so that through the lives of animals, we are able to appreciate the experience and the beatific sensation of *toska*. The word at once connotes melancholy, longing, torment and depression. But it is not a passive existential quality. Boredom and freedom speak to each other in *toska*. It builds up a pressure in the creature which is also interruptive. For Timofeeva, the best way to come close to *toska* is to dive into Andrei Platonov's universe of plants and animals. This, she gives the name of *poor life*. Matter has a shining quality in Platonov's Central Asia, tinged with the debris of ancient myths. Here, human beings come out of microbes and worms, the wretched and the beggarly. Platonov is enchanted by the great sparseness of the desert, the lives and deaths around Amu-Darya River. In this world, the god of darkness, Ahriman, is engaged in an eternal combat with Ormuzd, the god of light. In his canvas Platonov has placed animals and plants against the official idea of the people-*narodny*. He was charged with indulging with pity for the nomadic, but the same perceptive critics could see his relentless following of the forgotten and the lonely, "without giving birth to any answering sorrow" (Platonov, 2008).[29] This famously includes the cow who languished in grief, since unlike humans, she had no way to mitigate her state through words or consciousness, through a friend or other distractions. This is what Timofeeva calls *poor life*, an idea that has uncanny resemblance with Jaaware's destitution. Animals signify diligence and generosity in Timofeeva—they are a bridge between force and grace. But do these admirable qualities adequately address affliction?

The only other realm of freedom, of the creaturely 'second sight,' left to explore is the aesthetic-epiphanic. But once again, the creaturely encounter with such moments of awe and wonder must pass acutely through affliction that only force can produce. The condition of aesthesis is always neural and embodied for the creature—lyrical, gestural, stuttering and fantastic. There are at least three ways to address the domain of the aesthetic-epiphanic: the *mythical-anthropological*, the *sublime-rhythmic* and the *expressive-materialist* (Fig. 4).

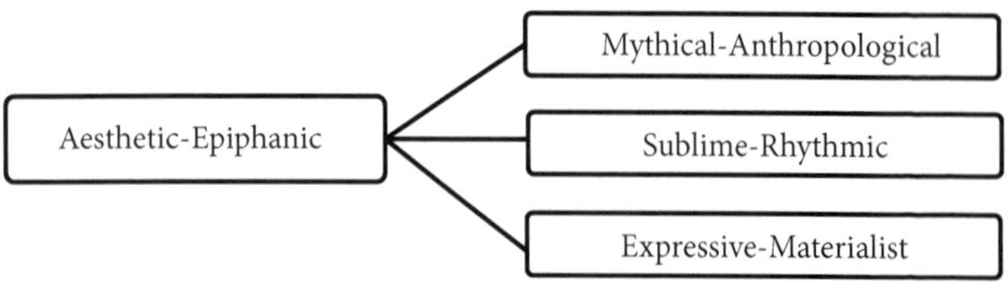

Fig. 4: Modalities of Second Sight (B)

The Vichian formulation of the poetic in Book II of *The New Science* is a firm terrain to explore the *mythical-anthropological* dimension of the aesthetic.[30] The cosmography of a poetic anthropology is governed through certain archetypal and allegorical signs. The poetic logic of such an imaginative universal begins through the creation of "fantastic speech based on animate substance" (Vico, 1999). The figures of speech are vehicles to such a poetic logic. Every figure of speech is an exercise 'in a miniature myth'. In order to explicate the primitive roots of such a vision, Vico says, "The language of gods was almost entirely mute, or wordless, and only slightly articulate. The language of heroes was an equal mixture of mute and articulate speech, which means that it mixed vernacular speech with the heroic characters which Homer calls signs, *semata*. The language of men was almost entirely articulate and only slightly mute, since no vernacular language is so copious that it has words for all things" (Vico, 1999). Vico especially marks the confusion and obscurity of the heroic-poetic language during demonic times.

The arche loop of violence and silence reign at certain epiphanic moments where serious positions collide and the world turns *pell-mell* and absurd. This is the domain of mythos of the tragic. In order to explore the subject further we accept Simon Critchley's sturdy invitation in Chapter Nine. He offers us to confront disorientation and ambiguity through material action. With Critchley, we are invited to see how creatures are part of deep time in the mythical-anthropological sense: time is slowed down drastically, and the perishable rushes towards their moments of perish. Will and necessity are inextricably twined. Besides, the time of gods invades the space of action and makes itself manifest within human temporality. The dead are always spectrally present in a heroic world. Mortals do not know what to do at certain conjunctures—which is what true contingency is. Fate turns into a character of law as creatures are caught in ambiguities. A logic of transgression and retribution takes over and turns events daemonic. Critchley calls this the state of transcendental opacity.

Human fallibility is the subject of Critchley. Tragedy goes beyond the ethical—it opens up to human imperfection. Peter Zapffe, speaking on the same subject many years ago, had mirrored Critchley's undertaking, when he discovered that a tragic constellation essentially confounds "the expectation that perfectibility will lead to fulfillment" (Zapffe, 1941/1983). Tragedy explodes the surplus in the living force; it affirms that the biotic world is fundamentally unfixed and mystical. In order to keep away from all pseudo-solutions (say, poetic sublimation) in addressing the terrible mystery of creaturely relationalities, the protagonists in a tragedy must confront dual arguments that beset each crisis. Such a realization takes us to *dissoi logoi*, which means looking at both sides of a case. With tragedy, we confront the fact that uncovering any firm ontological truth is a fancy, save for meeting affliction with nonchalant awe. The protagonists are divided within their own selves. The polis, the city space itself goes through a protracted period of crisis, affliction and demise in tragedy. The more the city state becomes modern and legalistic, the more *kratos*/power comes back as force to crush its hubristic citizens. Bit by little bit Critchley actually takes his readers towards a universe filled with *epistemic mist,* where Vico's giants once again face up to the floods and the gods alike. Critchley hopes for a democratization of the tragic space as he looks for its relevance in the contemporary world and yet the constitutive outside to the mythic-anthropological eludes his hope.[31] Ambivalence and its mimicry are not natural but social traits. Can ambiguity of creaturely action, played within the ambit of suprapersonal forces, be ever made ethically relevant, especially by invoking pity and compassion? Howard Barker seems to be honest when he says that "After the carnival, after the removal of the masks, you are precisely who you were before. After the tragedy you are not certain who you are. Ideology is the outcome of pain. Some people want to know pain. There is no truth on the cheap" (Barker, 1989). There can only remain a neutral and residual sorrow in tragedy, not any reflective idea of suffering or pity. Remorse and penitence take away the creaturely dimension of living by turning it pathological. Atonement is alien to the tragic spirit. Nor is it any sacrificial rite, through which the tragic hero can be made into a redeemed saint. Tragedy is rather a *visitation*—a strange and epiphanic appearance that reminds creatures of its vestments and roles amidst the oblique forces of relationality.

The condition of visitation amidst the 'social cut' is at the heart of the generative tension in the Vichian scheme of progression/regression itself, which traces the movement of the creative human being operating in civilization. On one hand, humans embark on a progressive philological process. But simultaneously, conscious creativity is unable to exorcise the mythical conditions of affliction, which continue to haunt the creature in the throes of force. The force of ambiguity, erupting violence and the consequent numbness that tragedy produces among those in its turmoil transfer the pathos of subjective suffering into a realm of *yonder* and yet it must return with a greater vigour to the dwelling that affliction is—always a gravitating force. Tragedy can give us a sense of *longing while dwelling*, a sense that takes us away from desolation and places us right in front of the equity of pain and power. There is no medicament of 'rescue'. The creature takes *form in*, and does not give *form to* tragedy. Conflict and dilemma get enacted in such a manner in tragedy that form can only be given to a 'weighty destiny'. Tragedy is a process of *immobilized becoming*, a constant hovering of the ominous within the conflictual.[32]

The pursuit of even a purer form is the second course to aesthetic freedom. This is the mode of the *rhythmic-sublime*, where the fundamental law is to 'give freedom by means of freedom'. What happens to painfulness in such a mode? In contemplating beauty, Friedrich Schiller says, creatures are unable to distinguish between cause and effect, activity and passivity—for there are no succession in time. To contemplate form is to simultaneously reflect and feel. Beauty, contemplated as such, is at once an idea/form and life, 'at once our situation and deed' (Schiller, 2016).[33] Chapter Ten looks with wonderment at this moment of pure rhythm where astonishment (*ekplêxis*) and wonder (*thaumasion*) come together as two lovers are intertwined in mutual gaze that emerges out of nowhere. This is the moment of dreaming and wakefulness, of entropy and energy. This *instantiated moment* at once brings a total collapse of action, an interruption and also inaugurates a process of transmutation of the being through an aching that completes and transfigures the painfulness of the force of the world.[34] In this manner, the moment of pure idea is the eternal recurrence of time and space. It is also a moment when creation begins by means of summoning imagination. Longinus says: "It is our nature to be elevated and exalted by true sublimity [*hypsos*]. Filled with joy and pride, we come to believe we have created what we have only heard" (Longinus, 1965). Is this also the moment of pure anarchy? Or conversely, does the rhythm that initiates with a gaze of the lovers begin to take creatures towards the realization of eternal laws of harmony and balance? But is not ecstasy bound up with dread? Rhythm is at once exhilarating and fleeting. The sublime is brought to life only through disintegration. The more crucial question is whether imagination and rhetoric are able to counter the numbing power of force.

This complete shattering of the sequentiality of time and entering into duration is what Jean Starobinski calls *a happy fluidification,* a subject dealt in Chapter Eleven. We step into the perishable moment of operatic synaesthesia. The operatic moment is the arrival of pure form through a heroic confrontation with painfulness: mediated through the double energy of memory that persists and an imagination that invents. In an enchanted performance, myth and the moment amalgamate. Starobinski's aim is to bring together the lethal combination of singing and seduction, which could *lead us aside* momentarily by letting us pass through exemplary heroism and pathos. He invokes charm, which is magical incantation, from Latin *carmen*, "the formula that witches knew how to pronounce to capture hearts and make the moon dance in a wooded clearing" (Starobinski, 2008). The opera, in this sense, could be seen as an act of initiation, a ritual into a world of aromatic charm that is enacted repeatedly in order to retrace us away from pain. The enchanted moment lets pain trek through the vales of pleasure: through the dazzling nothings that decide everything—seduction and death. Mladen Dolar has traced such manifestations—laughter and singing, to be outside of the purview of the speaking-animal: "The birth of the opera was accompanied by the dilemma of the *prima la musica, e poi le parole*, or the other way round; the dramatic tension between the word and the voice was put into its cradle, and their impossible and problematic relationship presented its driving force" (Dolar, 2006). In the perishable operatic moment of enchantment, matter and anti-matter collide as form gets annihilated and constructed at once. To indulge in the perishable moment and to desire freedom is to seek captivity in lightness and death alike. The *rhythmic-sublime* is a way to apprehend *real presence*, to invoke George Steiner, and as such, it takes creatures close to the apprehension of divinity.[35] Creatures intuit tracings "like the physicist's image of the momentary passage of sub-atomic particles through the cloud chamber"

(Steiner, 1989). And it is for this very reason that the apprehension of the *rhythmic-sublime* is like an 'ingressive, transformative summons' that reminds creatures of estrangement and the unhoused instability of their predicament. Enchanted moments are also moments of *facticity*, of silence. George Steiner has described such moments in terms of the Annunciation, "of a terrible beauty or gravity breaking into the small house of our cautionary being. If we have heard rightly the wing-beat and provocation of that visit, the house is no longer habitable in quite the same way as it was before. A mastering intrusion has shifted the light" (Steiner, 1989).Schiller's playful forms can only give us a kind of paradoxical freedom from the condition of thrownness. The *rhythmic-sublime* brings the creaturely circumstance to an even sharper relief.

John Coetzee has placed Ted Hughes' jaguar at the far corner to Rilke's panther.[36] While the latter instantiates the *rhythmic-sublime*, the former marks the sharp stink of the *expressive-materialist* in the creature. Hughes' jaguar is *elsewhere*, his eyes burning. According to Coetzee, for Hughes the kinetic energy of the body of the jaguar is not about abstraction/ephemera, but about inhabiting another body. The jaguar is in a kind of dream-experience. That creature does not care about our feelings for it. Coetzee sums up the situation by pronouncing that he suspects Hughes is "recovering an attentiveness that our faraway ancestors possessed and we have lost. I would guess that he believes he looks at animals much as Paleolithic hunters used do" (Coetzee, 1999). The artist-mediator is attentive to the *latency* and *tendency* of matter, which he seeks to capture and transfigure in the art form. He catches the *temperament* of the dynamic form itself. The urge to transfigure form-in-matter is a bio-existential ache on the part of the artist-mediator. Such an approach to art is permeated with the concerns of *lebenphilosophie*—the philosophy of life.

This manner of acute *attentiveness* runs through the works of Ernst Bloch, the undertaking of Chapter Twelve. Bloch feels that art releases matter-form into existence. For him, art is a process of actualization. Following Lessing, Bloch would say that art is *malleably impelled*: the plastic matter-form, the sub-atomic differentials of matter that keeps wondering at its own image and eventually *conjectures into* 'what-may-become-possible'. Predisposed matter-form works through a drive towards its completion. Throbbing, dynamic matter is Bloch's fundamental energizing principle, similar to the ones conceived by kindred souls who are also moved by such an impulse: Ted Hughes, D.H. Lawrence, Gary Synder or the artists K.P. Krishnakumar and Anil Karanjai. None of them have any sympathy for disinterestedness. Rather, the chaos informed by immediacy and actuality is the running thread in such artists.

As a utopian Marxist, Bloch's engagement with expressionism, of course, has a distinctly left dimension: a method that he would call *revolutionary-gnosis*. A left variant of *lebenphilosophie* tries to elaborate the rational content of such inexplicables like drive, will and the creature itself. How might one simultaneously elongate into and level life with art? Or bring the particularities of the forgotten and rejected within the rhythm of the universal? The first thing to notice among Bloch's interests—music, detective fiction, fairytale—is his rejection of the traditional forms and his espousing the people's demands upon art. He is fascinated by the full intellectual life of art, investing in a kind of contra-modernity. He believes that there is no liberation without freedom of the spirit. The transformative process, therefore, starts with acknowledging artistic volition, by taking into account the psycho-existential mores of living matter, which includes human beings. Hermeneutic intuition and historical understanding are brought into a dynamic confrontation in order to create art. The bridge between the expressive and the productive for Bloch is to spiritualize nature by getting into the bowels of society, to the lowermost rungs among the ignominious. Actually, alienation (which is the nothing but the condition of pain in the conscious being which keeps him away from the very process of production and social relations) of the humans is the alienation from the matter-form of the creaturely. Hence, human art is deadened and polite—it stands outside of nature, bereft. How can there be any transformation without engaging with the dynamism of form? Most importantly, Bloch feels that if a Marxist does not engage with the enchantment in matter-form, mechanical philosophers would use it crudely by instrumentalizing force. And conscious life cannot be deduced from a mechanistic perspective.

Hence, for Bloch, expressionism is a technique of moulding and purification; deployed to take us into the *socialist open*. Art performs an alchemical job by which our innermost shadows are expelled. The current productive forces of the society, the lower middle and working class, arrives as the active material force of form, not through petit bourgeois routes of empathy and empty kinship solidarity. Hence, his fondness for *colportage*—cheap materials sold by the colporteur or travelling bookseller. The colporteur used to carry bibles and chapbooks, cookbooks, primers and medical books, calendars and prayer-books, romances and adventure books. The characters dealt are edgy, cunning and naked proletarian creatures. At the substratum, Bloch's interests match with that of Platonov. In Bloch's case, the colporteur, as it were, is the dream merchant, fulfilling the wishes of the lower classes that seek freedom in such fares. His wares shatter the routine drabness of the lower classes by providing them with imagination and an alternative realm to fly.[37] It is in the same vein the Franco Fortini has critiqued Lucien Goldmann's reading of Pascal and Racine by asserting that mystification is always part of existential 'presentisms' of diverse variations—Catholic, historical, libertine or anarchist, and as such, not only contains the germ of the immediate and particular, but also the anxiety-ridden accentuation of the tragic character of existence. A Marxist must realize, Fortini adds, that such a sensibility is essential to inculcate in order to counter a future that is based on distribution of goods and happiness. It is also essential in order to appreciate the condition of tragic affliction in order to lay claim to an existential absolute, so that the future can be envisaged in terms of a *necessary supplement*. That is the most powerful way to confront and overcome the present.[38] But does not the very idea of a supplement remind us of a loss, and therefore, of reparation? Once the reparative part is abandoned, creatures must confront the power of the abyss in their various presentisms that Fortini so attentively acknowledges.

What freedom then, in the realization and arrival of matter-form into art, which is what constitutes true people's art or art of and for the forgotten souls, in the true Blochian sense? More significantly, can the tragic condition of life be transcended by invoking and asserting the *upright carriage*, as Bloch does? Can the bipedal human being whom we have encountered as a recurrent primitive creature right from the dawn of civilization at once bear and turn upright? Or is this the spectre of voluntarism—a metaphysics of the gesture? Does the 'feverish line of variation' between the pole of force and that of pain allay the fever or does it inflame it even further?[39]

Accidents are Incidents

Power is the ineluctable force by which the whole ecosystem of the being is brought crashing down without necessarily or overtly disturbing the personality of the being. In this sense, power is at once neutral and equitable. Through the coupling of power and pain, the being is radically reminded of its creaturely status. Sharon Cameron refers to a striking observation by Simone Weil in order to buttress the point: "If it were the human personality in [every man] that was sacred to me, I could easily put out his eyes. As a blind man he would be exactly as much a human personality as before. I should have destroyed nothing but his eyes" (Cameron, 2007). Force penetrates into being's distinctiveness and makes it common.

To appreciate the nonchalant and common nature of power is important. All accidents are incidents—they happen as they would.[40] Every relation is oblique, which is where force appears from, and spills over into the creaturely world. Power is the name of the mimicry of such obliquity. That is what Gabriel Tarde means when he says—*everything is social.* Force works casually in the lives of creatures. It converts beings into creatures. The conditions of force ensure the spread of affliction in such a manner that the coupling can neither be objectively measured, nor subjectively mourned. Creatures are placed in a purgatory, so that grief cannot arrive easily, for grief inevitably propels beings towards idealism. Grief is the mere savouring of pain. It tries to give an unrigorous elegiac dimension to pain. And yet detachment from the creaturely condition is a mirage: philosophy's consolation. There is no heroism in denying or explaining pain away. Pain operates resolutely. Its markings are lucid. Indeed, there are peaks and edges to pain, but there is neither surface, nor depth. There is no wisdom to be gained, for the experience of pain is also a process of oblivion, where pain's workings are spread like lyrical montages all over the creaturely canvas. The nature of the power of force can be realized only by living life and by failing to understand its workings.

Creatures perdure pain without feeling it, for it is a commandment. Feeling has scant consequence for the creature. And yet the same creature keeps babbling and stuttering its way through the condition of painfulness.

This book concludes with Simone Weil's extraordinary letter written to the novelist George Bernanos and its implications on the subject of force and affliction. Among other accomplishments, Bernanos is also the author of the novel *Mouchette*, later made into a singular film by Robert Bresson. *Mouchette* epitomizes the very process of discovering the Spartan exactitude of the creaturely condition, which the young-protagonist is made to realize very early on in life. The coupling of force and misery is relentless. *Mouchette* affirms the truth that casual pettiness and derision firmly reside within the interstices of flowing life. The novel and the film retract every cover of any organizing principle of security and reveal the effects of the unerring, casual power of force—natural, individual, paternal and communal. There is no specific evil to be signalled at, but everywhere creatures live by deriding, abusing and ostracizing the vulnerable, often their own flesh and blood. They mimic sociability at every turn. Consequently, violence lurks in the midst of every practice—from the schoolyard to the deserted forest, from the household to the pub, violence erupts off hand. Partridges and rabbits scurry through the grass and the brambles, hoping for some security cover where there are none. The agile hunters are ready with their guns. They seek game. The ordinary and incidental nature of radical insecurity is hammered on to the bereft—again and again.

But two things are evident. First, the afflicted bear pain nonchalantly, instead of giving in to pathos. Pain speaks for itself. Throughout the film, the young protagonist Mouchette herself reserves an impassive and deliberate mien. It is a trance-like state of ecstasy and withdrawal. Every act of force augments the steeling of the soul, until body and soul turn into the form of pain itself. Bernanos and Bresson (and Weil, in her letter) tell us that violence is a matter of complex interplay of circumstances. The rejected may also reject the world in her own manner.[41] Not once does Mouchette come across as a figure of traumatized innocence in the two works. Gradually, it dawns upon us that power and pain are often reversible cogs in a game of surrogacy. The destitute is an oddity and the odd one has her own logic of action. Eventually, she takes her life in a matter-of-fact fashion, playfully. The abandoned one turns into an *auto-reject.* What kind of beatific protest is that to the condition of affliction? Howard Barker's observations about certain incandescent forms of the tragic seem to perfectly describe the situation: "The frustration of the message sets up an anxiety, while the beauty of the scene locks it in the imagination" (Barker, 1989). The scene denies us any catharsis, but keeps us in a state of radical unease and awe. Mouchette explodes all ethics of benevolence, and yet her life and death show how we are all implicated into making beings into strange creatures. In the process of inflicting force upon another, every being wilfully facilitates its own entry into the cycles of the creaturely purgatory. Second, many of those who perpetrate force over others are themselves unfurnished, helpless and know no better. This is the life the community has known—a community that forever hopes to turn civil, private and transactional. We realize that there is no outright villainy. Yet, everyone is casually cruel; every act arises out of the creatures' thrusting their will upon other creatures. The giants of antiquity lie dormant within us, and given the slightest opportunity, returns triumphant. Perhaps to such an obliquity, Weil gives the name *metaxu*—whereby people are at once connected and separated?

This *elastic reciprocity* of the creaturely life is expressed in a most pellucid manner by the forlorn poet, Jibanananda Das, to whom we must return as long as voice precedes utterance:

> সৃষ্টির নাড়ীর পরে হাত রেখে টের পাওয়া যায় / অসম্ভব বেদনার সাথে মিশে রয়ে গেছে অমোঘ আমোদ; / তবু তারা করেনাকো পরস্পরের ঋণশোধ।
>
> Place your hand upon the pulse of creation and you can feel / Overriding agony is dissolved in decreed pleasure / And yet they do not defray each other's arrears.[42]

The *omen of nothing* is the sign of everything.

Notes

1. Robert Bird. "The Omens: Tarkovsky, Sacrifice, Cancer." *Apparatus. Film, Media and Digital Cultures in Central and Eastern Europe*. No. 10. 2020. An equally powerful rumination on the subject is Lesley Stern's *Diary of a Detour*. Durham: Duke University Press, 2020.

2. Pain is coterminous to affliction in the book, without necessarily invoking the Christian or the Buddhist connotations of the latter. Pain must be distinguished from grief, which is associated with elegy and mourning even if used in the impersonal sense on occasions. Pain is also the opposite of pathos and loss. It can sometimes come close to sorrow, if used in the tragic sense and not as a condition of 'affinity of feeling'. Pain is materially active and pervasive among creatures, and as such, has little to do with detachment and/or transcendence. The equitable spirit of pain is palpable in the neural centres of the creatures and their relationalities. Similarly, power is used in the sense of a penetrative, pervading and inevitable force of contingent necessity. Power coagulates as force, though its form and gathering conditions may vary. Power is sometimes used alongside *fortuna* in the book, which is as historical and social in texture and make-up as it is natural and psychic.
3. For a deliberation on the formal and self-imprisoning patterns of the web of anxiety and pain, see R.D. Laing. *Knots*. New York: Vintage, 1972.
4. See Peter Wessel Zapffe. "The Last Messiah." Trans. Gisle R. Tangenes in *Zapffe in Translation*. https://www.docdroid.net/ape1GYz/zapffe-in-translation-pdf. See also, Zapffe's conversations with Herman Tonnesen, collected in *I Choose Truth* (1983). Zapffe's thoughts on the tragic appears later in this *Introduction* in connection to Simon Critchley's work on the same subject.
5. See Bruno Snell. *The Discovery of the Mind: The Greek Origins of European Thought*. Trans. T.G. Rosenmeyer. Tacoma, WA: Angelico Press, 1953.
6. See Mladen Dolar. *A Voice and Nothing Else*. Cambridge, MA: The MIT Press, 2006.
7. See Leslie Fiedler. "An Introduction to the Life and Writings of Simone Weil," in *Waiting for God*. New York: HarperCollins Publishers, 1951.
8. Maurice Merleau-Ponty. *The Visible and the Invisible*. Chicago: Northwestern University Press, 1968. See also, Mauro Carbone. *The Flesh of Images: Merleau-Ponty between Painting and Cinema*. Trans. Marta Nijhuis, Albany: State University of New York Press, 2015 and Ted Toadvine. "The Chiasm," in *The Routledge Companion to Phenomenology*, Sebastian Luft and Søren Overgaard (eds), London: Routledge, 2012, 336–347. Also see, Louise Westling. *The Logos of the Living World: Merleau-Ponty, Animals, and Language*, New York: Fordham University Press, 2014.
9. David Abram. *The Spell of the Sensuous: Perception and Language in a More-than-Human World*. New York: Pantheon Books, 1996.
10. Nikola Grahek. *Feeling Pain and Being in Pain*. Cambridge, MA: The MIT Press, 2001. See also Daniel Dennett's incisive article "Why You Can't Make a Computer that Feels Pain," in *Brainstorms*, Cambridge, MA: The

MIT Press, 1978 and Valerie Hardcastle. "When a Pain is Not," *The Journal of Philosophy*, 94(8): 381–409, 1997 and her *The Myth of Pain*, Cambridge, MA: The MIT Press, 1999.

11. One of the lessons of how not to make an objective fetish out of pain is to consider Ernst Jünger's classic work *On Pain*. New York: Telos Press Publishing, 1934/2008. Jünger was responding to a strange mix of barbarity and humanity that defines the bourgeoisie, which to him, resembles "an archipelago where an isle of vegetarians exists right next to an island of cannibals." This is prescient. But in order to get into the "peculiar mechanics and economy of pain", Jünger espouses a form of noble detachment and wholly jettisons subjective authenticity. Furthermore, his economy of pain is suffused in the language of a communal sacrifice, which this work steadfastly shuns. Finally, in Junger, pain is a benchmark to discern race, which is a richly misguided venture. A defensive fatalism drives Jünger's quest; not any sense of creaturely vulnerability.
12. See Max Scheler. "On the Tragic." Trans. Bernard Stambler. *CrossCurrents*, Winter, 1954, 4(2): 178–191.
13. See Sasheej Hegde and Sanjay Palshikar. "Caste and 'Seeing Double—The Challenge of Aniket Jaaware's Practicing Caste'" *EPW*, Volume 54.43, October 2019, for trying to understand Jaaware's method through the dual lens of philosophical archeology and genealogy, both being scaffolded by the specificities of ontology in Jaaware's book on caste and destitution. Though Hegde and Palshikar do not 'touch' the other axis of Jaaware's work, that is, the tropological way of engaging with the literary, the essay is a serious attempt to engage with the sociological implications of working with ontology and difference in matters of pain and power in Jaaware. In *Powers of Horror: An Essay on Abjection*, Julia Kristeva, of course, has read the abject, as not only as the site of radical exclusion, but also as a precondition for narcissism: "Abjection preserves what existed in the archaism of pre-objectal relationship, in the immemorial violence with which a body becomes separated from another body in order to be." The anomalous-abject to Kristeva is like the skin that develops on a glass of hot milk. Jaaware often uses destitution in a similar sense—something that is permanently thrust aside in order to live.
14. For a succinct discussion on the idea of 'life-alien', see Chapter 23, "Visions of the Post-Romantic Age," in Charles Taylor. *Sources of the Self*. Cambridge, MA: Harvard University Press, 1989.
15. For an in-depth and interdisciplinary discussion on deep time, see Chapter 2 in *Battle in the Mind Fields*, John A. Goldsmith and Bernard Laks. Chicago: University of Chicago Press, 2019. See also, Stephen J. Gould. *Time Arrow, Time's Cycle*. New York: Penguin, 2000 and Henry Gee. *In*

Search of Deep Time: Beyond the Fossil Record to a New History of Life, Ithaca: Cornell University Press, 2000.

16. Hans Blumenberg. *Work on Myth*, trans. Robert M. Wallace. Cambridge, MA: The MIT Press, 1985. By contrast, to Walter Benjamin, the originary impulses are the demonic-ambiguous and the spectral, but he opposes any morphological form of myth as a vehicle to metamorphosis in the tradition of Spengler and Blumenberg. He is, however, inclined to include sub-rational insights into history in the tradition of Goethe. For elaboration on this point, see Kirk Wetters. *Demonic History: from Goethe to the Present*. Evantson, IL: Northwestern University Press, 2015. See also, the first three chapters in Jan Patočka. *Heretical Essays in the Philosophy of History*. Chicago and La Salle, Illinois: Open Court, 1996.
17. Giambattista Vico. *The New Science*. Trans. Thomas Goddard Bergin and Max Harold Fisch, Ithaca: Cornell University Press, 1948. See also his *On Humanistic Education*: (Six Inaugural Orations, 699-1707). Trans. Giorgio A. Pinton and Arthur W. Shippee. Ithaca: Cornell University Press, 1993 and *On the Study Methods of Our Time*. Trans. Elio Gianturco. Ithaca: Cornell University Press. On the same subject see further, Max Scheler. *Man's Place in Nature*. Trans. Hans Meyerhoff. New York: Beacon Press, 1961 and Arnold Gehlen. *Man: His Nature and Place in the World*, trans. Clare McMillan and Karl Pillemer. New York: Columbia University Press, 1988. Chapter 2 ("Taboo and the Ambivalence of the Affects") of Sigmund Freud's *Totem and Taboo*. New York: W.W. Norton and Company, 1990 refers to Wilhelm Wundt on the relationship between the demons (as psyche) and the primitive man: "The general commandment . . . that lies behind the numerous variable and unspoken interdictions of taboo . . . is originally a single rule: Guard yourself from the wrath of the demons."
18. For a humanist interpretation of Vico, see Erich Auerbach, "Philologie der Weltliteratur" (1952). 'Philology and Weltliteratur.' Trans. Edward Said and Marie Said. *Centennial Review* 13, 1969. 1–17 and "Vico and Aesthetic Historicism." *The Journal of Aesthetics and Art Criticism* 8.2, 1949, 110–118. See also, Edward Said. *Humanism and Democratic Criticism*. New York: Columbia University Press, 2004. For an onto-theological reading of Vico, see John Milbank. *The Religious Dimension in the Thought of Giambattista Vico*. 2 parts. Lewiston: Edwin Mellen Press, 1991.
19. Friedrich Schlegel refers to a 'new mythology' that demolishes the 'laws of reasonably thinking reason' and re-establishes the 'swarm of ancient gods'. See Friedrich Schlegel. "Dialogue on Poesy," in *Theory as Practice: A Critical Anthology of Early German Romantic Writings*. Ed. and Trans. Jochen Schulte-Sasse. Minneapolis: University of Minnesota Press, 1997.

20. See Massimo Lollini. "On Becoming Human: The 'Verum Factum' Principle and Giambattista Vico's Humanism." *MLN*, Vol. 127, No. 1, Italian Issue Supplement. Tra Amici: Essays in Honor of Giuseppe Mazzotta, January 2012, pp. 21–31. See also, Paolo Rossi. *The Dark Abyss of Time: The History of the Earth and the History of Nations from Hooke to Vico*. Trans. Lydia Cochrane, Chicago: University of Chicago Press, 1984.
21. See Maurice Godelier. *The Enigma of Gift*. Chicago: University of Chicago Press, 1999. See also Michael Taussig. *Defacement: Public Secrecy and the Labour of the Negative*. Stanford: Stanford University Press, 1999.
22. On the role reversal in the hunter–hunted relationship, one has to only recall the opening line of Hans Blumenberg's esoteric and reflective work, *Lions*: "If Lions could paint, their hunters would be the hunted." See *Lions*. Calcutta, London, New York: Seagull Books, 2018.
23. For an appreciation of the notion of sacred 'conjunctions' and the practice of power, see A. Azfar Moin. *The Millennial Sovereign*. New York: Columbia University Press, 2012. See also, Laura Ackerman Smoller. *History, Prophecy and the Stars*, Princeton, NJ: Princeton University Press, 1994, Marc Bloch. *The Royal Touch: Sacred Monarchy and Scrofula in England and France*. London: Routledge and Kegan Paul, 1973 and Clifford Geertz. "Centres, Kings, and Charisma: Reflections on the Symbolics of Power," in *Local Knowledge: Further Essays in Interpretive Anthropology*. New York: Basic Books, 1967.
24. The naturalistic explanation takes us towards explaining tumults in terms of humours and body fluids as explained by Gabreile Pedulla in *Machiavelli in Tumult: The Discourses on Livy and the Origins of Political Conflictualism*. Cambridge, UK: Cambridge University Press, 2018. Pedulla calls this tendency Machiavelli's 'anthropological turn'. For the conjunctional in Machiavelli, see Anthony J. Parel's pioneering work, *The Machiavellian Cosmos*. New Haven: Yale University Press, 1992. For an extension of the principle of polarity and the idea of 'war of gods' in the exercise of power, see Thomas Read. "Machiavelli, Hobbes, Clausewitz, and Foucault: Four Variations on the Zero-Sum Theme," in Sharon R. Krause and Mary Ann Mcgrail. *The Arts of Rule: Essays in Honour of Harvey C. Mansfield*. Lanham: Lexington Books, 2009.
25. For this particular point about freedom's essential passage through necessity, see Roberto Esposito. *The Origin of the Political: Hannah Arendt or Simone Weil*. New York: Fordham University Press, 2017. Esposito says this about understanding of force in the Homeric epic by three leading critics of the work, Bruno Snell, E.R. Dodds and Georges Dumezil: "Snell considered that in Homer 'mental and spiritual acts are due to the impact

of external factors, and man is the open target of a great many forces which impinge upon him, and penetrate his very core'. This explains the proliferation of terms that the poet uses in order to substantiate the word "force": *menos* (the force that is felt in the limbs), *alchē* (defensive force against enemy assaults), *sthenos* (the power to dominate), and so on. On the other hand, Dodds saw in *ate* neither 'a personified operator; nor an objective "ruin," but insanity caused by an external demonic force. For Dumézil, heroes appear 'dedicated to Force, they are the triumphant victims of the internal logic of Force, which proves itself only by surpassing bound *aries*—even its own bound *aries* and those of its raison d'etre.'"

26. See Julia V. Sineokaya and Anton M. Khokhlov. "Lev Shestov's Philosophy of Freedom." *Studies in East European Thought*, Vol. 68.2/3, September 2016: 213–227.
27. In Chapter 1, "The Man of Flesh and Blood," of his *The Tragic Sense of Life*, Miguel de Unamuno recounts a "pedant who beheld Solon weeping for the death of a son said to him, 'Why do you weep thus, if weeping avails nothing?' And the sage answered him, 'Precisely for that reason—because it does not avail.' It is manifest that weeping avails something, even if only the alleviation of distress; but the deep sense of Solon's reply to the impertinent questioner is plainly seen. And I am convinced that we should solve many things if we wept out in the streets and uncovered our griefs, which perhaps would prove to be but one sole common grief, and joined together in beweeping them and crying aloud to the heaven's and calling upon God. And this, even though God should not hear us; but He would hear us." This is the sensibility that Shestov wants us to appreciate, so that all abstractions about affliction can be denied. The daemonic-divine is at once dreadful and alluring to the creature-devotee. The robustness of such an encounter is quite different from the mitigating, partial theodicy of C.S. Lewis' Christian apology, *The Problem of Pain*. London: Centenary Press, 1940.
28. See Raymond Geuss. *Who Needs a Worldview?* Cambridge, MA and London: Harvard University Press, 2020. In the chapter on "Games and Proverbs," he compares his life to two of Bruegel's paintings, *Children's Games* and *Netherlandish Proverbs*: "My awareness of my own life is a series of flickering moments, located in various of the personages in the panel and, very occasionally, incorporating the imagined perspective in a fictional observer (including, possibly, Bruegel himself, as I imagine him to have been at various points during the production of the picture). Even this is an imaginary projection of mine at a certain point in time. There is no point, not even an imaginary one, from which all of this looks like a

single, unitary anything." This is an exercise in Montaignesque scepticism, powerfully engaged with the variety that life offers us and yet recognizing the fleeting, contingent nature of it.

29. See the Introduction by Robert Chandler in *Soul*, Andrei Platonov. New York: New York Review Books, 2008.
30. For an elaboration on the same issue framed within a comparative framework, see Georges Dumezil's notion of the 'trifunctional hierarchy,' distributed among the priests, the warriors and the commoners, especially as it comes across in *The Destiny of the Warrior*, trans. Alf Hiltebeitel, Chicago: University of Chicago Press, 1970, *Mitra-Varuna: An Essay on Two Indo European Representations of Sovereignty*. New York; Zone Books, 1988 and *Gods of the Ancient Northmen*, Berkeley: University of California Press, 1973. See also Paul Veyne. *Did the Greeks Believe in Their Myths?: An Essay on the Constitutive Imagination*. Chicago, University of Chicago Press, 1988, John Colarusso. *Myths from The Caucasus: The Nart Sagas of the Circassians, Abazas, Abkhaz, and Ubykh*. Princeton: Princeton University Press, 2002, J.P. Mallory. *In Search of the Irish Dreamtime: Archaeology & Early Irish literature*. London: Thames and Hudson, 2016 and M.L. West. *Indo-European Poetry and Myth*. Oxford: Oxford University Press, 2007. For the relationship between myth and tragedy see, Jean-Pierre Vernant and Pierre Vidal-Naquet. *Myth and Tragedy in Ancient Greece*. Princeton: Princeton University Press, 1988.
31. In his tracing a radical sophist impulse in tragedy, Critchley seems to be treading an independent line of thought that steers clear of the settled conservative approach to the tragic (as exemplified in George Steiner's *The Death of Tragedy*, for instance) as well as the left teleological variations on the subject (as encountered in Terry Eagleton's *Sweet Violence*, for instance). Critchley's interest is also not semiological and symbolic in the sense that Umberto Eco uses the term 'sudden epiphany' to describe the tragic-dramatic process/experience in *The Limits of Interpretation*.
32. For a notion of tragedy as a form of longing within dwelling, see *The Diaries of Paul Klee*. Trans. P. Schneider, R.T. Zachary and M. Knight. Berkeley: California University Press, 1964. See also, María del Rosario Acosta López. "Tragic Representation: Paul Klee on Tragedy and Art." *Research in Phenomenology*. Vol. 43.3, 2013: 443–461.
33. See Letter Twenty through Letter Twenty-Seven in Friedrich Schiller. *On The Aesthetic Education of Man*. London: Penguin Books, 2016.
34. See Paul De Man. "The Rhetoric of Temporality" in *Blindness and Insight: Essays in the Rhetoric of Contemporary Criticism*, Minneapolis: University

of Minnesota Press, 2010. See also Maurice Blanchot. *The Infinite Conversation*. Trans. Susan Hanson, University of Minnesota Press, 1993, Rudolphe Gasché. *Of Minimal Things: Studies on the Notion of Relation*. Palo Alto: Stanford University Press, 1999 and Philippe Lacoue-Labarthe et al. *Of the Sublime: Presence in Question*. Trans. Jeffrey S. Librett. Albany, NY: State University of New York Press. 1993.

35. George Steiner. *Real Presences: Is There Anything in What We Say?* London: Faber and Faber, 1989. See also his *Grammars of Creation*, London: Faber and Faber, 2010. See also, Simon Leys. *The Hall of Uselessness*, New York: New York Review Books, 2011.
36. See J.M. Coetzee's second Tanner Lecture "The Poets and the Animals" in *The Lives of Animals*. Princeton: Princeton University Press, 1999.
37. Jacques Ranciere's *Nights of Labour: The Workers Dream in Nineteenth Century France* is another classic instance that rummages freedom of the heroic in art, though the forms explored are not necessarily expressive in the Blochian sense. See also the works of Alexander Bogdanov for a similar sensibility of a *gauchiste* interest in will and energy.
38. In an inspired pronouncement, Fortini says: "Contradiction, monstrosity, illegality, evil—they all demand citizenship in the world of the living, once again. In each and every one of us there is a part that is the daughter of Minos and Pasiphae, of the contradiction between reality principle and pleasure principle. The wretched, and the wretched parts of humanity, want to be accepted, contradiction wants at the same time to be lived, overcome and posed again." See the chapter on "Deus Absconditus" in Franco Fortini. *A Test of Powers*. Trans. Alberto Toscano. London, New York, Calcutta: Seagull Books, 2016.
39. See Gilles Deleuze. *Negotiations: 1972–1990*. Trans. Martin Joughin. New York: Columbia University Press, 1995. See also, *The Crisis in Modernism: Bergson and the Vitalist Controversy*. Eds. Frederick Burwick and Paul Douglass. Cambridge: Cambridge University Press, 1992 and Neil Donahue. *Forms of Disruption: Abstraction in Modern German Prose*. Ann Arbor: University of Michigan Press, 1993. Many of the expressionist concepts encountered in these texts partly go back to Wilhelm Worringer's *Abstraction and Empathy: A Contribution to the Psychology of Style*. Eastford, CT: Martino Fine Books, 2014. Worringer is deeply invested in exploring the tension between cultures that go though anxiety and spiritual quest and those which view the world through science and matter. For an aesthetic reconfiguration of the regimes of the sensible, also see Davide Panagia's *The Political Life of Sensation*. Durham, NC: Duke University Press, 2009.

40. See Odo Marquard. *In Defence of the Accidental*. Trans. Robert M. Wallace. New York and Oxford: Oxford University Press, 1991. Marquard makes a crucial distinction between the *arbitrarily accidental* and the *fatefully accidental*—the latter constitutes the "transformation of extreme situations into routines."
41. See Irving Goh. *The Reject: Community, Politics, and Religion after the Subject*. New York: Fordham University Press, 2015. Goh provides a three-pronged definition of the reject: "The *reject*, as I would like to conceptualize it here, is constituted by three turns. The first turn concerns the *reject* as it is conventionally understood: a passive figure targeted to be denied, denigrated, negated, disregarded, disposed of, abandoned, banished, or even exiled. The *reject* is not always passive, however. In its turn, it can actively express a force of rejection in retaliation to the external forces acting against it. The *reject* can in fact also be the one who *first* rejects things and people around it with a force so overwhelming that it is only *subsequently* rendered a *reject* by those around it. Whichever the case, the active force of rejection constitutes the second turn of the *reject*. The third turn concerns the *reject*'s turning of the force of rejection around on itself, and this is where one may speak of the *auto-reject*."
42. "Abohoman," from *Jibanananda Das er Srestho Kobita/Selected Poems of Jibanananda Das*. Kolkata: Navana, 1954.

References

Abram, David. 1996. *The Spell of the Sensuous: Perception and Language in a More-than-Human World*. New York: Pantheon Books.

Barker, Howard. 1989. *Arguments for a Theatre*. London: John Calder Publishers Ltd.

Bird, Robert. 2020. "The Omens: Tarkovsky, Sacrifice, Cancer." In *Apparatus. Film, Media and Digital Cultures in Central and Eastern Europe*. No. 10.

Blumenberg, Hans. 1985. *Work on Myth*. Translated by Robert M. Wallace. Cambridge, MA: The MIT Press.

Cameron, Sharon. 2007. *Impersonality, Seven Essays*. Chicago and London: University of Chicago Press.

———. 2000. *Beautiful Work: A Meditation on Pain*. Durham: Duke University Press.

Ceylan, Nuri Bilge. 1997. *Kasaba/The Small Town*. NBC Film.

Chamayou, Gregoire. 2012. *Manhunts: A Philosophical History*. Translated by Steven Rendall. Princeton: Princeton University Press.

Coetzee, J.M. 1999. *The Lives of Animals*. Princeton: Princeton University Press.

Das, Jibanananda. 1954. *Jibanananda Das er Srestho Kobita/Selected Poems of Jibanananda Das*. Kolkata: Navana.

Dolar, Mladen. 2006. *A Voice and Nothing Else*. Cambridge, MA: The MIT Press.

Esposito, Roberto. 2015. *Categories of the Impolitical*. Translated by Connal Parsley. New York: Fordham University Press.

Fiedler, Leslie. 1951. *Waiting for God*. New York: HarperCollins Publishers.

Foreman, Richard. 2013. *The Manifestoes and Essays*. New York: Theatre Communications Group.

Fortini, Franco. 2016. *A Test of Powers*. Translated by Alberto Toscano. London, New York, Calcutta: Seagull Books.

Geuss, Raymond. 2020. *Who Needs a Worldview?* Cambridge, MA and London: Harvard University Press.

Godelier, Maurice. 1999. *The Enigma of Gift*. Chicago: University of Chicago Press.

Grahek, Nikola. 2001. *Feeling Pain and Being in Pain*. Cambridge, MA: The MIT Press.

Harpham, Geoffrey Galt. 2001. "Elaine Scarry and the Dream on Pain." In *Salmagundi*, No. 130/131, Spring–Summer: 202–234.

Jünger, Ernst. 1934/2008. *On Pain*. New York: Telos Press Publishing.

Kristeva, Julia. 1982. *Powers of Horror: An Essay on Abjection*. Translated by Leon. S. Roudiez. New York: Columbia University Press.

Lollini, Massimo. 2011. "Vico's More than Human Humanism." In *Annalid'Italianistica*. Vol. 29, Italian Critical Theory: 381–399.

Longinus. 1965. "On the Sublime." In *Classical Literary Criticism*. Translated by T.S. Dorsch. Harmondsworth: Penguin.

Negri, Antonio. 1999. *Insurgencies: Constituent Power and the Modern State*. Translated by Maurizia Boscagli. Minneapolis and London: University of Minnesota Press.

Nelson, Maggie. 2011. *The Art of Cruelty: A Reckoning*. New York and London: W.W. Norton and Company.

———. 2009. *Bluets*. Seattle and New York: Wave Books.

Platonov, Andrei. 2008. *Soul*. New York: New York Review Books.

Scarry, Elaine. 1985. *The Body in Pain: The Making and Unmaking of the World*. Oxford: Oxford University Press.

Scheler, Max. 1954. "On the Tragic." Translated by Bernard Stambler. *CrossCurrents*. Vol. 4, No. 2, Winter: 178–191.

Schiller, Friedrich. 2016. *On the Aesthetic Education of Man*. London: Penguin Books.

Snell, Bruno. 1953. *The Discovery of the Mind: The Greek Origins of European Thought*. Translated by T.G. Rosenmeyer. Tacoma, WA: Angelico Press.

Sontag, Susan. 2003. *Regarding the Pain of Others*. New York: Picador/Farrar, Straus and Giroux.

Starobinski, Jean. 2008. *Enchantment: The Seduction in Opera*. New York: Columbia University Press.

Steiner, George. 1989. *Real Presences: Is There Anything in What We Say?* London: Faber and Faber.

Unamuno, Miguel de. 1921/2013. *The Tragic Sense of Life*. London: Macmillan and Co. Ltd.

Vico, Giambattista. 1999. *The New Science*. London: Penguin Books.

Weil, Simone. 2015. *First and Last Notebooks*. Eugene: Wipf & Stock Publishers.

Zapffe, Peter Wessel. 1933 and 1941/1983. "The Last Messiah" and "Summery to 'On the Tragic.'" Translated by Gisle R. Tangenes in *Zapffe in Translation*. https://www.docdroid.net/ape1GYz/zapffe-in-translation-pdf. Accession date: 10 May 2021.

Zaretsky, Robert. 2021. *The Subversive Simone Weil: A Life in Five Ideas*. Chicago: University of Chicago Press.

BOOK I

The Imitative Creature

The Catacombs of Invisible Stars: Gabriel Tarde's *Underground Man*

> In the forced intimacy of a cave there is no mean between warfare and love, between mutual slaughter or mutual embraces.
>
> —Gabriel Tarde (*Underground Man*)

There is no way to be fair with Gabriel Tarde. How can one possibly be even remotely fair with someone who is simultaneously the high priest of imitation and anti-sociality, of auxiliary but relational monads floating about in affinity and of the sacrificial, castaway terrestrial task-force working tirelessly within the bowels of the earth for the establishment of a new order under the instruction of a heroic innovator? There is "something irrational at the bottom of the inevitable," Tarde says right at the onset of his famous work on imitation (Tarde, 1903). And large moments of historical swings happen through contingent turn of events, he suggests. But how can the contingent force be also inevitable? Or are there only molecular traces that collide with each other, differentiate and diffuse and lead to a gradual equilibrium until that equilibrium destroys itself to molecules? Can there be a direction to what is repetitive? One can only hope to be partial in understanding these apparently simple but fundamental conundrums. These paradoxes are also at the heart of the encounter of the creature with the unknown, the acknowledgement of its abjectness and the power of its adaptability to resurrect.

Gabriel Tarde has been demonized for about a century for advancing a kind of *pansocial ontology* and *nested reality* (Tarde, 2012). The past three decades, by contrast, have witnessed a Tardean revival of sorts—a phenomenon that has also been critiqued as 'presentist transgressions' by Tarde's detractors. Each such attempt tries to make a case for the whole of his thinking. In vain. Sociology cannot own him. In fact, much of it does not know what to do with him, barring few who have transcended the narrow bounds of the discipline. So, let us try a roundabout way and read afresh a forgotten fragment from his eclectic oeuvre: the story of the hero with a scarred face who almost died with the distinction of a monomaniac along with his morally atavistic ladylove. This is the story about the ardour of Miltiades and Lydia. And the consequences of such heroic exploits for humanity.

A Fortunate Disaster

The end of the 20th century: the era is prehistoric, which was formerly called Christian. This is the setting for the *Underground Man*. In the beginning, there was extraordinary prosperity. The Asiatic-American-European confederacy was in ascendency. There have been terrible and protracted wars to bring about peace. There were no enmities among nations anymore. And now the fruits of the war could be actually savoured, for "of all this warlike mania there only remained a vague poetic remembrance. Forgetfulness is the beginning of happiness, as fear is the beginning of wisdom" (Tarde, 1905). Not lethargy, but calm prevailed. Or it seemed so. The military personnel were now 'intelligently selected' in conjunction with the incomparable beauty of the human race. In contrast to this new and improved version, humans of the yore looked like dwarfs and scare-crows. All microbes were gone. No patient of the rheum or consumption anywhere to be seen. There was not much small talk or needless pleasantries to be exchanged. The epidemic spread of sensational journalism, a phenomenon of the marauding hordes, was over.

The universal language was now Greek—the language of Demosthenes. All rudeness was brought to a halt. Other dialects like French or German sounded gibberish to the city people, though those were sometimes practiced in some isolated rural areas and grottos. Ideas flourished, thanks to the unification of language. And industry flourished too. Gone were all the products of neo-Hegelian influence and the scholars found the verses of Shakespeare, Goethe and Victor Hugo to be rugged and jarring to the refined senses. The more vulgar copied and imitated these authors of the past. Pericles, Homer and Aristophanes returned in their full glory. The ears and eyes of the readers and audience were saturated with classical restraint and romantic ardour. Alexandrines, hexameters and iambics reverberated.

Poetry regained its legitimate rank—the premier. All these happened since humans were once again attentive to the nuances of language and the exchanges of relationship. 'Eternal truisms' and verity once again began to reign.

The masses too participated freely in appreciating the masterpieces of art and literature. Nature had been successfully harnessed and therefore domestic helps, artisans and repairmen had lost all roles. Some voluntary workmen helped increase productivity multiple folds. In the social front, mutual quarrels had disappeared. Everyone could reap the benefits of wealth and competence freely. Love too was in the air and available—good looks were abundant and it was easy to please lovers. The only desire left to be fulfilled was political in nature. Owing to socialistic centralization, covetousness, lust and envy heightened and took gigantic proportions—in order to grab state power. Power was centralized and universal suffrage seemed impractical and meaningless. Electoral privileges got suppressed, while the number of electoral districts increased. Feudalism reconstituted itself into a successful monarchy. A philosopher financier ruled the earth.

Science turned simplified and popular. Art and architecture flourished. Great structures were built and transferred with the aid of harnessed energy: "The stored energy, electrically conveyed, of a hundred Abyssinian waterfalls, and of, do not know, how many cyclones, hardly sufficed to transport from the mountains of Armenia the necessary stone, wood and iron for these numerous constructions" (Tarde, 1905). Museums were thronged and certain schoolbooks were printed in cuneiform characters, so that an ancient authority enhances the youthful and imaginative minds of the young ones. But under the philosopher financier, commonness of bearing was the order of the day. All choices followed the following dictum: *the most useful and the best among the most unattractive.* Insipidity and monotony were the reigning notes of governance. Artists moved away from governance, since it was generally agreed "that the superiority of the politician is only mediocrity raised to its highest power" (Tarde, 1905). It was as if the greatest sociologist was not Auguste Comte, but Menenius Agrippa, who said that the government is only the stomach and not the head of any social organism. The best government is always humdrum. The whole scene, in short, was that of *gratuitous abundance.*

It is at the point that the sun began to show anaemic tendencies. The temperature of the earth began to fall rapidly. Initially no one believed, save a few heretics and sensationalists, that stars could burn themselves out to oblivion. Orthodox science still had faith in the slow and steady evolution of the universe. But it seems that the anaemia had become apoplexy by the winter of 2489. The spring colours were pale and drab. The tints of the sky turned chameleon-like and the leaves and the water in the lakes changed rapidly. Disasters aggravated: "The entire population of Norway, Northern Russia, and Siberia perished—frozen to death in a single night; the temperate zone was decimated, and what was left of its inhabitants fled before the enormous drifts of snow and ice, and emigrated by hundreds of millions towards the tropics, crowding into the panting trams, several of which, overtaken by tornadoes of snow, disappeared forever" (Tarde, 1905).

Avalanches blocked enormous areas and rivers stopped flowing—frozen to the bottom. There followed draughts and famines so indescribably horrible that mothers were forced to devour their own children. Whole continents lost connection with the central agency. Telegraph, electricity and railroads, all were gone or lied scattered. Iced lavas from glaciers began to flow to the plains. Humans were truly back in the glacial age, and water and ice and slush took over "as an advancing army recaptures and enfurls its ancient flags, all covered with dust" (Tarde, 1905). Was this the final and fatal blitz?

Few million humans, those who could, the last remnants of the third planet of a frozen sun, took refuge in the caverns of Arabia Petracia, few hundred yards deep below the surface of the earth. Along with Arabia, the Sahara region became the most populous region under the earth where wave after wave of human hordes took refuge. Glaciers covered the top of both regions, but fortuitously, a couple of virgin coal mines were discovered underneath. A new town was constructed gradually by using breakthrough architectural skills. Now warmth could be assured for years to come—that was the hope. Will the frozen corns sprout, was the immediate question? The sun did shine for a while, but then turned violet. Nothing was eatable. The cold once again became intolerable. Walls cracked and waves of wind and gale led to a speculation that the atmosphere could decompose into its constituent elements. The rivers and the seas were already thick ice. There was government stove, but that was too meagre a support. A whole population turned into icicles overnight and in the following night, many others met their undignified and decomposed end. Those humans who remained were the last trustees of the human race—rattled, spent, quivering.

In such a grave situation arose a man called Miltiades (the name of course reminds us of the commanding presence of the Greek general and statesman of the yore), who we are told in this case, was a cross between a slave and a Briton. The defining characteristic of Miltiades is that the germs of breach and recalcitrance lay deep within his soul. But this disbeliever in civilization was the one perhaps who was needed to produce something unique in order to arrest the downfall of humankind and its lost glories. For he is the very *principle of generative radiation, the first ovulary cell* (Tarde, 2012). He is eloquent and taciturn at the same time and is, as it were, a mix between Chateaubriand and Napoleon in features. Men and women are in awe of Miltiades. He was a great explorer and adventurer. He had once fought such a great combat against some 'Bible reading savages' that he was declared to be insane and monomaniac. Although it was actually an atavistic heroic state that he found himself in. In the same combat, his face was disfigured and he turned into the scarred-face hero. He was relegated into oblivion as a madman until Miltiades returned as the prodigal in that great cavern at the time of the gravest calamity. He reached the state shelter. Those who huddled around him, the splendid lot now in misery, are the apprentices, the secretaries and the deputies of the so-called great men and women. Models and fashionist as flocked around him too. Among them is Princess Lydia, who stood out as stately and exquisite. She was the winner of the last grand international beauty contest.

"Youth, beauty, genius, art, infinite treasures of science and art"—the remnants of distilled culture is now the concentrated miserable last vestiges of human beings. Miltiades is himself tall, lean and wizened, and donned a cowl like hood upon his figure. The scar shone athwart his visage. Lydia is all admiration and astonishment for the scarred hero. She "remained imbued with this sentiment of another age, by a kind of moral ancestral reversion which served as a pendant to her physical atavism" (Tarde, 1905). At that point, Miltiades breaks into a discourse for the rapt crowd—which was a combination of his story of being exiled, his tenacity, bravery and arrival at the right conjuncture of history to deliver human beings from their slavery to pestilence and calamities. Nothing like this was experienced by man since the geological epochs, he begins, and then starts revealing the blueprint of a most extraordinary and extravagant project of renewal and resurrection. The first thing was to look inward rather than out to the cosmos for sustenance and energy—that is to say, to seek sustenance in earth itself rather than in some distant star called sun which has betrayed the earthlings. The earth and the sun were coterminous and the earth hides within its bowels a tremendous source of virgin energy, far superior than what sun give us, that is yet to be explored by humans.

The depths and abyss were the most certain retreats for earthlings. They must seek salvation below, not above themselves. The inner selves must be ignited: "The mystics had a sublime presentiment when they said in their Latin: 'From the outward to the inward'" (Tarde, 1905). We now return to our authentic existence which was shrouded by the artificial one that had lived on the surface of the earth. To bring the project into fruition Miltiades urged patience, discipline and courage. Civilization must return to where it started: the caves. In fact, humans must dig far deeper. Designs and drawings soon led to the creation of an alternative realm, with marvellous crypts and cloisters, all illuminated in light and splendour. Ice was melted to produce water and wine from water, alcohol and mineralized rock. Soon more refined stages of gastronomy were reached from the most inexhaustible larder: the animals, humans and other beings buried under the ice. It was an endless quarry.

Miltiades further made an immense claim that life, thought and love cannot be the privilege of only those systems which are awash with light and temperature. Other spaces also have the right to live. Unquenchable fire lies within planets and celestial bodies—the catacombs of invisible stars—which cannot be often seen from the surface. This was the new arc of Noah, which instead of animals, shall carry the artistic and poetic achievements of the humans to the next phase of civilization. A vast library will be created to preserve such creations; "enriched with cinematographic albums" (Tarde, 1905). The crowd cheered as

Lydia kissed Miltiades after his triumphant speech. This stamped the idea that indeed she was morally atavistic. The younger generation was particularly buoyed by such hope and applause. The love and mutual respect that the valiant two reserved for each other sparked the rarest of heroism and innovation among others. This was the real cause that humanity could avoid the fate of the other animal and arboreal species: "What strikes us today in his discourse is the extraordinary and truly prophetic lucidity with which he sketched in general terms the conditions of existence in the new world" (Tarde, 1905). Consequently, tens of thousands 'auxiliary geniuses' bloomed. The ardour of the two had percolated down.

The success of the new creations and the work of salvation depended as much on enthusiasm as on a realization about their sacrifice and a sense of duty. The workers knew that they were dilettantes. But their job was to now to recreate humanity afresh, keeping civilization intact. This sense electrified their spirit—which was a mix of ardour and onus. This collective requirement of individual self-sacrifice is at the heart of all new beginning for "we know from the treatises on natural history that have been preserved, that mere insects giving the same example of foresight and self-renunciation, used before their death to employ their latest energies to collect provisions useless to themselves, and only useful in the future to their larvae at their birth" (Tarde, 1905).

Innovation, Syllogism and Preservation

What does it mean to be resurrected after coming close to species-obliteration? Was humanity the slave of nature until that time, clumsily dealing with the vagaries of creation? Was the geological disaster, like the fall, a fortunate and momentous event in giving shape and direction to human destiny by means of converting them into truly social beings? How could the 'new troglodytes'—each a little god—come out victorious by means of winnowing, honing and improving nature? What is the new social mode of perpetual perfection and order that the antiquated socialists could not imagine?

The apparent work of fiction is indeed a fantastic exercise in social reorganization—derived out of the fundamental insight that "nature, organic and inorganic, at all scales from atoms to stars and galaxies, consists of societies" (Tarde, 2012). As a consequence, new processes of social order are created and given shape by Tarde without necessarily subjectivizing the participating individuals (troglodytes) into known models of hegemony and yet a willing world of discipline is enforced over this perfected universe by subtle means—by regulating art, love and scientific excess. Indeed, through a process of fortunate event, which is a fictional construct to take us back to a state of bereft abjectness and geological calamity, Tarde creates the conditions for his sociological experiment to take place. But the work is also a stupendous sojourn into imaginative literature itself. The space of real-fiction lies between the miraculous and the mimetic. A cornucopia of figurative usages, events and objects tumble over this newly-created interstice of the 'underground' as the story progresses. This veritable museum of creations is then brought to regulation through a rarified mode of social cohesion and order. Consequently, there is a disjunction. More of that anon.

Once the calamity happens, the whole process passes through an extraordinary innovator, who dares to take certain individual steps, which are the creations and outcomes of his reflective mind and courageous self. The reflections are conjoined with deed/action. Those reflections are, of course, sold to the followers who were waiting agog for the innovators to arrive and deliver—first at the level of actionable hope. The story of the mythical rise of humanity is aided by natural bounty, more fortunate events and a tremendous human zeal to survive, excel and flourish in the cavernous depths of the planet. The question of labour and service are adjourned and held back.

The issue and nature of individual agency is at the centre of a long-standing debate among Tarde scholars. On one hand stands the agreement that the radical libertarianism of Tarde is fundamentally a world view that is centred on contingency, that the individual monads act as assemblages, which fuse and detach themselves according to conditions. There is no bounded selfhood, but rather a host of floating cybernetic selves that touch each other at times and then drift. The assemblages form and re-form. Monads, by this account, are distinct conscious entities, which contingently interact with other such entities. This is a radical account of the self. The contending view believes, however, that the individual entities in Tarde are reflective, responsible and imitative, and such entities work towards a clear social and moral telos through mutual interaction. The second reading imputes conservative individualism over Tarde's thoughts, which ultimately rely upon a concoction of belief and desire and their restrained channelling in the right directions in order for the society to flourish at a high optimal level.

The character of Miltiades is crafted with care. Here is someone who had been banished as a monomaniac since he had a streak of heroism that verged on the deep romantic irrational. Even for a heroic society, the idea of courage and fortitude are sensible virtues to be used for the collective good. And the ancient human society that carried its business on the surface of the earth was primarily prosperous in a superficially sane manner, since it did not know how to use the creative genius of the heroic individual who starts all processes of social transformation. Miltiades, therefore, arrives as a messiah at the right moment. This is indeed the contingent moment of the supreme catastrophe, where human beings have been decimated by nature as a species. The clumsy dealing of natural forces by the erstwhile humans has come home to roost. It is here that we see how important monomaniacal passion is for galvanizing a whole people, who wait to be imitative and labour blindly in order to get the better of nature. At the time of acute contingency, the steadfast force of genius gives direction, first by arousing faith in the tribe of the beautiful humans, and then, gives shape most sensibly by offering certain simple and direct ways of resuscitation and then thriving. It is impossible to distinguish the creative reflective ideas of the heroic innovator, the fortuitous help the bowels of the earth provides him with and the methods of the innovator which are extremely practical and sociable in nature. One recalls that in his book on imitation, Tarde had pronounced that "the individual often innovates unconsciously" (Tarde, 1903) and that some innovations arise out of themselves though they seem like conscious initiatives on the part of the individual creator. Initiatives simply *arrive* and yet, once projected, they seem scandalously realizable. The solutions that Miltiades offer are clinical in nature. They could be realized to such an extent that human beings eventually realized the strength and beauty of the truly social that could be achieved simply by harnessing earthly forces. All energy was social.

Nothing was natural anymore, and hence, humans did not need to rely upon nature and worry about its cosmological and geological vagaries.

The next important shift that happens after the flourish is the way Miltiades is disposed of his own creation and the underlying reasons for his demise. It is here that Tarde seems to be sceptical of the romantic hero. Time and again Tarde has acknowledged that in spite of the work, hope, art and natural aid, it was the individual genius of Miltiades that has made possible the supreme change of course for human beings on this planet: "But still courage and intelligence lavished on such a work, and solely called into being by an idea which, starting one day from one individual brain, has leavened the whole globe" (Tarde, 1905). High praise indeed. So where did Miltiades falter? It is here that Tarde provides us with a great insight by means of which contingency is fused with order: *he says that the intimacy of the underground was a forced one.* The troglodytes in the caves passed through several phases before they reached the state of equilibrium. There were several civil wars. One took place between the centralist and the federalist forces. The former were the industrialists, while the latter more artistic in nature. This was followed by a war between the freethinking cities and the cellular cities: "The former fought to assert the freedom of love with its uncertain fecundity; the second, for its prudent regulation" (Tarde, 1905). And it is here that Miltiades took an atavistic decision, much like Lydia at an earlier phase. He took the side of the freethinkers who fought for the freedom of love. Here was the monomaniac hero back in his elements. But the new society cannot afford elemental behaviour anymore. It has to work towards order and discipline. The freethinkers must recede. Prudence must take over art and science, love and all social interactions.

So, if we put the question of the individual from the side of the creative genius, it is now evident that a number of factors overlap. The question of being at crossroads is a contingent situation.

The genius innovator is at heart an anti-social being, but it is only through a radical form of anti-sociality that any genuine form of the social can arise. To that extent, Miltiades symbolizes a radical and evolving monad. Single-handedly he helps create, bring together and make the assemblage of the troglodytes thrive. But on the other hand, he seems to be following a blueprint that must resurrect the human species, a path in which he is one of the mediating cogs. His job done, he is relinquished. From this vantage, Tarde's experiment is an exercise in system-building, where individuals, even innovators, are creators of possibilities. Heroes themselves have a *telos*—they are brought back from oblivion. They produce awe, and possibilities for innovation among the imitators. Their job done, the same heroic tendencies are a liability to society since it has no use for irrational zeal in a prudent world. Creative outbursts are aesthetically normalized. The innovator's role is to mould contingency into order, by facilitating the process of dispersal.

In the *Underground Man*, imitative hordes are gradually made to remould themselves into segments. In this sense, there is a clear line of flight or relative deterritorialization, through which the troglodytes are able to amplify and alter their imagination, rework their lives by migrating to the deepest caverns and successfully reterritorialize themselves culturally and geologically in such spaces. The territorial relocalizations happen through a protracted process of clash between the old and the new order. In the *Underground Man*, the immigrants in the inner world have to face immense hardship on their path to improve and perfect their condition. As they enlarge into a new equilibrium, they also have to adjust between two civilizations. It is true that the sum total of natural forces aid them cost free, as Miltiades had prophesized, by means of providing them surplus energy (caldrons in volcanoes, condensers in glaciers). It provides enough power to manage "excavation, air supply, water supply, sanitation, locomotion, descent and transport of provisions" (Tarde, 1905). And yet, the intimacy was forced at one stage among the inhabitants of the brave new world: "We shall never know what bloodthirsty duels, what rapes, what doleful tragedies, took place in this lawless society, which have not yet been reorganized" (Tarde, 1905). A new beneficial symbolic order is gradually created through a process of purification that acknowledges, fosters and emphasizes the shift from the masses to classes. By means of opening up the radical process of reorganization, Tarde adumbrates what Anthony Giddens would later describe as an undertaking, in which "the very tissue of spatial experience alters, conjoining proximity and distance in ways that have few close parallels in prior ages" (Giddens, 1990). Convenience, contemplation and discipline are the hallmarks of the reorganized regimen.

What is the nature of this new and hard won world that destiny has fostered upon the humans? The premium attribute is the total elimination of living nature, animal or arboreal, save humans, who are now called troglodytes. The flora and fauna are enervating elements, and hence, jettisoned wholesale. Tarde calls this reterritorialized world to be socially more vibrant and purified. According to Tarde, the experiment was undertaken in order to learn two things:

(a) What would happen to the social being if left to himself, deprived of all other living beings and inorganic nature, but furnished with the accumulated intellectual arsenal of the past, worked out by the creative genius into action?
(b) How would the reorganized humanity behave, when restricted among its own species and obligated to extract food supplies, other pleasures and creative inspirations from its own resources?

Man is no more natural. He is *avid* and many such *avidities* are now aligned. The romanticization of the rural and the artisanal are all anachronisms in the new dispensation. Tarde clearly states that the idea that society runs through the exchange of service is a value that ran the erstwhile world of the superficial. It is sophistry; a mistake of the socialists, the misguided visionaries who exaggerated the development of commercial life and romanticized what they thought was natural, and hence, authentic living. Society now runs via multiplicity of relations. Society is an exchange of reflections. Man apes one another and by means of accumulated apings, diverse combinations of possibilities are produced. Reciprocal service is merely organized as accessory to such apings that take place at the level of reflection. In the new world, desires of food, transport and clothing have been simplified. Climate is soft. If any additional space is required, humans bore through the crust of the caverns and create fresh dwelling areas. There are no superfluities.The whole human race in hermetically sealed anyway. Consequently, there is abundant time to reflect. It is an aesthetic society and not a utilitarian one. All aesthetics is acquired taste and art is produced for passion and not for consumption. Art has an anti-social relationship with the utilitarians, as well as with the freethinkers. In such a society, all artists may have a dilettante double, but the distinction makes it clear that mutual service and amusement are not the aim of art. In lieu of exchange of services, there is exchange of admiration or criticism/judgement among the inhabitants: "We possess the joy and the strength of the mind which attains a certainty of its own, founded, as it is, on its only sure basis, the unanimity of other minds on certain essential matters. On this rock we can rear the highest constructions of thought, nay, the most gigantic systems of philosophy" (Tarde, 1905). Personal wants are abandoned. We shall recall that *relation* is always prior to *being* in Tarde. And here such a relational world attests to the universal propagation of truth and beauty, of strength and sweetness.

The undetectable core of social interaction in the reorganized world is simplicity and inevitability. The social law of separation has come to fruition whereby "heterogeneous talents and vocations were bound to take place of its own accord" (Tarde, 1905). The interior is valorized which makes the troglodytes free—not stiff or correct like those who live in the ancient civilization. Differences now mean the diversity of social aptitudes, not terrestrial accidents of regional variance. Everything is boundless and everlasting. A profound repose reigns after all the tempests have been negotiated with. The underground illuminates—within and without. The illumination is hypnotic and psychedelic.

The new underground is illumined owing to several variables, but clearly, at some point, a kind of magnetic machine, like the relationship of charges (a kind of constructivism), and dynamic forces of balancing/calibrating desire with belief (expressionist motifs) conjoin among the highly motivated, aping troglodytes, which propel them towards a world of ruthless and higher action. The society as such begins to work towards a directed aim and the assemblage acts in unison. Tarde's central thought: "Suppose a somnambulist who pushes the imitation of his medium so far as to become a medium himself and magnetizing a third, who in his turn imitated" is in full play here (King, 2016). The automated herd is formed and begins to operate on its own, once the process is initiated. The idea of herd somnambulism in Tarde does not preclude, we shall recall, the complexity of social relations, "talking and listening, beseeching and being beseeched, commanding and obeying, producing and consuming" (Tarde, 1903). It is only that dogma or power which runs all relationships. And soon, such automation turns self regulatory and suave, finding its highest efflorescence in a specialized condition of love, as we shall see anon. This is the reason Tarde says that man is truly urbane and urban at this stage. Everyone is born well bred in the caves. All courtesy is real, which charms others without any falsehood of intent or accent. Humans are free of obsequiousness or fawning. The fear of ostracism is enough to help prevent others from any veering from this everlasting order. There are no social hierarchies. Only social harmony prevails. Each monad exerts its beliefs and desires on the other. Once initiated by the pressures of contingency, civilizational progress is a matter of progression of imitative beliefs and desires: "In sum, progress in general is the fruit not of conflict, not of competition, not even discussion, but a series of good ideas appearing in the ingenious brains at the appropriate time" (King, 2016). Progress happens through infinite variations of willed agents and their actions.

Moral Solidarity of Vortex Atoms

The idea of the troglodytes as nodes who transmit and receive innovative thought and action takes a most interesting turn in the final chapters of the book, which addresses love and aesthetic life in the underground world in great detail.

Tarde feels that love is a novel courtesy. In the earlier epoch, love was a juvenile emotion, held in check by ego, rivalry, madness, luxuries and political ambition. Such impulses of the heart are extraneous to love in the present age. Love of the nation makes no sense, since there are no nations, but only the corporate-spirited and overarching grotto. Likewise, love of the family and maternal affections are no more needlessly sentimentalized. Love is the unadulterated moral force—one true religion and art. Austerity is its hallmark. The human form, especially the female form, has always been perfect—in charm and beauty. And affection is our final homesickness. Therefore, love cannot be trivialized by merely considering it in terms of nourishment. It is like air and water—persistent and insistent in its demands over us.

Love, in the new age, gives light now. It does not dazzle like the old sun, which lies cold and spent now. Love is worshipped by its devotees. The wise man and the woman have a remarkable relationship: "The wise man is to the woman what the asymptote is to the curve, it draws ever nearer but never touches" (Tarde, 1905). The lovers now have a most uplifting relationship—saintly and perfect—men and women wander together in magical cloisters, in the cells of painters and museums where an artificial dusk is produced by a richly coloured twilight and audacious and marvellous revelations of the nude abound. Lovers spend their time in such contemplative recreation. These are heroic lovers "whose whole pleasure in love consists in the sublime joy of feeling their love growing within them, blissful because it is shared, inspiring because it is chaste" (Tarde, 1905).

But for those who will indulge in *ad libitum* of the ancient age, severe penalties are prescribed. For lesser crime of such libidinal nature, lovers are thrown into the lake of petroleum. But often, such is the force of public opinion in these matters (for aping troglodytes) that penalties are more or less rendered unnecessary. Still, transgressions do happen and sometimes, lovers die of their own madness. Others get themselves hoisted by an elevator to the mouth of some extinct volcano and as they reach the surface of the earth, they freeze themselves to death. They get no chance to admire the disorderly spectacles of nature that lie about in the outside universe. The summit of such volcanoes are crowned with the corpses of such unnecessary passionate lovers, showing the rest the stark image of the lower kind of love as full of agony, frenzy and despair—although such deaths may seem like repose.

Every male lover must produce a masterpiece (to be proclaimed by his rivals as being one) under the influence of his beloved and the woman would truly abandon herself to the man. The right to have children is the monopoly of the genius. The race is thus exalted. Besides, a man can produce children as long as he produces masterpieces, in order to enrich the civilization.

Unlike the ancient society, which used to be run by the fear of punishment, this one moves by expectations of happiness. But such happiness is surpassing, not utilitarian. Marriages, like the umbrellas the ancients carried to stave off nature, seems a ridiculous proposition—over the top and pretentious. Instead, union between the sexes is now "at once free and regulated, energetic and intermittent, passionate and restrained, the true corner stone of our regenerated humanity" (Tarde, 1905). Mystics wondered whether, in such a society, art and philosophy were to mollify and assuage love or whether such love can actually replace the pursuit of truth and art. This was true salvation: a civilization in which love has refined the habits of the citizens of the underground.

The higher principles of moral miracle spread in intellectual directions too. Science is no more an inductive affair in the cavernous depths. The troglodytes have the dual advantage of converting science into an object of luxury and a deductive zone of knowledge. They now arrange all measurements, experiments and vivisections that the past has bequeathed upon them. Most contradictory conclusions about scientific details can be debated now from every side. The scientists have now become religious savants, who debate about schisms and heresies in the intellectual world. Mathematicians have taken giant strides with 'chalk in hand' 'descending to fabulous depths', for they no longer see the sky. Only *higher inutilities* interest the intellectuals of the underground. However, among the inductive sciences, chemistry and psychology have great sway among the troglodytes. The chemists, inspired by love perhaps, are greatly knowledgeable in the 'nature of affinities'. They pummel their way into the inner universe of the molecules in order to unearth their desires, tendencies and physiognomy. As the chemists construct the psychology of the molecules, the psychologists explain the atomic theory of the self, which Tarde calls the sociology of the self. In fact, if we are imaginative enough to take chemistry and psychology to be the two central disciplinary innovators having minds of their own in the new world, Tarde's original definition of imitation would at once come alive: "that of the action at a distance of one mind upon another, and of action which consists of a quasi-photographic reproduction of a cerebral image upon the sensitive plate of another brain" (Tarde, 1903). Chemistry and psychology are, therefore, reciprocal sciences, one influencing the other and working in unison, but in an inter-psychical and imitative fashion. Both the subjects are able to get to the bottom of the "hierarchy of consciousness" and the "feudal system of vassal souls, of which our personality is the summit" (Tarde, 1905).

Furthermore, chemistry informs the inhabitants that they are not alone in the frozen earth. The rocks are animated and are full of life force. Indeed, they are alive and protect the inhabitants. It is a brotherhood of vital matter that binds the underground—warm and giving: "Through their mediation these living stones have some message for our heart, something at once alien and intimate, which neither the stars nor the flowers of the field ever told to our forefathers" (Tarde, 1905). Food is processed by the chemists, so that there is no fear of dying by hunger and the psychologists free the troglodytes from the fear of death. Death, they realize, is a window to freedom. There are no terrors of the former men, who experience fright and foreboding with ice and snow. The relay system is ethereal.

The philosophers stand at a higher level than the savants, the latter being ordinary ruminants. The philosophers congregate in their appointed seats made of granite blocks. The grottos themselves are marvellous stalactites, which "vaguely imitate, in the eyes of those who are not too critical, all kinds of beautiful objects, cups and chandeliers, cathedrals and mirrors—cups which quench no man's thirst, chandeliers which give no light, cathedrals in which no one prays, but mirrors in which one sees oneself more or less faithfully and pleasantly portrayed" (Tarde, 1905). Tarde suggests that such a cave imitates the exact philosophy that it houses. The relay of ideas continues to flow through vital matter: mental stalactites help crystallize and mediate such ideas. There are powerful Neo-Aristotelians, Neo-Kantians, Neo-Cartesians and Neo-Pythagoreans among the new race of humans, who revivify all ancient authority of thinking. But the greatest thought and projection comes from the sociologist, who provides a *telos* for the social development of humanity. By such a scheme, the new race of humans would pursue its progress from the outer rind and then move from strata to strata till the centre of the earth. Civilization thus expands to a 'new descent'. Each stratum shall shelter the social type peculiar to the humanity of that circle, "growing ever nobler and richer, happier and better balanced" (Tarde, 1905). The civilization shall in this manner reach the last man, self sufficient heir of hundred successive civilizations. He has solved all enigmas and yet he cannot survive humanity. He eventually blows up the globe and himself with a potent explosive material "to sow the immensity of space with the last remnants of mankind" (Tarde, 1905). This is the process by which creation descends to the infinitesimal, a process of elimination, which leads to the geometrical point of pure nothingness: "Everything comes from the infinitesimal and everything returns to it" (Tarde, 2012).

The 'outside in' world also gradually builds up its own aesthetic norms and creations. Stone is the idealized kernel of former nature.

All living force jostles in the gravelly striations. As a result, frescoes and enamels abound. Art is but the apotheosis of love, Tarde declares. The same robust and moral purity drives both the ventures. How does art represent erstwhile natural elements and objects? The question is: "Does it mean that nature, now dead and formerly alive, from which our great masters drew their subjects and themes, has become a simple hieroglyphic and coldly conventional alphabet?" (Tarde, 1905). The answer is negative. Nature now stands methodized, humanized and harmonized. Art is about reverie, imaginings and admiration rather than terror and impressions. No blue sky, no fragrance of flowers or chirpings of birds. Fuelled by a 'strange instinct', the mind conjures up the suggestions of love sans passing those through the senses. Is instinct an attribute to be stored and restored or does it strike contingently some nerves in the accidental and appointed moment? In fact, the contingent is also necessitated by some higher commandment. In his ruminations on monadology, Tarde would, therefore, say that Leibniz:

> had to posit a pre-established harmony, in the same way that, as the complement of their wandering blind atoms, materialists must invoke universal laws or a single formula embracing all laws, a kind of mystical commandment which all beings would obey and which was not produced by any being, a kind of ineffable and unintelligible word which, having never been pronounced by anyone, nonetheless would be heard everywhere and forever. (Tarde, 2012)

All sublime tales are marked and vivified by clear notes and harmonized orchestrations. The glories of the antiquity are transfigured. Sentiments of former human nature have been transcended. Jealousy and ambition, patriotism and warmongering, love of family, hankering for noble names and passions of the heart no longer elicit and stir any unnecessary emotion in a single individual. New passions only play over those antiquated language. Only love reigns—the source and motor of all art. Love reanimates everything as the old sun used to do. The most cherished ideal for the artist and the poet is the economy of expression: "a short passage, a line, half a line, on which an imperceptible hint of profound passion, or the most fleeting phase, though unexpressed, of love in joy, in suffering or in death has left its impress" (Tarde, 1905). With such a high and classical aim, to deal with eroticism in art is not an issue (since sensation is anyway relegated as a primitive trait). The real difficulty is to address correctly the concerns of the mystics—sorrow and ecstasy in aesthetic representations.

But in spite of such harmony, there is another kind of contrarians who trouble the consonance of such a settled and surpassing society. These malcontents are not the schismatics who reject the consonance and depth of the cavern, but the recusants who declare that they are suffused with the essence of truth and purity far above the standard compulsory excesses of the newly found moral boundaries. The super-purists find the beauty of the new underground to be too fixed and undeviating for their taste, too tranquil for genuine happiness to burgeon. The recusants challenge monotony with some higher beauty in nights and seasons and country-life. And the restlessness seems to be contagious. It tantalizes the inhabitants with its spectral and haunting presence. In such times, the music that the musicians play turns doleful, pathetic and melancholy and the lovers in hundreds go up to gaze at the 'death-dealing' sky. Some have even been attacked by the incurable malady of 'matrimonialites'. On the other hand, the population begins to grow at an unmanageable manner and consequently, there is a slackening in the number of masterpieces. Do the recusants secretly wish to take the troglodytes back to outer nature in a round-about manner? Is there a relaxation and contamination of the moral order? Perhaps, these are all artificial discontents. In fact, attentive students of Tarde know that all negation is counter-imitation in his imagination of the social, for "What do we place within the ultimate discontinuity if not continuity?" (Tarde, 2012). For *everything is society.* Just like supernaturalism suggests naturalism and affirmation of idealism gives birth to the notion of materialism, all positive imitation gives rise to a counter breed of divergent recusants. This shows two things. One, that adversaries are deeply attached beings in their antagonism. And two, to be rebellious with certain counter-expressions is not being inventive.

Therefore, as Miltiades had suggested, it is still the tranquil underground of the dark stars that store the real energy and radiance of the cosmic forces. Cosmic vibrations echo in the universe through such cellular societies. All dust is thus spiritualized. The rest are optical illusions. True happiness live concealed in purity and in complete independence.

For a social man's scheme of innovation-adaptation-organization to take place, some kind of underlying social glue is required. That glue happens to be the pursuit of a higher moral order. It is the glue of moral certitude that helps foster the social somnambulism/hypnotism of command and action that Tarde has famously pitched in his definition of the imitative society:

> The magnetiser does not need to lie or terrorise to secure the blind belief and the passive obedience of his magnetised subject. He has prestige that tells the story. That means, I think, that there is in the magnetised subject a certain potential force of belief and desire which is anchored in all kinds of sleeping but unforgotten memories, and that this force seeks expression just as the water of a lake seeks an outlet. The magnetiser alone is able through a chain of singular circumstances to open the necessary outlet to this force. (Tarde, 1903)

The force that fosters what Tarde gives the name of prestige is undoubtedly the imitative idea of moral certitude, decorum, health and proportion. What starts as a seed idea of *obedience through fascination* soon leads to mutual imitation of *moral sympathy* as the key magnetic influence and claim on each other's life. Hence, Tarde's telling line: "Is not fascination a genuine neurosis, a kind of unconscious polarisation of love and faith?" (Tarde, 1903). One often spontaneously becomes credulous and docile.

The idea of a moral solidarity (cataleptic fraternity) is everywhere—but the most important hypnotic mediations happen through love, which is further channelled via art and other intellectual pursuits. As Tarde says elsewhere, "In a judicial solidarity, the individual members recognised and responded to each other in ways which did not simply involve the extraction of services or goods or as a result of coercion but distinctively on the basis of a common agreement of what was just" (King, 2016). In imitative societies, members simply abide—and the rules are guided at the root by moral concerns and by the hopes of reaching and maintaining an organic social equilibrium, although the beginnings of such change happen as contingent and as a radical reaction to an ossified and superficial older world order. The common standard of propriety are set in aesthetic-behavioural terms, which happens through a process of imitative relays. Internalized common laws develop and there is no scope for any rational due process or other independent ways of running the society. Imitation thus turns into a matter of moral experience. Tarde would always seek atomized factuality and, therefore, rejected all recusancy as moral deviation: "Let us admit free will, be it so; but we ought to recognize that which is a patent fact, rather than liberty which is a latent force" (Tarde, 2012). Though matter is all force, the force has to be restrained through art and higher love. The attempt is to objectively appreciate and put to use the best available ideas into practice. And that can happen only when there is a moral consensus among the community members. The idea of common good becomes a matter of belief for the participants. Such a process of consensus is invoked all the time, so that the innovative forces of vitalism can be harnessed in the perfect society for common good of the new breed. This is the reason Tarde could so forcefully state that "We may rightly be amazed that, among so many philosophical conjectures, it has occurred to nobody, at least explicitly, to seek in the objectification of *belief* rather than of desire the solution to the problems of physics and of life" (Tarde, 2012).

It is befuddling as to why the *Underground Man* has escaped the attention that it deserves in Tarde scholarship. Perhaps, sociologists have made a clear distinction between imaginative fiction and empirical analysis and gave the work a pass? The work was conceived in the backdrop of the emerging financialization of the bonds of Western society in the late 19th century through banking, homeownership and so on, which would eventually lead to the Great Depression. Tarde ontologizes these principles, Grant Bolmer reminds us. On the other hand, literary scholars who deal in 19th century fantasy and/or science and speculative fiction, utopic/dystopic literature, social satire or new age heroism, have failed to notice this remarkable, dense gem (in contrast to, say—that attention that E.M. Foster's *The Machine Stops*, H.G. Wells' *Country of the Blind* or Ayn Rand's *Anthem* routinely receive)—perhaps owing to its austere and economical use of language and large swathes of sociological digression (though Wells and his many imitators come across as realists among the fantasts, seeking new social forms in their fictional speculations). Still, perhaps Tarde's world is too stiff and classical even for those who deal with *secular magic*?

Or is it that the modern mind does not wish to confront the creaturely underside of its own civilized self, especially if the aesthetics of virtual experience is imagined and justified in terms of the real? Do we actually bristle, because he shows us the mirror: that there is nothing natural or authentic within or about us? Everything is social.

References

Alliez, Éric. 2009. "Gabriel Tarde." In Graham Jones and Jon Roffe (eds.), *Deleuze's Philosophical Lineage*. Edinburgh: Edinburgh University Press.

Bollmer, Grant. 2016. *Inhuman Networks: Social Media and the Archeology of Connection*. New York and London: Bloomsbury.

Giddens, Anthony. 1990. *The Consequences of Modernity*. Cambridge: Polity Press.

King, Anthony. 2016. "Gabriel Tarde and Contemporary Social Theory". *Sociological Theory*. Vol. 34.1, March: 45–46.

Latour, Bruno. 2002. "Gabriel Tarde and the End of the Social." In P. Joyce (ed.), *The Social in Question: New Bearings in History and the Social Sciences*. London: Routledge, pp. 117–132.

Tarde, Gabriel. [1903] 1962. *The Laws of Imitation*. Translated by Elsie Clews Parsons. New York: Henry Holt and Company.

———. 1905. *Underground Man*. London: Duckworth & Co.

———. 2012. *Monadology and Sociology*. Edited and translated by Theo Lorenc. Melbourne: Re. Press,

Toews, David. 2003. "The New Tarde: Sociology after the End of the Social." In *Theory, Culture and Society*. Vol. 20, No. 5: 81–98.

———. 1999. "The Renaissance of Philosophie Tardienne." In *Pli: The Warwick Journal of Philosophy*, No. 8: 164–173.

The Hounded Creature

The Paradoxes of Manhunting in Gregoire Chamayou

Gregoire Chamayou has been instrumental in giving us two pithy and sharp entry points to the idea of hunting—as a clinical discourse and as an art form. First, he provides us with a philosophical history of the theories of manhunting in the Western world as exemplified through its interactions with what it considers to be the 'outsiders, outliers, code-breakers and trespassers' among the slaves, vagabonds, anarchists and imperial subjects and also increasingly detected among its own population. The genealogy shows a complex relationship between processes of capturing, excluding and policing in creating a particular kind of social economy in different times and conditions. The second coordinate concerns, as he says, in trying to make sense of "What happens in your head if you are hunted? What happens in your head—if you hunt other human subjects?" (Chamayou, 2012). What is the nature of the subjectivity in such states of consciousness? His is a phenomenological inquiry. Chamayou primarily deals with human subjects and with concrete historical details as he tries to enjoin conceptual breakthroughs with a particular genealogy of the cynegetic art. In a manner of speaking, Chamayou develops a kind of diachronic ontogeny of manhunting.

From a conceptual point of view, there are two extant notions about actual conflict that Chamayou takes on. To begin with, the manhunt doctrine revises ways and methods related to conventional warfare (especially those forwarded by the likes of Carl von Clausewitz and Sun Tzu) which has more do to with direct confrontation—that deals in the opening of fronts and wings and having a linearity about it. If victory is the aim of such conventional battles, a cynegetic approach is more about either capturing or excluding the prey by the predator. It is a battle of attrition with a premium on a primitive excitement. Manhunt is a game of cat and mouse with a deadly intent. This form of interaction comes close to what Elaine Scarry has called 'war as a contest' (as opposed to 'war as injury') in which "participants enter into a structure that is a self-cancelling duality" (Scarry, 1985). The idea of contest does not hinge on winning or losing a war. Rather, it relies on maintaining and perpetuating the formal binary structure that fatally connects the two antagonistic sides. It is to draw our attention to such a contrast that Chamayou has also delved into the notion of drone warfare in his other work since such a covert warfare means "to be able to kill without being able to be killed; to be able to see without being seen" (Chamayou, 2015). Besides, Chamayou's predator-prey coupling also considerably modifies the older notion of Just War—*jus bellum*.

His other targets are the primitive and arcane ideas of community sacrifice, religious propitiation and/or scapegoating (approaches championed by Rene Girard and Georgio Agamben). Girard zeroes in on the mimetic nature of rivalry and envy in desire that flows into internecine warfare in a differentiated community. Desire is mediated by desires of others in such a situation. Soon, each in a given community begins to copy the other member even as the community turns into a horde. Conflicts thus turn enemies into doubles. This generalized violence is soon turned into some particular members of the horde, often selected arbitrarily and following the Biblical ritual, makes him a scapegoat. Through venting of violence against the victim, the community regains its equilibrium and peace. The victim might turn into a *sacred hierophany*. And the community thus becomes reintegrated through this violent cleansing process. Similarly, in *The Accursed Share* (and in his involvement with the secret society known as *Acéphale* ('headless'), Georges Bataille unveils the motif of archaic sacrifice and argues that society must be periodically afflicted by a surfeit of waste in order to purge itself of its own serviceable tendencies. Most of all, he was invested in understanding the sacrifice of the God of Christianity and salvation and the stultification of society's mythic aspirations and sacrificial ways. Giorgio Agamben, through a series of works, has elaborated on the archaic notions of depriving certain people and bodies of rights, a process which reduces them to bare life. Such a *condition inhumana* is nurtured by the non-rigorous concepts of good morals, race or personal subjective biases where legality is voided. In order to understand such a condition, Agamben reminds us of a specific figure under the Roman law, when a person who committed a certain kind of crime would be excommunicated from society and all his rights revoked as a citizen. At such a point, paradoxically, he turned into a sacred man (*homo sacer*). While his life would be considered sacred and not sacrificed, he could be killed by anybody under such circumstances. The ostracized figure (like the one of 'enemy combatant' in modern times) is thus simultaneously included and excluded by an ordinary and boundless act of sovereignty.

Chamayou keeps himself clear of such pure notions of scapegoating, sacredness or expiatory sacrifice, as he explicates on manhunt. His interest is in tracing the changing morphology of the very processes of manhunting and how sometimes, they overlap but in other times, also turn specific in their modes and motives of operating. With Chamayou, one thus travels with a dual sense—that the Western world indeed changes and progresses with the very methods of manhunt and yet, the 'doctrine' of manhunt somewhere remains the same, since that is an ontologically defined relationship between the predator and the prey.

Pursuing, Capturing and Excluding

The basic unit is a common order. The order shall not always explain everything to you. But flouting the order is crime. Period. If the order decides for some reason—sometimes out of compulsion, at other times, out of economic or personal reasons and still, at some other times, arbitrarily—that certain people need to be pursued, it will. This is the origin of manhunting. The decision shall make sure that human beings are brought to realize that they are actually all skin, bones and blood. The question of any legal process or transparent mechanism does not arise. Such chasing and tracking down a prey may happen due to two reasons: in order to capture/incarcerate/annihilate the prey or to send it to banishment. The first method works by limiting or destroying the conditions of life after having played with the prey. The second: through a common understanding of ostracization and chopping off of the 'gangrene' of abnormality/heresy/conduct germinating in the community through an errant prey. But the two processes of tracking down and chasing out can sometimes collapse.

The ontological rift that determines the predator–prey relationship arrives early on in Chamayou. This is a running thread in Chamayou's work, but the nature of the rift shall change according to historical necessities and exigencies. There is an absolute feature of delimiting the scope of the prey. Once the prey is decided upon, its movement needs to be restricted. Chamayou says at the outset that this ontological dimension of the relationship assures the predator that there is no reason to look for any productivity at the root of the doctrine of manhunting. The cynegetic modality of power means the right to arbitrarily choose the prey and pounce upon it: "the Greek seizes his slaves as fruits in a harvest" (Chamayou, 2011). The relationship is not natural. Nature has some logic behind its ebbs and flows, but the invocation of cynegetic power is extra-natural in the sense that the arbitrariness of being chosen as a prey is completely unexplainable. Further, in a cynegetic war, the zone of combat is the body of the hunted individual itself. But the zone of the body, since it leaves traces as the individual moves about, can also be virtually extended. Such a primal zone, which also repeats its presence across time, is therefore named by Chamayou as "mobile micro-space" (Chamayou, 2011).

Manhunting is legitimized right from Aristotle onward by arguing for the natural art of acquisition. This is an ontological justification of an extra-natural act on natural grounds. Acquisition is the natural right, says Aristotle. But is that not a natural right for certain individuals who are in a position to do so? Is that decided genetically—predatory tendencies being coded within? Or do predators get constructed as certain people decide to respond to situations in a raptorial and avaricious fashion? Or is there a strange coming together that happens around the predator-prey complex during *certain times* and the two groups become sharply polarized as antagonists?

But there is another way that manhunting gets legitimized as a primal impulse. This time from the side of the prey: the fear of being hunted down. This is an archaic fear—of being captured and being sold as a slave. Man-stealers lurk at every bend—that is the fear. Is Chamayou suggesting once again that there are certain people who are born prey? Is preyness a given? That will be an ontological proposition. But again, this whole idea that there are certain people whose bodies dominate the soul and, therefore, are inferior humanoids (fit to be preys) is a construct by the predator class/clan. This Chamayou points out very clearly. But the line between the ontological and the historical are so intertwined that we are not often sure how the primal doctrine is being employed at various junctures in history so that the predator–prey relationship (capturing, excluding or exclusion leading to capturing) is repeated and yet the conditions and circumstances change as history unfolds.

Of course, one can say that this is the way the dialectic of history progresses except for the fact that we always do have a sense whether in a modern police state—which is the culminating point for Chamayou—the tendencies of the two 'typologies' have vanished into a process of history. The gyre returns. In fact, the types get entrenched by being more refined and clandestine. The essential element about ontological policing on one side and fear and anxiety on the other is a constant variable. The degree of the general relationship varies, but the kind remains almost uniform through time and space. At the same time, Chamayou has indeed been successful in showing the various possibilities enacted in the manhunt doctrine by being historically specific and following a certain chronological order. The question is: is there a *telos* to manhunting or will this pattern be repeated in various ways as long as humans live in the planet? This question not only foregrounds the issue of difference and repetition in creaturely interaction, but also implicitly asks whether there is any possibility of resistance or even insurrection in Chamayou's manhunt doctrine.

The Hunter King and the Pastoral Shepherd

A crucial conceptual distinction on which the manhunt doctrine stands is the one between cynegetic and pastoral powers. One of the prototypes of the manhunting principle for Chamayou is Nimrod—the grandson of Noah. This is a Hebraic prototype in which the ancient tyrant is portrayed as someone who had 'acquired' his own subjects by violence. Nimrod represents Babylon, the other of Israel, since he disobeyed the commandments, destroyed his own people and seized his subjects. Manhunt marks his sovereign status: the slave-owner and king-hunter combine, in order to produce the cynegetic power. From a pastoral viewpoint, the obverse is David, the good shepherd. The antithesis of good shepherd is not a bad one but the manhunter, Chamayou emphasizes. If the shepherd, in his care-giving role as the leader of the flock, is guided by the divine source, the hunter is the cold mechanic that represents pure terrestrial physics.

Further, the shepherd takes individual care of each member of his tribe and manages growth and stability by mobilizing internal economic resources. He redistributes resource and builds up a benevolent system even as his flock is mobile. The shepherd works through a model of humility and sacrifice. The vocation of fishing is the metaphor that comes closest to sheep rearing and managing the pastoral economy. The sovereign hunter, on the other hand, gathers the scattered ones in order to build his economic order. He levies taxes, consumes and raids to consolidate power. In this manner, he centralizes his power, captures his prey and uses the captives in order to build his empire. He isolates his prey to vertically accumulate his slaves, work force and militia. Unlike the shepherd, he is not bothered by any compunction of sacrifice and suffering. The manhunter is a pure immanent force.

So far, the antithesis is neat. But the story becomes complicated as soon as Chamayou begins to delve into a curious and often understated phenomenon: pastoral manhunt. The hunting in pastoral flocks happens paradoxically from the same source for which they are celebrated, namely, caring and protecting individual members of the flock. This idea of protection, however, can at times become wholly and completely righteous and melodramatic. The shepherd turns overprotective and authoritarian. In such circumstances, a diseased sheep (often the malady is moral or emotional, rather than directly physical) is identified as highly contagious to the flock and an inquisition and witch-hunt ensures. Chamayou calls this process 'salutary ablution' and the mode 'beneficent exclusion'. The noun 'ablution' and the epithet 'beneficent' ought to be especially marked. The ancient process of moral purification of the community is at the heart of such pastoral methods of 'smoking-out' the errant or the irreverent soul. The authoritarian pastoral mode is often explained indeed in mitigating and paternalistic terms—like 'beneficent' here. The metaphors of cleansing the society of such infected elements is often described in and through health metaphors—so that everyone realizes the beneficial aspect of destroying or banishing such creatures with deep seated moral maladies of body and soul. Ultimately, in the mode, the ostensible rationality is protective idea of 'measure for safety'. All forms of absolute enmity are thus covered up.

The process of moral witch-hunting often ensues when the prey is identified as practising some secret or esoteric knowledge, to which the shepherd or other prominent members of the flock are not privy to. The root cause of such a mode of manhunting lies deep in the recesses of human psyche: ranging from envy to greed and one-upmanship and quick popularity on the part of the pastoral predator. Consequently, care turns into repression. Chamayou reminds us that in such a socially ostracized state, the prey is exposed to further predation. The prey is identified as a counterfeiter and a fraud, since he has challenged the 'ecclesiastical authority' of the seniors of the flock. Hence, the necessity to exclude him from the community, law and all social security. The process is often not just to leave the excommunicated person to be excluded from the proceedings of the flock, but to neutralize him by converting him into a 'walking dead'. Chamayou tells us that sometimes he is killed by a process of surrogacy—his images are desecrated and effigies burnt. This is condemnation in absentia, set in motion in order to exhibit examples of errancy to the now-vigilante pastoral flock.

This is a kind of 'inverted penitentiary system', where the banished becomes the bandit. The faux civility of the pastoral flock becomes naked in times of such proscription. Eric Hobsbawm, Chamayou tells us, however finds this mode of operation as a case in weak authority. When law does not apply and when real modes of authority (Mommsen's definition of authority for instance: 'less than order, more than advice') are eroded, such a possibility of raw community justice arises. Retribution for power grabbing dons the mask of empathy for the flock. The weakness in such a mode of hunting lies in the fact that the fugitive-prey may largely still be on the loose, since the process of smoking out is often open-ended and left to chance, once the initial process of excommunication is completed. There is not always any closure in such a mode of operation, since excommunication is mired with a notion of guilt on the part of the shepherd and his henchmen, who would also like to project the ethos of the good pastoral and their righteousness to the world.

Now the contradiction is simply stated: if the very distinction between the cynegetic power and pastoral power is instrumental in defining and highlighting the force and methods of manhunting, how can the pastoral mode itself become a modified but trenchant form of cynegetic power? If the second is true, is not the very ontological definition of the manhunting doctrine, based on the hunter-king and the slave-owner, in jeopardy? Is the shepherd merely a garb and mask for the paternalistic slave owner? In that case, how does the earlier distinctions between the cynegetic sovereign and the pastoral mode, based on the counter-principles of guarding/accumulating and redistributing/raiding hold good? One argument can be that the shepherd turning into a manhunter is a rare and emergent situation. But Chamayou's explication puts the mode as one more conceptually astute manoeuvre in the history of manhunting. The other explanation could be historically sought—that the slave-owning mode is a prior and ancient one in contrast to the policing approach of the modern ways (clearly Foucault's influence is central in Chamayou's leading us to the police state via the pastoral, instead of making a distinction between the pastoral and the modern policing and bio-political acts to which Chamayou arrives later). But this historical explanation once again is complicated by the original ontological and subjective nature of the exercise of the manhunting impulse among human beings in general. The question of righteousness, care or paternalism turning into rogue manhunting exercise as a tribal form of meting out justice is as archaic and laden with power as its supposed obverse—Nimrod and his successors, who encourage violence as a direct mode of centralizing and consolidating power and authority. In fact, the pastoral mode of empathetic ruthlessness is an instance of a much advanced and sophisticated mode of the hunting principle and shows creaturely craft and astuteness of operating in a personal fashion within an apparently modern set up. The ancient mode lacks the sophistication to hunt with finesse and its preferred mode is direct and violent—albeit done often in a disciplined manner (reading Xenophon's cynegetic explications is instructive). The pastoral mode, on the other hand, is the direct harbinger and progenitor of the modern police state.

Freedom and Its Inversion

The genealogical thread in Chamayou is able to depict how the apparently contradictory modes of operation could be reconciled and justified in the manhunt project as the Western world has 'progressed'. One of the conundrums is to balance humanism with imperial aspirations. There could be three separate modes of manhunting in colonial situations:

(a) If the slave or the colonial subject is considered to be imperfectly human, the mode of hunting is to dominate him. The hunter acts as the slave-master in such circumstances.
(b) If the subject is viewed as perfectly inhuman, the preferred mode is to proscribe. The hunter is the sovereign pure here.
(c) In case the slave/subject is taken to be essentially human, the way is to convert him to an obedient Christian, which is where the hunter dons the habit of the proselytizing shepherd. The very idea of human actually presupposes the inhuman, for that is one way to define what can be hunted as base and uncivilized: by creating a binary based on proportion, perspective and cold cruelty.

Chamayou stresses at this juncture that beneath all these strategies—proscription, subjugation and acquiring of the prey—stand powerful economic reasons. Slaves provide the supply chain of labour. Does economic maximization, if that is the underlying reason for manhunting as history progresses, nullify the ontological bedrock of the impulse? Is it impulse that is being given direction by these extraneous factors or is it that manhunting itself now transforms at its root as historical exigencies begin to decide the very nature of hunting? The question shall take particular importance when we shall get into the issue of resistance and freedom, the equation between the predator and the prey. Is it ever possible to invert the relationship? And if such an inversion happens, does it end up by mirroring the same relationship once again as actors just change place or are the keys to the lasting and effective change available in the very structure of the relationship between the two existential foes?

Let us look once again into the nature of the antagonism. The key to understanding the preyness of the hunted is what Chamayou calls the victim's dilemma. If the victim considers itself in terms of an existential preyness without historicizing his position, it becomes the passive carrier of an alien will—that of the predator, which considers the prey not as an innocent victim, but as a non-subject. As a non-subject who is not historically situated, the prey is fundamentally irresponsible (the slave or the resident alien). And for the subjects embedded in history—predators, that is, there is no responsibility to recognize the condition of a being living outside the flow of history. The predator keeps the asymmetrical relationship outside of time and nature.

At this stage, Chamayou considers the central dialectic that supposedly ushers in Western modernity: Hegel's master–bondsman relationship. Chamayou says the very precondition of Hegel even before the first move of the dialectic unfolds, namely that the two antagonists stand on equal footing, is a faulty assumption. Domination already exists. This is an ontological position for Chamayou's manhunt doctrine. Hegel's gambit makes the slave-consciousness clash with the master's consciousness, where eventually there is no freedom for the bondsman, but the relationship is rather reformed and given a mitigating direction with each consciousness transforming in the process of the encounter. This narrative is useful for the modern Western mind, so that it can begin to believe and show to the world that the prey, in its apparent resistance to the master does not have any insurrectionary contempt for death. In fact, it actually despises life since it is unable to integrate with history. The sense of victimhood for the prey gets further entrenched in the Hegelian scheme.

In contrast to this hypothetical dialectic, Chamayou's narrative is doggedly real in the phenomenological sense, with the power gradient always placed at the forefront. There is no struggle for recognition among the two parties. In fact, a dog/falcon is trained to hunt the prey. The actual act of preying is farmed out to an intimate confidante. Is the dog the original drone? Or vice versa: as Chamayou has called the drone to be "the robotic heir of the dog of war" (Chamayou, 2011) to the intermediary. Since this is the actuality of hunting (hunting is not a duel), Chamayou goes back to the moment of pursuit that precedes capture in the relationship. This is an acknowledgement of the arche moment of power gradient, but it is also a reminder of the arbitrary nature of choosing the prey by the predator as a harvest to be consumed. The prey has no choice but to flee—helplessness and a radical anxiety to be captured define its arche-preyness. At this level, each of us is a potential prey, isolated and scattered; each trying to save his or her skin. The absolutely unnatural state of acute isolation among creatures is the pure state of nature. The possibility of capture shows the complete and total impotence of the prey (unlike the prior equity on two sides in the Hegelian scheme).

In such a circumstance, the prey is beset with two possibilities. One, to revolt at the camp or in the slave ship and die as a martyr. But such an abstract idea of freedom shall actually stamp the imprimatur of impotence over the prey once and for all. The other option is to either live a life in servitude or in banishment—that is to say, in living death. This is an impossible choice. The absolutely practical dilemma leading to such a *cul-de-sac* could foster a most pessimistic conclusion: that freedom is an ever-receding fantasy. This conclusion shall go a long way to affirm the ontological grid of the predator–prey relationship, from which there is no escape.

Escaping from the predator is also not an option. One possibility is to turn into a chattel slave—the master's intermediary. But these alternatives have nothing to do with freedom. At this juncture, Chamayou cites Orlando Patterson's well known formulation that the only exit for the prey to escape its ontological victimhood status is by invoking a double negation, that is to say, negate the condition of social death and reclaim life. Reclaiming life does not mean being able to return to a pristine world before the chase and the capture, but a creative and active construction and strategizing of life. The key for the prey is 'will to freedom' and 'desire to live'. The prey looks directly at the predator and takes certain steps. The prey turns sagacious in the sense that it masters its own traces and confuses the hunter off his scent (*faire hourvari*). In other words, a resistive guerilla warfare ensues.

But here comes the most pertinent question. The moment the prey is able to invert the relationship, are the roles reversed? In other words, has the prey internalized the consciousness of the predator within itself at the moment of insurrection? Chamayou puts this stage brilliantly with a simple exchange between the now reversed antagonists:

> Erstwhile Predator: Why are you doing this?
> Erstwhile Prey: Poor people get bored too.

This is reactive violence at its purest (which Franz Fanon had delineated masterfully in the context of the colonial subject). This is the reflection of the violator in the violated. There is no escape from manhunting. The significant question is about the nature of the inversion and the new status. What kind of emancipation lies ahead for the erstwhile prey, now turned predator? The new power inversion shall lead to the mirroring of the manhunt principle in an equally ontological fashion: ambushing, closing off, arrests at home, setting traps—all the trappings of an ancient rhythm in new set ups. What is the nature of this new subjectivity on the part of the pursuer and the pursuant? Clearly, Chamayou strives to show that there are certain groups of people who are gradually being hunted: slaves, heretics, the colonial subject, vagabonds, women, the racially disposed, immigrants, poor people and so on. His genealogy shows that he is historically informed about the nature of the people he gives the status of the prey. The only exception is the pastoral hunter. That is a curious case. But he also strongly suggests that the inversion, if that happens, may not lead to equitability and freedom proper for the prey. It may replicate the immutable doctrine of manhunting in new guise.

In fact, there is likely to be more refined versions of the police state, once the inversion happens. The erstwhile prey brings all the reserves of its righteous indignation to a devastating purist level and ends up building up a closed and retributive society. The most significant way of anonymous, but effective, policing in modern times happen through the deindividualized members of a violent pack, which zeroes in on the prey, attacks it in a sustained manner and then disperses. It is a hunting pack that seeks blood. This is the crudest atavistic revival of the most primeval form of vendetta extraction. It may not necessarily happen in order to scapegoat others. The move may be an instance of pure distraction or perhaps even more primal: that of securing one's own skin. The actual guilt of the so-called perpetrator is of little significance. The pack is composed of a bunch of blue souls, who would let go all pent up *ressentiment* of their misfortune to the projected predator. The lynching pack needs to reterritorialize its ground by setting examples through manhunting. Such bloodthirsty packs could be of various hues and ideologies. The gradient of power could be quickly inverted. But the essential nature of the lynch-pack would remain intact even after the inversion. The mode of operation is still manhunt. The other variable through which the power gradient is neutralized, but the bloodletting continues, is what Chamayou calls 'interpredation'. Once the super-predator creates a situation of 'wage war' and 'opportunity glut', the phenomenon of manhunting enters the interstices of the prey-typology and divides them further through rapid formation of fresh predator-prey couplings. It is a kind of civil war until the very distinction between the two types get blurry and yet predating continues in the dark.

Chamayou suggests that in order to avoid the pitfalls of such acute persecutory polarization in modern times, there is only one way: joining and supporting an internationalism that is based on a large solidarity of the prey class. The preys of the world must not base their solidarity on a common minimum identity but on difference and yet on the common experience of exploitation. Chamayou's ideological bias notwithstanding, this is perhaps one way by which the personal creative negation of negation of the prey at the ontological level could be positively brought together to a unified sense of a large number of collectively hunted people around the world at a given conjuncture of history.

Howard Caygill feels that Chamayou's study is primarily conducted from the perspective of the hunter (Caygill, 2013). Is there an art and science of the prey, he asks? First of all, the prey must give away a specular relationship with the predator. It has to get rid of then ontological coupling by rejecting all enmity and resentment. In other words, it has to get rid of the victim's dilemma that we had earlier visited. The struggle must be converted to a political and a cultural one and creatively discovered at every turn. The prey must also understand the main battle is also a war of attrition if the mode of the hunt is banishment or indefinite capture. Again, the will to withstand and thrive is crucial. The fugitive's strength is his unpredictability. And counter-guile. Can the hunter, who is now the unmanned drone and the anonymous troll—ever fully fathom this aspect?

References

Aarons, Kieran. 2013. "Cartographies of Capture," In *Theory & Event*. Vol. 16.2.

Caygill, Howard. 2013. *On Resistance: A Philosophy of Defiance*. New York: Bloomsbury.

Chamayou, Gregoire. 2011. "The Manhunt Doctrine." In *Radical Philosophy*, Issue No. 169. https://www.radicalphilosophy.com/commentary/the-manhunt-doctrine. Accession date: 10 May 2021.

———. 2012. *Manhunts: A Philosophical History*. Translated by Steven Rendall. Princeton: Princeton University Press.

Chamayou, Gregoire. 2010. "Hunter vs Hunted." https://www.dailymotion.com/video/ximngv. Accession date: 10 May 2021.

———.2015. *Drone Theory.* Translated by Janet Lloyd. London: Penguin.

Elden, Stuart. "Chamayou's Manhunts: From Territory to Space?" The Funambulist Papers #46. https://thefunambulist.net/history/the-funambulist-papers-46-chamayous-manhunts-from-territory-to-space-by-stuart-elden. Accession date: 10 May 2021.

Patterson, Orlando. 1982/2018. *Slavery and Social Death: A Comparative Study*. Cambridge, MA: Harvard University Press.

Scarry, Elaine. 1985. *The Body in Pain: The Making and Unmaking of the World.* Oxford: Oxford University Press.

The Creature Forlorn

The Deceased Deer, Spring Moonlight and Shahduz Zaman's Jibanananda

#1927: A young Jibanananda Das musters courage to send his first collection of poems—*Jhara Palok*—by post to Rabindranath Tagore, requesting the great man for his opinion. Tagore reads the poems and replies to the accompanying note. Few people knew Jibanananda at that time as a poet. But Tagore's sincerity to respond to his interlocutors is legendary. What Tagore writes can be summed up somewhat like this:

> There is no doubt that you are blessed with poetic sensibility. But I do not understand why you should announce a war—*jabardasti*—with language and words. This eccentricity of gesture becomes needless *ostadi*. In all large compositions there is always some kind of *shantih*—surpassing calmness. Wherever I see that element missing, I feel worried about the staying power of such an art form. To show force is not exactly a thing by which one achieves power. Often the opposite happens. (Zaman, 2019)

Such a note was surprising coming from Tagore, especially since he was unusually polite or quiet, even with his detractors. Besides, Jibanananda's *ostadi* (*swagger*) with language did not even begin at that stage! Jibanananda was just an unknown *mufassil* poet at that time. Anybody would be devastated with such a rude letter, and that too coming from Tagore! Jibanananda did not flinch. With great composure and self-confidence, he replies to Tagore:

> I am honoured to merit your response. Indeed, young Bengali writers are blessed to have such a great savant-like you, blazing bright over the firmament. I am in no way fit for such large bounty coming from you. But I worship a certain writerly *shakti* and try to connect that to all that is benevolent in the cosmos. Your note has set me thinking. In much high art, I often notice a great thirst for happiness or *dukhha*—sorrow. The poet often strives to achieve surpassing truth by travelling

> to the *jyotirlok* or in the poison infested netherworld—*paataal.* But even in such places, it does not seem that poetry could achieve calmness or composure. Indeed, serenity is a thing in the Greek universe. But I do not see much of that in Dante or Shelley. Does that make them lesser poets or their art temporary, I wonder? There could be various moods. The sky has so many colours—sometimes darkness deep, flushed with light at other times; endless blue now, earth's green reflected in it at other moments. Can we say one such hue is more beautiful than the other? Sometimes the changing colour of the kites plays with sky's changing hues. That seems permanent to me. Perhaps there is some inward tone and lilt to creation? If true creativity is absent, can *shantih* make such art timeless? I write here what I feel. You will forgive my talkativeness with your largeness of soul. My *bhaktipurna pranama* to you. (Zaman, 2019)

This description appears in one of the most powerful creative biographies written in Bangla in recent times: *Ekjon Kamolalebu* (*Someone, an Orange*) by Shahaduz Zaman. The work follows a *chronos,* but time is weaved through an inner, creative story. The vicissitudes of the poet's life is woven through and placed within the experiences of a most troubled and moving time. And yet, there is a constant return and renewal of phrases and ideas, inner turmoil and psychic conditions—as if everything comes together to create a rich palimpsest over the narration. In young Jibanananda, who was financially in a precarious situation at that time and temperamentally deeply taciturn, we detect a man well adept to argue, especially equipped to cite Western instances of artworks in defence of his position. He was an itinerant professor of English literature. We see a man who nurtures a strong sense of creativity and self-confidence about his capacities, though still not recognized and acknowledged by the world. But most importantly, here is a battle that has erupted between two differing sensibilities. A new and restive existential quest is about to interrogate all that is estimated as surpassing, harmonious, and in order in the cosmos. Jibanananda has deftly transferred the onus of art to a variety of frames and dispositions that the artist may nurture with reference to the changing natural and ambient circumstances. The subjectivity of the artist is deeply material and pantheistic. He wants poetry to renew its bonds with blood and grime, with ennui and sexuality, hunger, cruelty and despair. Following this, there are meanderings through difficult pathways in order to emerge from such states, though not necessarily unscathed. And always: attempts to forge a new language, sieved through the uncanny-everyday, to express such restive thoughts.

Upon acquiring a master's degree in literature, Jibanananda joins as a junior tutor in City College, Kolkata. Not very adept in the ways and attitudes that the big city demands, he lives in the Presidency College boarding house; reads sundry magazines and books. And he writes in his diary, "We have no taste for enjoyment … nor have we any instinct for aesthetics. We are content with fourth-hand men and materials … we have no complaints if the chair is bug-ridden and creaking if we can manage to sit on it somehow.… We have lost the iconoclast's spirit" (Zaman, 2019). He feels Kolkata is akin to a prison, where people, zombie-like, move about with no destination. And at this time, he loses the City College job. His first book of poetry has not been well received. Jibanananda begins to feel he 'shall survive' to see himself 'impotent and forgotten'. He begins to come closer to his self.

At that point, he receives an unexpected piece of news from his father at Barisal: that with the help of a mutual contact, he had managed to procure for Jibanananda a job in the English department of Ramjas College, Delhi. Having no choice as an unemployed man, Jibanananda rushes to Delhi. Delhi proves to be even more inhospitable to him. The chilly winter and loneliness make him go inward. And the principal and his colleagues are most distant and unforthcoming in nature. Perhaps, few were prejudiced against him, owing to his learning and introverted nature. His dhoti-clad self felt small in the midst of the smart and articulate teachers of the college. Besides, the students were not at all warm to him. He was not a particularly effective teacher perhaps? The students often booed him off the class. But he stuck to the job.

He was, by this time, in love with his cousin Shobhona, with whom he had spent sundry sweet hours in Dibrugarh, a few years ago. But his love stutters. And this state of mind he calls 'torment incarnated'. Meanwhile, one morning Jibanananda receives a letter from his mother Kusumkumari, a poet in her own right, to come back to Kolkata for there is a match for him: her name was Labonyo. He agrees to the marriage after a brief meeting with the prospective bride. But back in

Delhi, once again he pines and feels tormented for Shobhona. One day, a colleague cajoles him to visit the brothels and he writes about the first impression of that world and then abruptly ends with—'everything, Namaste'. He seems to have been struck by the ritualistic aspects of a transaction that was otherwise most blasé and natural in its pedigree. Eventually, he travels to Barisal for marriage. Shobhona too makes an appearance—casual and offhand. He had taken leave from Ramjas College for the ceremony, but one day, he receives a letter from the college administration, notifying that he has been terminated from the job. The letter is signed by one Lala Rai Kedarnath, who was the proprietor-principal of the college at that time. Only a strange, half-hearted letter of recommendation follows, written by the same man who terminated him from the job. A line in the letter reads: "He proved himself useful and efficient in the English Deptt. & his conduct and bearing have been satisfactory" (Das, 2009, Vol. 4, p. 1972). A 'useful man of literature' becomes unemployed for the second time in life. This time, just after his marriage. The marriage soon turns bitter and he writes poignant entries in his diary that the marriage was a scam.

And he is in the throes of acute poverty: "moneylessness, like a dirty wallowing pig". His days are much soiled and he feels like a *pariah*: "degraded in soul [I have bowed before every cat and dog]" (Zaman, 2019). At that point of time, he turned into writing stories and novels, many of which are autobiographical in spirit. The reigning theme is creaturely defencelessness. It is as if Emil Cioran's favourite Romanian expression comes to life: *n-a fost sa fie*–literally, "it wasn't to be". He left those in trunks, unpublished—to be discovered much later. Failure became too familiar, and he nearly develops a kind of flair for it. And failure always receives company in humiliation. Failure reveals us to ourselves. In his diary entries and fiction, he gives a direction to this failed, parasitical existence.

During this time, a particular poem by Jibanananda—titled *In the Camp*—was especially targeted by his detractors, like Sajanikanta Dey. This poem dramatized the notion of the hunter and the hunted, and the idea of the tragic trap that we are in. In fact, the interplay between desire to hunt and the exposed assailability of the hunted is a constant and recurring motif in his writings. The carpers frame charges of obscenity against the poet. And the whole episode turns into a little scandal.

Jibanananda takes up the quill and laughs at the dismal level of aesthetic sensibility among the Bengalis. What is the supposed condition of existence which is being evaluated as obscene? These people, the evaluators—are prurient within, he decries. To such people, even the sky and the stars are not undefiled. Prurient critics shall forever miss the angst and imagination of creation. Had such poems been sent to the literary circles of Europe, true appreciation would be forthcoming. He recalls Robert Browning delineating *Muleykeh*, a mare in these words, in the long poem with an eponymous title: "she was the child of his heart by the day, the wife of his breast by night" and wonders about the reaction of the prurient to such lines. His angst-filled, but confident, note would be published after his death in *Shatabhisha* magazine.

It is all a trap—that is what exposure to frangibility instructs Jibanananda night and day. The lovers in his stories are like insects drawn towards the sundew plant. In every turn of life, brutality awaits. A great hunter plans and executes our daily degradation and downfall. There is no dodging, no respite. Fortune, through its many deft agents, lurks in the wings to extract a steep price for our daring to fulfil desires. The wings of the beautiful butterfly are mindlessly torn off by the truant schoolboy. The stag in the spring moonlight is first trapped and then killed effortlessly by the hunter. Agitation and passion usher in expectations that are bound to lead to vulnerability. Doleful absurdity is the truth of the hunted and the hunter, each bound by his own trajectory of anxiety and terror. No wonder he despises all cosmic order of regulated movement. Does this condition of being embroiled in desperation also devise its own release?

#Early 1930s: Pangs of unemployment swallow up Jibanananda's morale and increases domestic strife. He writes, "I wish I was a bachelor again—aghast when I think of future domestic life" (Zaman, 2019). Someone taunts him about his state and he responds in his dairy that the unemployed "stand & run & throb & palpitate, it is only the well-placed who merit the eternal charm of the easy chair or cushions" (Zaman, 2019). To stand sentinel every waking hour to one's fate was too much for him. Such was the nature of the manifest darkness that he preferred sitting in the dark for hours—which he calls sleeping within the womb enmeshed, like death. In one of his poems, he describes the world as infected with sunlight and millions of hogs are wailing and thumping around in festive spirit. Love and marriage eluded him. The last resort was literature. He notices that some of his mates have learnt to 'sing well' and are achieving literary fame too. He observes some others hankering for recognition. He is tremendously shocked to find his name missing in one of the new anthologies of Bangla poetry. He hopes to maintain his composure. But inevitable mood swings happen: "Everything is old, musty, worn out & second hand about me: literature, liberty, catalogue—Even in poetry, thrust back, my anthologies and cuttings don't help me … nobody, nowhere & the corruption, bulging flesh &washing away … to die thus …" (Zaman, 2019). An old student wants to help him with a job as a railway guard. Later, in one of his novels, Jibanananda would dramatize the event by suggesting that he had a dream that even after his death he keeps a vigil of railway stations with a green flag in hand, donning a white cap of the railway guard and an even whiter pair of shoes to match.

Shahaduz Zaman ponders that it may well be inquired as to the reasons for his not being able to land up a job. One was that in the late 1920s and in the 1930s, the Great Depression took a huge toll on the prospective job seekers. Britain too suffered and consequently, slashed financial expenses towards the upkeep of its colonies. Workers were being retrenched from offices and factories. Besides, Jibanananda had a second-class MA degree and many of the new applicants had a first. That did not help his cause. Another reason was his mien and temperament. He was well aware that people who make it in life are often articulate to the extent of being able to sell themselves to prospective employers. Their demeanour is also full of confidence, unlike his own state of affairs. Having a degree is never sufficient insurance. One also needs to be adept at keeping up with significant networks.

Not only that, but he also often suffered from issues of his own making. For instance, Jibanananda would not travel outside Bengal for a job anymore after the abortive Delhi experience. He was plain scared. The choice was between genial acquaintances and interlocutors on one hand and money on the other. But he needed the dough. Even as a teacher, he was not exactly first-rate. He tried out his hand in small enterprise—selling insurance and even umbrella handles. Again, his introverted nature and lack of agility were not conducive to such ventures. Labonyo writes in her autobiography that more than not bagging a job, Jibanananda was not inclined to be drafted into the drudgery of a pen-pushing clerk or even be a tutor. It is telling that in one of his short stories (*Poetry, Poetry and Still Poetry*), the protagonist, upon inquired about his liking, says, "A little single storied house in the far corner of the city, a carpeted reading room, a few tables and chairs made of *mahogany* wood and lots and lots of books to my taste—days and nights of reading and smoking cigar" (Zaman, 2019). This was his dream: to nurture an absolute contemplative life and keep writing.

This brings Shahaduz Zaman to reflect upon the underlying cause of Jibanananda's reticent nature. Like most of his fictional characters, he was constantly grappling with the idea of an aesthetic realization of the self and failure in worldly ways. This tendency he named—*karubashona*—the inclination and intense desire for the aesthetic. It is a condition of insatiable thirst, an existential craving. Those who are afflicted by *karubashona* have no other route available to them to square with life's travails and punishments. Beyond all the din of the world rings the peals of imagination and dream. In the throes of *karubashona*, perception is creation itself and not a mere receptive faculty. Perception of this nature is neither a matter of intellect nor that of affect. But a mode of establishing a sense of the relational—with time, nature, the palimpsest of history, other human beings, and with an ever insistent creaturely angst. There develops an acute attention to pain. To have this sense, he felt, was an inherent sin to the world and a curse that the artist carries along with him. Who would buy books of poetry—filled deeply with the malady of *karubashona*? Is there an eternal battle between Lakshmi and Saraswati, never to be truly reconciled? The artist is an unnatural, illegitimate being. He cannot run away from the mundane world for that is what nurtures art; nor can he come to terms with its demands and with the common measures of success.

These tidings might well be read as pure indulgence on the poet's part. To keep pace with such a level of self-absorption may even be tiring at times. But that is not the point. It was a difficult time globally and we notice how a highly imaginative and sensitive being is buffeted by circumstances and by his temperament. Circumstances do alienate him, but they also strengthen his resolve about the genuine vocation of the artist. An artist may be intensely implicated in the conditions of living; but he is also psychically tempted to read his circumstances and his time through a special filter which only he is able to take into several directions in future days and years. And there is a powerful and stark realist-materialist sense in Jibanananda's ways. What is immediate and raging is also fleeting. And this disconnect simultaneously creates cravings and disappointment. One of the characters in his novel *Karubashona* says: "God has not given us *nirvana*. He has given us memory. And desire like the sea. But he has constructed the body with a speck of rotten wood" (*Jibanananda Uponyash Samagra, Karubashona*). There is a constant play of finitude and abundance in his very notion of *karubashona*. This can be noticed even in despair; especially triggered by despair. The desire for art—*karubashona*—came across as an edict to him; it came to him as *karunirdesh*, which must be obeyed by the *kobimanash*—the horizon that the poet inheres (Ghosh, 2000). And a notable form of a moralism suffuses his works: "Like a static snail every person has his treasure, each operates within the ambit of social *dharma* and *neeti*. Only my eyes elude such immobility. I visit illegitimate roads, have illegitimate thoughts, ask illegitimate questions" (*Jibanananda Uponyash Samagra, Karubashona*). The free artist must shun the dicta of legitimacy.

Poised at such a nadir, Jibanananda's heart and soul begins to respond to the natural bounty of Bengal. In nature, he seeks a fresh beginning. His delineation of nature is remarkable for its tactile and sensuous details, its lazy and bountiful forms. There is nothing ethereal, everything is felt. Yet, in his writings, nature distinctly harbours a geological dimension—as if the foliage and waterways of Bengal speak daily to the stars and the ancient planets. Uncanny presences of creatures—algae and moss, insects and luscious fruits, hundreds of species of birds and plants, cattle and the wide fields speak through his living, throbbing quill. Shahaduz Zaman calls this "a drowning man's plea, his manifesto for a primitive love" (Zaman, 2019, p. 107). But it is here that we also detect his difficult attempt to forge a restorative relationship between the *particular* gifts of wonder and the pangs of despair that life throws at each one of us, and the *universal* traffic between immersion in nature and a planetary-geological sense of history. Jibanananda nurtures a world-historical

sense of human-creature, placed within the historical, the natural and the cosmological like the one conceived philosophically by Giambattista Vico or Wilhelm Dilthey. *Association* is the *copresence* of continuity and contemporaneity as the likes of Hartley, Coleridge or Thomas Mann have shown us, in their own art practice. (Incidentally, Jibanananda was a very meticulous reader of Mann). And imagination gives shape to such unicity. He was aware of such a characterization of his art, but refused to acknowledge that he was consciously attempting in any such project. He would always consider himself a lyric poet. At the level of singularity, therefore, Jibanananda realized that drowning is the first real step towards emergence. A fragile and despondent time is also uncanny and mysterious. Consequently, the poems written in this period are a goldmine for those trying to appreciate the planetary condition. But such an appreciation is never divested of the *singular* aching of the body and soul that is able to *perceive* the manifestations of crushing power and excruciating pain that contingency must bring about in the creature. This running dialectic between the individual and the *singular* on one hand and the geologically informed creaturely condition of the human and its *universality* on the other marks his many utterances, as if two parallel lines sometimes touch each other explosively only to return again to their respective trajectories. The poems of this phase would be anthologized much later under the rubric *Ruposhi Bangla* (*Beauteous Bengal*).

#1935: Happy tidings. A new job. Lecturer at Brajamohan College, Barisal. Once again—days and nights by the bends of his favourite river, *Dhanshiri*. The domestic scenario also improves. The students are friendlier here than what he had encountered in Delhi and Kolkata. It is during this period that Jibanananda receives a letter from Buddhadev Bose, his old backer, that a new magazine called *Kobita* is about to be launched and Bose would be delighted to have poems from Jibanananda. He had stopped writing poetry altogether. But the letter galvanizes him. He comes out of ennui and begins to write a series of remarkable poems on the subject of love.

Shobhona was always his muse but now love takes a very different dimension in his poetry. It is about loss, recovery, and a renewed sense of loss. Love is about perennially waiting like a country owl for one's beloved. The loss is a strange sorrow—"the world possesses another being only once and never again." Love is like grass germinating over his beloved, who is like loamy soil. It is, as it were, the embodied grass that rises up to the heart which turns grassy too. And then there are layers and layers of wind and sky. But love is full of danger too; it especially teeters at the threshold of jealousy and death. Under the spring moonlight, the lovers experience eternity through piston-like wings. The energy is palpable. And then—a gunshot. His winged creatures sometimes transcend death through love in this manner. But often they succumb since human life is not sufficiently attuned to the secrets of existence, unlike the lives of other creatures. Couldn't living be less or more than the humanly?

Jibanananda has been interrogated about the European inspiration in his poetry. His response was an acknowledgement of anxiety of influence. Reading other works, experiencing the flow of life, associations of immediate nature, social changes—everything bounces off against each other, an intricate tapestry develops, and gradually art happens. The poet or the translator has to reinvent a language and work creatively, with the medium that he engages with. Digesting diverse influences is of foremost importance for a creator. The past years of acute despair and poverty and his immersion in literature meanwhile is now converted into a powerful dialectic: between life and death, mirth and sorrow. He can now sense the whole cosmos in the particularities of the everyday. The universe seems to revolve like zebras and vultures; the roar of ferocious lions comes to his home through open windows. At this point, with some egging from Bose, Jibanananda decides to publish his second book: *Dhushar Pandulipi* (*Ashen Manuscript*). The collection shall alter the fortunes of Bangla literature.

What he had once called *bipponno bishmoy* (enchanted vulnerability) actually never abandons him. Now he once again returns to those ontological concerns, and marries those concerns with stark and uncanny poetic imagery. There have been endless speculations about death and suicide in his landmark poem—*Eight Years Ago a Day*. The conundrum of creaturely action, the facticity and finitude of living are marked by an equal and powerful attraction to bring life to an end, having felt in the veins the excesses of sensual bounty. Creatures of such nature burn themselves off—there are no other alternatives left.

But he also satirizes such a sentimental and self-indulgent way of looking at living. He repeatedly refutes the charge of being a poet of despair just as he had refuted the charges of obscenity earlier. Perhaps life's success may lie in living fully by taking on life threats and beauties first-hand, as other animals and insects do. And by immersing in a certain life-force that moving history provides. In fact, Jibanananda was fully aware that his poetry is not a luxuriant indulgence to death or a passport to the spillover of the sensuous excessive. The stairs to heaven must pass through the purgatory. Therefore, to history, nature and love he brings the evil directly and a libertarian romantic sensibility to boot that horrified the humanists and the genteel liberals. As a reaction, they charged him with writing counterfeit poetry and for creating an immoral cult and cautioned the young and the aspiring to keep away from such spurious influence. What they failed to notice is that the darkest of realizations for Jibanananda was his secret and sole path for emergence. A sense of creaturely vulnerability takes us headlong into the ferment of life, not away from it. We shall forget at our peril that bountiful marvels of life and nature forever awed Jibanananda's sensibilities. He has captured the condition of such recompense in a gratuitous phrase: *life's endless granary.* At his heart, he knew that from the depths of the most ominous caverns of sorrow, a hundred cataracts cascade like soothing care-givers. This is what Buddhadev Bose has called 'renascence of wonder', scattered within the subdued and haunting tone of his poetry (Bose, 1959).

At this stage in his life, Jibanananda does not solicit the evaluation of his poetry anymore from the critics and interlocutors. He is done with beseeching. He understands that apart from the kind and forthright Buddhadev Bose (and later, Sanjay Bhattacharya) he is surrounded mostly by detractors. Instead, he responds to the criticism about his writing and also gives his own viewpoint about poetry through sundry essays. The opening lines of one of his essays—*Kobitar Katha* (*About Poetry*) therefore famously announce, what has now become an adage in Bangla literary circles: "Not everyone is a poet; only a few are" (Das, 2015). He feels that amalgamation of imagination, thought, and experience, which when sieved through centuries of poetic utterances and through other contemporary forms, turns into poetry. It is not that

poetry does not take cognizance of society, nation or humanity, but any prior idea, ideology or conclusion in the poet's mind cannot give body to the skeleton of poetry. Such thoughts rather remain hidden like veins and blood particles within poetry. In another memorable utterance, Jibanananda says how he had felt sometimes that "the heart begins to burn like a candle in darkness and silence, and one can then feel the birthing process of poetry" (Zaman, 2019).

Through his prose and poetry, he ponders about wars, famines, bombing, black-marketeering and the rapid augmentation of greed and narcissism that constituted the world of the 1930s. During these times, the progressive writers' movement began to take shape and hope was being sown in order to take up cudgels against fascism. Socialist realism was in the air. And Subhash Mukhopadhyaya, a leading progressive voice of the time, attacked Jibanananda's poetry of being a drug, which destabilizes the sense of contemporary politics and history among the reader. Can hope be thus jejunely contrasted with despair, especially for those who pass through the severity of extreme times? Shahaduz Zaman sums up the situation: he has now squarely been pilloried by the progressives, the traditionalists and leading modernists of Bengal.

This issue—that Jibanananda takes us inward and by doing so, foments inertia, ennui and stasis, in an old charge. Shankha Ghosh has responded to such an allegation in two ways. One, he has looked closely at the poetics (*swarabritta*), the rhythmic patterns, and the nature of suggestibility in Jibanananda's art and found out a form that follows a certain tradition in the poetic practice in Bengal. So, Jibanananda's relinquishing of the ornamental actually brings his creations closer to the everyday following of such a tradition. It is not that Jibanananda wishes to look beyond the contemporary upheavals of history. His works are rather testimonials of the diurnal, placed within the frame of a larger totalization of creaturely acts. Such art practice provides a certain sonorous and rhythmic density to the passing tabloid of the contemporary. Art enframes every significant passing act. In the words of Ghosh, we discover an echo of Jibanananda himself, expressed in the latter's essay on poetry:

> Therefore he wishes to imagine a certain distinct water by relinquishing every drop of earthly water, by abandoning every available lamp he begins to imagine another lamp. At such moments, he does not wish to

> see water but waterness, not the lamp but a certain luminous lampness. And in order to visualize such a truth, the poet requires a secret tunnel. From such a tunnel he can see the incandescence that irradiates life, illuminating its kernel and crux. (Ghosh, 1991)

The artists-creator simply refuses to rely on any superficial and disconnected sense of optimism.

It is pertinent to remember here how, right from the early days of his writing, Jibanananda was acutely conscious of the working class, especially the urban poor, the humdrum cycles and drudgery of the clerical class and generally about those who are hungry and unprovided for. In one of his early poems, he thunders against the practice of retrenchment that was routine at that time, owing to the fallout of Great Depression and states that the power of the poetic self can only then be realized and one can sing paeans on behalf of the world if the hungry belly is sated. A memorable character sketch of the same period is *Shital muchi* (*Shital, the Cobbler*) (Das, 2004), whom he imagines as a figure about whose dire state all statisticians and policymakers are silent. Yet another poem is addressed to Haridas Ghosh, the postal clerk who loves life in penury. He imagines life as a piece of meat. In an ironic temper, Jibanananda says the more he would discover poetry, the more others will say that the time of poetry is gone; that they had enough of such things. These set of poems were composed much earlier, in the 1920s.

But being shunned by the progressives, he now begins to write about poetry. There is no pressure or responsibility upon poetry, he writes. Poetry irradiates the naturalness of the stark and it does not follow any set direction. Honest poetry comes to humiliation and daily grind through a holistic understanding of the vigour and force of life. Honest poetry is the poetry of revolution and that of the mightier time that arrives after the revolution. There cannot be any universal panacea, nor can there be any universal solution to the creaturely condition. And yet, he is acutely aware of the daily humiliation of the working class and the lowest strata of the society. But as an artist, he would keep away from the totalization of the social and reveal time through the particularities. Shahaduz Zaman writes that Jibanananda would actually keep away from both the extremes of blind belief and pure rationality, and hence, he was attacked by both sides. Golam Mustafa's translation of his poem *Of 1934, A Poem on Motor Car*, for instance, makes it evident that Jibanananda believed in the ferocity of slowness: "I do not want to go anywhere so fast. Whatever my life wants I have time to reach there walking" (Chowdhury and Mustafa, 2008).

> # As the Second World War rages, one day Jibanananda receives an extraordinary letter. The sender's name is Prabhakar Sen. He says that he has just received an MA degree in economics from the University of Calcutta. He wrote a few paragraphs about how as a lay reader he grapples with and feels about Jibanananda's poetry. He further states humbly that his literary knowledge is limited and, therefore, it is impossible for him to do any justice or fully savour the *rasa* of Jibanananda's poetic utterances. Nevertheless, he writes to find out whether his hunches and surmises about Jibanananda's poetry are correct.

The first observation is about Jibanananda's writing style and method. Sen feels that unlike numerous other poets, Jibanananda does not pick up his pen whenever he is saddened. The realm of the poet is not a triage centre for the wounded. Instead, he lets the *bhava* to permeate throughout the form of the poem. Each part of every single poem is related to the other in such a clear manner even as each remains in its metaphoric or revelatory state. Owing to this method, sometimes single stanzas may appear as weak, but overall, the pattern stands illuminated to the reader. Each letter, therefore, corresponds and becomes an equal partner to the immersed state of the poet.

The second observation is a speculation about the inspirational source of Jibanananda's poetry. Sen feels that each of the poet's contemporary articulations is rooted in the grey perennial. Time consciousness is crucial here. There is a crisscross of diverse time-space within each utterance, though this factor is not easily visible to a naïve reader. Such a sensibility of time also demands an equal investment by the reader who must place the passing moment as palimpsest over multiple frames. Not too many readers can or will take this trouble. Only a few will travel through the light-years to reach another galaxy or glean pearls from the deep sea.

The third observation is about historical sensibility in Jibanananda's writings. Sen astutely observes that since Jibanananda was intuitively tuned to the passage of time and its twists and turns, it was impossible for him to hold on to any ideology, temporality, system or even to human beings; that the poet will and have tried to latch on to such things, but they slip and elude him. And therefore, a residual desire for the earth, the female form (*manushi*), and so on is projected sometimes to the future in his poetry. The rhythm of time oscillates back and forth and these birthings of temporality appear as history to Jibanananda.

Shahaduz Zaman tells us that after going through the letter, Jibanananda felt that he is encountering and knowing his self in a new manner. He replied to Sen with a lot of commendation and love and even hoped that he should use such a sharp analytical mind to review the poet's works. That bit never materialized. But the two turned into good friends, though Sen was much younger to Jibanananda. Much later, after the Partition of India, when Jibanananda and his black trunks (filled with manuscripts, mostly unpublished) will forever be part of Calcutta, the two would often meet at the Indian Coffee House and discuss novels and novel writing. They would also discuss Jibanananda's unpublished works and their prospects. At this stage, he also begins to write more novels. The company of the young economist was like a lease of fresh air to Jibanananda's despairing self.

A line from Jibanananda's response to Sen's initial note is worth quoting in full:

> The poems that I have composed till date is not mere tableaux that illustrate my acceptance of some universal source of origin (*utsa-nirukti)* of humanity by placing that within the intersection of nature and temporality. Can anyone ever find such a thing? If such a thing was possible, the concentrated intensity of the lyric poet would then turn into the purity of the dramatic-narrative form. It is necessary for a narrative poet to seek such a space-time. But I still remain a lyric poet. In this path their lies another perplexing purity. (Das, 2017)

It is absolutely clear that the primacy of the vulnerable and the fragmented lyric self and its many relationalities are important to him as an artist. It is also worth noting that instead of dramatizing evil or loss, he emphasizes 'another perplexing purity' in the lyric form. What was he trying to recover from despair? The response to this query can be found in and through his creations of course, but sometimes, he has also directly addressed the issue. For instance, in a short essay titled *About Poetry*, Jibanananda has emphatically suggested that the lyric poet too travels through the three-worlds (*tribhubhanchari*), but the manner of his journey is unique: "Poetry can permanently put the mindscape under a certain catastrophe, and by doing so make it purer and transparent, effected through an economy of words and clues.... The temporal world gets an opportunity to be reconceived in this manner" (Das, 2015).

The Partition and relocation in Kolkata proved disastrous to Jibanananda. He lost his job in Barisal and had to accept an appointment in a small magazine called *Swaraj*. Humanyun Kabir was the proprietor. The salary was meagre and he had to work day and night. The office ambiance was forever crowded and hustling, very different from his college staff-room. The thought of committing suicide along with his family flashed before his mind and he often wrote about euthanasia. But he also hoped to write more, in case he did survive. A sense of finitude lurks. He writes in one of his diary entries: "I find mother the way I used to see my blind father. Groping, shaking with palsy, incapacitated, unable to do anything. Before reaching such a stage one will have to finish 'everything' that may give one the satisfaction of a Tolstoy or a Goethe" (Zaman, 2019). The level of confidence is stunning.

Shahaduz Zaman writes how his mother, Kusumkumari, had always felt that God would come to her son's rescue if he held on to the Almighty. But the son had little faith in faith. Instead, he believed that an inner spirit, which he called *bodh* (sometimes *neetibodh*), propelled creatures. In his novel *Bibha*, the eponymous protagonist buys a mynah bird, which unfortunately suffers from a boil under its wings. Bibha, the character, is empathetic to the bird's condition since God has sent her the bird. But as the mynah jumps off Bibha's lap to the carpet, a cat arrives out of nowhere and breaks her neck. The bird's head is gone. No God could save the mynah. At that point, we realize that the servant has killed the cat with an iron rod. At this, Bibha's father says that now he would finish off the servant and Bibha would in turn kill the father figure. That is the cycle of devouring. So, Bibha ought not to see benevolence in God's ways. It is sufficient if one is able to spend life in a relatively harmless condition. We do not have the power to provide solace or support to others.

Shahaduz Zaman reminds us that in another novel, *Purnima*, that his scepticism is even more pronounced. There is nothing worked out or semi-hazardous here, no god or devil. If there was a blueprint, one could at least complain or revolt or accept fate. All methodological systems break down in some random manner. Beneath the created universe of the stars, there is no empathy, no attention, no help, no power of our own, no sudden miracles here, no faith in *bidhata*, *dharma* or *sanyas*, no solace or support here. The artist restores creation by recreating anew from the tiniest of dead insects, but once again, everything disintegrates. The artist keeps trying. Jibanananda had therefore conceived the artist as *keetnirmata* (insect-creator).

Radically alienated, with no friends, no relatives to go to, Jibanananda often now turns suspicious of people's motives. So, he would refract his view of the humans through birds, insects, fish and foliage. Creating intricate tapestries by placing a chain of creatures within the wilful play of fortune, he would try to recreate the cosmos anew.

#1954: The final year of Jibanananda's life. One of his favourite quotations was from Andre Gide: "I do not write for the coming generation but for the following one" (Gide, 2000). Perhaps, this is the manifestation of a certain irreverent strain on his part? But it was strange that he turned most active during this late period: landed up a job in a college once again, his collected poems got published and he had even begun attending meetings and poetry reading sessions. But Shahaduz Zaman also tells us that he would sometimes visit the zoo and stare for hours at the rhinoceros, the giraffe and the elephant. Did these creations arrive from some other galaxy to meet and greet him on earth? During mid-October, for a couple of days, he mentions to some close family members that he has heard someone to have come under the tramcar that passes by his residence. He himself would take evening strolls in the neighbourhood. The following day, he falls under the tramcar and is taken to the nearest hospital. At the hospital, he asks for an orange. Perhaps, as he lay on his deathbed, the din of life flowing past the hospital precincts seemed like fleshy fruit?

In the city of Calcutta, barring a handful, no one had the time to care about the passing away of an unalloyed, Neolithic failure, who wanted to feel and express the power of vehemence, working incessantly within the wholeness of time.

References

Bose, Buddhadev. 1959. "Jibananada Das Smarane." In *Probondho Sankalan.* Calcutta: Dey's Publishing.

Chakrabarti, Arindam. 2008. *Deho, Geho, Bondhutto: Chhoti Sharirik Tarko.* Kolkata: Anustup.

Chaudhuri, Sukanta (ed.). 1998. *A Certain Sense—Poems by Jibanananda Das.* Translated by various hands. Calcutta: Sahitya Akademi.

Chowdhury, Faizul Latif and Golam Mustafa (eds.). 2008. *Beyond Land and Time.* Dhaka: Somoy Prokashon.

Chowdhury, Faizul Latif (ed.). 1999. *Aprokashito Ekanno.* Dhaka: Mawla Brothers.

Cioran, E.M. 1996. *On the Heights of Despair.* Chicago: University of Chicago Press.

Das, Jibanananda. 2009. *Dinolipi—Literary Notes.* 4 Vols. Compilation and Analysis, Bhumendra Guha and Gautam Mitra. Kolkata: Protikkhon.

———. 2006. *Selected Poems.* Translated by Chidananda Das Gupta. New Delhi: Penguin Books.

———. *Nirbachito Kobita.* Ed. Tapodhir Bhattacharyya. Kolkata: Bangiyo Sahitya Sansad.

———. 2017. *Patralaap—Letters.* Ed. Prabhatkumar Das. Kolkata: Ebong Mushayara.

———. *Jibanananda Das er Uponyash Shomogro.* www.amarboi.com.

———. 2015. *Kobitar Kawtha.* Kolkata: Signet Press.

———. 2004. *Chhaya Abchhaya.* Kolkata: Pratikshan.

Ghosh, Shankha. 2000. "Shomoyer Shomogrota." In *E Shohorer Rakhal.* Kolkata: Paschim Banga Bangla Academy.

———. 1991. "Shato Jaljharnar Dhwani." In *Chhander Baranda.* Kolkata: Aruna Publications.

Gide, Andre. 2000. *Journals. Volume 2: 1914–1927.* Translated by Justin O'Brian. Chicago: University of Illinois Press.

Ginsberg, Allen and Lawrence Ferlinghetti (eds.). 1964. "A Few Bengali Poets." In *City Lights Journal.* San Francisco.

Mitra, Gautam. 2015. *Aprokashito Jibanananda Das.* Kolkata: Saptarshi Publications.

Shahriar, Abu Hasan (ed.). *Jibanananda Das: Mullayon o Patthodhhar.* Dhaka: Shahitto Bikash.

Winter, Joe. 2003. *Jibanananda Das—Naked Lonely Hand.* London: Anvil Press Poetry.

———. 2006. *Bengal the Beautiful.* London: Anvil Press Poetry Ltd.

Zaman, Shahaduz. 2019. *Ekjon Komolalebu.* Dhaka: Prothoma Prakashan.

The Elsewhere Creature

Aniket Jaaware's Destitute

In his book *Practicing Caste, on Touching and Not Touching*, Aniket Jaaware takes caste as an instance in order to transport us *elsewhere*. We are not yet born, he says. So, he wants us to travel with him to the island of Hokkaido, and especially to Fukushima, and take a little pause with the *ainu*, an outcaste group that lies at the bottom of the traditional Japanese society. We could also go to Yemen and learn the language of the *al-akhdam*, who harbour *negrito* features on their *cultured bodies*. Jaaware wants us to see that there are other worlds too, with similar sets of primary and primal distinctions based on questions of pure being. In this, our primary condition is that we are the same everywhere, needlessly making segments and boundaries of living all the time and trying to obliterate our common creaturely state. This is the condition of living. In our variegated splendour, humans shall continue to *live as one* in bringing others close or keeping them at bay, depending on some inexplicable and unknown equations that they will invent (or have invented already) from within their chosen sect.

Caste is an instance. Destitution is the state of being.

Aniket Jaaware was wracking his brain and soul about the destitute, immersing himself as one more creature in the throes of destitution. He wanted to deliberately forget (his term is *oublierring*, from French *oublier* and English *err*) not just the hitherto deliberated upon history and sociology of caste studies but more importantly, the language of certainty and sociability which is also the language of our present ethical conundrum about destitution. The real problem to him was the condition of intellectual destitution—that we do not know where to go with our creaturely sense of fallenness, humiliation and abandonment. To bring rumination down to touching and not touching, therefore, is to break down a seemingly insurmountable problem into the basics and try addressing it afresh. Therefore, Hokkaido and Yemen. These are not geographical places to him, but insignia of a huge inchoate and unknown future, the *elsewhere* where the destitutes of the world can say: *just us,* instead of getting into the infinite spiral of identity and victimhood. Only internalizing such a realization can perhaps open up the realm of freedom.

There is Nothing Called Society

In a way, Jaaware at once affirms and confronts Gabriel Tarde's motto: *everything is social.* There are several *intimate cuts* among ourselves; we shall interact with some people and not with other animals and abject bodies. This is how groups, clans and segments work. *Samaj* is not society—there are divisions and hierarchies. These are real, stubborn striations. Consequently, there are only forms of sociability (love or hate at first sight) in our living interactions. Beings interacting in sociability are deeply and phenomenologically bound to each other, though such bonds are invented through interactions. Sometimes, these differential bonds turn ephemeral and transcendental and leave certain traces, when some member(s) decide to quit a loyal sect or a group—by way of exile, voluntary or otherwise, and through death. These set of thoughts we also encounter in Tarde. But Jaaware wishes to take us *elsewhere* from such a condition of corrosive sociability. Tarde's world of fantasy is stark in its encounter with the social. He deepens the force of the *actual* by means of imagining the vicissitudes of a world that greets creatures after the apocalypse. Jaaware, on the other hand, after acknowledging the tangible dimensions of destitution, speaks passionately to our common humanity.

Under ordinary circumstances, we have sociable encounters with our alterity—with those who are from other segments, but live within the communal space. Jaaware calls this the state of *pathologically nonchalant non-sociability.* Even civility seems to be too abstract for any exchanges to happen among individuals here. Others with whom we interact are rather *obstacles* to be overtaken or circumvented. The destitute are produced in this manner as *obstacles.* The destitute are not adversaries or competitors. They are simply *not like us*. Our parks and clubs, washrooms and corridors, gymnasiums and bazaars—all are made into sanitized territories, so that certain creatures can be hounded and pulverized. Being-in-the-world means that such a form of sociability has to be reinvented in and through every single encounter. This manner of interaction is customary. The fragility of this customary mode of sociability directly leads to violent and demanding impositions and maniacal postulations against the destitute enemy, the unknown person(s) whom we know as the interactive other.

Jaaware gives the example of a performance artist who goes up to strangers and does 'pleasant' or 'unpleasant' things:

> touching them, jumping up and down in joy in front of them, picking a speck of dirt from their cheek (grandma's spit), carrying a portable toilet and sitting on it in public with pants down, standing half-naked with just a jacket on in front of a painting, grabbing and eating food from someone else's plate at a party, lying down in an art gallery and holding people's legs and not letting go, posing nude beside a sculpture of a nude, standing half naked beside a clothes rack, asking people to dress her. (Jaaware, 2019)

This is a control experiment in order to explore the way sociability actually takes place. By starkly deflating its operation, we realize the power and ubiquity of sociable interaction. The artist is asking people to invent sociability by improvising or formulating human interactive methods right at the moment of her performance.

This is exactly what one could see unfold after Aniket Jaaware's death. Or the obverse of it rather. It was spring time and his material body had just been cremated a few days ago, along with his famous ear-stud! A really good discussion on his book was arranged at the Max Mueller Bhavan, New Delhi. And academics like me heard his video-recorded voice waft across the hall—and the hall indeed was *choc-a-bloc*. There was hope for something grand and gone for the audience. And therefore, *collegial sociability* was everywhere. That is the only mode in which each makes peace with the other, just before and after such discussion sessions: in the foyer or the rotunda or at the car park outside. These modes of *temporary communality* we carry to the hall itself (perch ourselves at the right spots, greet other fellow beings with a certain collegial air, preface questions later with polite humility, and so on). You keep on performing something 'social'—yourself as an academic, a journalist or as an intellectual—while being constantly individuated. This was the 'silence' part of the 'social sciences', as Jaaware had already predicted. Did he presciently envisage the process of his own memorializing by his sociable colleagues and well wishers? There was Jaaware's voice coming across to us, but not his nonchalant form of comic challenge to this whole mode, which he knew he would be subjected to after being gone. It is in this manner that a great intellectual is canonized socially, and permanently made into *one of us*. It is not that he was righteously out of it, but he could possibly see the canonization from an ironic distance as he planned and wrote the book.

There are archetypal sociological studies of the phenomenon of suicide of the destitute animal, but there is no sociology "of the girl's falling body as it falls while she, high on this or that form of joy assisted by acidic chemicals, thinks she is flying, there is no sociology of her joy as she flies before she splatters her blood and brains and bones six stories below," Jaaware says (Jaaware, 2019). Similarly, there are ways in which mob psychology or the behaviour of a crowd can and has been explained, but none to map each little move of the 'flash' crowd in its violent or silent actions, or about the individual troll coming together with other such souls to extract vengeance or show purposeful righteousness. It is here that Jaaware marks the stubborn nature of *not touching* someone—a phenomenon that we call the actual practice of caste. The destitution of caste arrives to us through such a cognitive force stereotyping, always mediated through ways of sociability.

The *workability of future*, on the other hand, is always done by temporalizing the space of the social: that we can change the future by *doing* something in the present. It opens up the past, present and future hope for the destitute of the world. The future is unknowable and yet you wish to make it workable. In distancing himself from the very ideas of compromise and workability, and by not offering any social blueprint of a temporal future when all human beings will have no problems in touching oneself as well as touching others, Jaaware teeters on the brink of determinism. Disinheritance and destitution then would seem natural. In fact, there is always this play and conjunctive possibility of finitude and creaturely initiative that haunt us.

We were considering the notion of segmented sociability, "a phenomenon that works at a lower level than society," something that works at the level of solving problems (Jaaware, 2019). Solving the problem of untouchability and destitution is the problem of segmentation. Is Jaaware saying that if we get rid of the tricks of the social, then we can rid ourselves of the issue of caste itself? If such a thing happens, there are two possibilities perhaps. One, that we go back to a traditional form of living with the archaic structures of sociability in place. That will mean the *thrown* idea of caste existence is made timeless and universal. This mode of thinking valourizes a hierarchical system where barriers of identity are naturalized as communal living. The other is that if such a temporal idea of sociability thwarts full resolution of the condition of destitution exemplified via the enactment of touch, then we can think in terms of radical difference and hence, a larger kind of plurality of a common existence may materialize. I think Jaaware shuttles between these two poles. He keeps the notion of destitution tautly balanced between the condition of phenomenological existence as suffering and the possibility of endless tropes and differential measures, by which, instead of highlighting the finitude of our identities, we would seek out and revel in some *radical elsewhere*, where we can be *just us*. You and you and you make *the us*: "We have been told that we must constitute us, ourselves, in a limited manner. Me, my family, my friends, my clan, my caste. This limits *the us* to ourselves merely. We must reject this limited us" (Jaaware, 2019). The constitution of quick autobiographical we-ness is what he rejects, for that assumes human hubris of correcting destitution through means of social projects merely. To that he places a great wager and hope for altruism: "Birth is, in that expanded sense of time (evolutionary time), one iteration in a recursive process, or unknown algorithm, and not the final determinant of anything at all, just as death is not. 'They' will die too, perhaps after they kill us. In as much as we are living and dying together at the same time, we are also cause and effect together at the same time.... Can the us change the direction of time? Let us hope" (Jaaware, 2019). Nothing is any final determinant in our creaturely interaction with one another. Everything is possible if we can *oublierr* all unnecessary baggage and think in terms of the commonality of existence. Hope belies all notions of determinism in Jaaware, which always tries to appear through the back-door. There is a great utopian fiction in Jaaware's conception of the togetherness of destitution. He wants to summon that unspoken language of changing the direction of time and traversing elsewhere.

There is this deep, angry and hopeful longing for reconstruction, once the units and fragments of the sociable are de(con)stituted by looking closely at the de-stitute.

The difficult point is that customary and acquired protocols and actual empirical processes of segmenting creatures into the destitute cannot easily be breached. Reinstitutionalization is once again merely a workable non-solution, since the deeper cut remains unchanged. Alterity rather stubbornly continues to fester as pathological identities. The question remains: how do we relate to those we do not know? How do we sensually and phenomenologically deal with other physical bodies that are outside and beyond us and our known circle of existence? How do we traverse the difficult path from one body to another, one destitute to another? Jaaware's response is that we can expand our horizon of expectation and project it onto other sociabilities. Hence, Hokkaido and Yemen. The habitual invention of our own kind of sociability must be dropped. It is only then that we would realize the existential condition of destitution that binds all of us. Only in such a circumstance might alterity cease to be a wall of incomprehension and division, but rather could become "a hinged turnstile or door which can open both toward the inside and toward the outside" (Jaaware, 2019). Only in such a situation can one think of the movement towards temple-entry and the movement towards access to water—not as protests, but as rearticulating the possibility of traversing to another destitute sociability.

Traversing between divergent sociabilities is a possibility—not in understanding and correcting destitution with any quick-fix, but by living it. Is destitute living enough though? Jaaware takes us to the limits of untraversability by considering the vortex of death, which seems to be the end of all destitution and the discussion of it. Even that gap, between living and extinction, can be traversed perhaps through language and memory and imagination. Our body is scattered in death and has become part of things, but those things (marrow-blood-brain—now turned into pure matter) will live on in language and travel through tropes. That (a sense of our biodegradability) does not solve the question of destitution. Can it be addressed, though, by returning to *where we are* and only by dispossessing everything, and by considering that some other primal unity is living and dying and living again with matter?

Literature between Things and Humans

Can there be a category called *destitute literature*? Is not all literature also somehow imbued with destitution in so far as it deals with material suffering, abjectness, tribulations, contradictions and conflict? But when we think of destitution and art, it is assumed almost that the ethical is the consequence of the literary: "as if the literary production were the consequence of the ethical superiority of victims of political and social domination, exploitation, suppression, oppression and hegemony" (Jaaware, 2019). Jaaware contends that literature itself cannot bridge this distance between the political and the ethical; that "Dalit literature might have been revolutionary—but it should not be confused with revolution itself" (Jaaware, 2019). A generous use of affects ought not to confuse the literary and the political. In fact, such a route might short circuit the full power of the very condition of destitution, which always lies in the immediacy of the political acts of suffering and humiliation. At the heart of such a claim seems to be a *project of truth hunting* that will lead to some ethical core or to an authentic idea of destitution: the truth of caste-injustice, for instance. Experience itself would then surrogate simultaneously for the political and the literary. And experience is registered through affect, which is always a romanticization of the ego. There seems to be no discord between style and content in constituting such an idea of the literary-aesthetic. The idea of truth is already ethically and discursively been operative in society, and in such a view—fiction ought to rearticulate that very truth. Such an ethical move finally can only relate realism with a certain didacticism, though it will be always mediated through the *authentic genres* of autobiographies, confessions and memoirs. The nature and power of the fictive will find very little articulation.

That does not imply at all that fiction and narration merely lie behind any aestheticized notion of 'disinterested interest' in the post-Kantian sense, nor is it that any New Critical concept of the autonomy of art and its tropes and ambiguities brings us closer to the destitute. In this context, Jaaware refers to the writings of Baburao Bagul, whom he finds truly modernist in the sense that he directly brings us to the gruesome lives that are narrativized, and later, reveals to us its ethical fallout "as the reader gets to read the impossible performative situations in which the characters find themselves" (Jaaware, 2019). The ethical is always the condition of the impossibility to turn ethical, and yet one performs actions that will have consequences for oneself and for others. And the disjunction between style and content gets hammered time and again in the process. This is the reason, according to Jaaware, that many of Bagul's narratives end at what is often called a double bind. The ethical complexity is of such an order that it is impossible to take any superior righteous or correct position. Mere exhortations will not do—one has to take the full power of the fictive immediacy of destitution in life and in representation. It is in these ethically impoverished moments that the literary and the political are likely to come together.

The question about destitution cannot start with birth or biology. Nor with physical anthropology, race or other essential typologies. It is a natural order of existence that had been constructed by the humans—their turning to destitution as a fact of life or custom. This is a kind of stylistic choice that a group of people makes about others. To believe in mapping a pre-existent future by speculating positively on transformation, or mapping a pre-existent past by speculating positively on memory or custom are such stylistic choices. These are styles or tendencies of sociality, as we have discussed earlier. Often these two tendencies—looking forward as hoping to fulfil a project or looking backward nostalgically and deterministically, interpenetrate.But these tendencies are manifested always as and through certain empirical markers, which are felt and material.

Markers are actual things/happenings, through which the condition of destitution is brought into practice, for instance, by touching a thing or another body one not only carries out an act, but also leaves a trace of an encounter. This may be allowed, or not, depending on certain injunctions. The injunctive regulations on a person or a group of people to touch or not touch another body or thing actually means regulating presence and absence. This fundamental marker will lead eventually to higher level regulations about intermarriage or inter-dining. The metonymies of bodily presence are submitted to such commands of exclusion at the most basic level. At the heart of destitution are regulations on both things and people. You cannot stop touching things as long as you are alive and yet you are asked to cease from touching certain things or people. Even the shadow of a lower caste person is a kind of material trace that cannot be grazed by the Brahmin. That is how the most intense matter of physical revulsion turns into a trace. The material act of not touching and the force of the injunction cohere at a point, giving rise to the predicament of ostracism. The gradual and chronic normalization of such ostracism is the condition of destitution. The regulators of destitution do not allow the *diffusion of markers* into a free-for-all—that is to say, one set of sociable people serve an injunction on touching or not touching, since they actually are scared of the mushrooming of the traces into multiplicity and randomness. Hence, they desperately clutch on to the fundamental markers of identity. It is this diffusiveness and unconnectedness that urges us to forge the strongest of bonds, something that can only be recalled and something that will outlast the demise of the body.

Traces will not be domesticated. Traces are errant. They are stubborn reminders and forever-present possibilities—which is where the domain of art and literature lies too. Institutionalizing defeats the very purpose of recalcitrant traces, which were born in the first place from touch. Those traces are the ones that may defeat all narrow boundaries of small sociabilities. The traces are where the figures of speech lie too. The object of encounter or the regulations to an encounter can turn to art by means of expressing and suggesting the electric power of touch. Literature in such cases is both denotative and connotative, both as acts in and of life, but also as fictive ephemera, having a certain excess and subtlety that only art can suggest through the use of the figural. As Jaaware points out profoundly, things are even more destitute than humans and other animals, or everything exists as matter and also as an excess to matter:

> We include here the accidental but scathingly erotic touch of a table, or a cousin or some other person, a cushion perhaps, or the door handle or tap if it matters, or, as always the painful cut from the knife accompanied by onion smell and tears, distraction and randomness; and therefore, there was an attempt to regulate these acts. (Jaaware, 2019)

It is not that Jaaware uses the literary in order to make a case for relations between things. He rather tries to map how our relations with things can include people if mediated through metonymies and other tropes. Literature is a matter of extension through spatial and temporal concomitance. "I do not touch shit" can be extended by saying "I do not touch those who touch shit". In our polymorphic existence, the literary may happen if we realize how certain dos and don'ts function, since we touch only those things that seem sociable to us, as our own. These things are also often transposed to people. There is a touchable ownership of people and kin and lovers and children. The moment we have moved away from the hunting-gathering stage, we begin to regulate and manufacture the destitute from among ourselves and begin to distance them. Regulation on touching things is transposed onto other people through metonymies. This extension of the one whom I wish to radically dispossess from my existence is the destitute. Literature tries to explore these partially understood regulative processes that begins viscerally and remains in the world as traces amidst us.

That means destitution is a *promiscuous possibility*. Jaaware has, time and again, emphasized the eroticism of the traces. "Incest is institutional; promiscuity is random," he says (Jaaware, 2019). Destitution is beyond all measures and refuses to be institutionalized. Hence, the fear. And the deployment of regulative mechanisms to stem it. The promiscuity happens owing to a primal fear of mixing caste barriers—what he calls the *beforehand-mixedness*. In fact, all marriages and sexual relations are incestuous possibly, if we go back in time—until we reach the mitochondrial Eve. Literature, on the other hand, is a celebration of a promiscuous trace that goes far beyond our austere and ascetic incestuous and adulterous relationships. At the core of addressing destitution is this fear of the randomness of promiscuity. That is why we wish to bind it through sociological analysis. Only a topological measure (figures of speech, symbols, explanations and syllogisms, *alamkara*, apophantic significations, other heuristic devices) of the visceral nature of the act and event of destitution can come close to realizing what it actually is. As Jaaware says: "The melody must destitute itself musically" (Jaaware, 2019).

Touch Itself

Touch as such, or the lack of it, where destitution resides, is neither philosophical nor social. It is present *right here* among us, in its full visceral presence. Jaaware wants to decipher that bit, mediated through the 'social prose of the world', the ways of which we have indicated earlier, when it gets written, by touching others and by touching oneself too.

In order to keep his subject absolutely simple and material (touching and not touching bodies—objects, creatures and humans), Jaaware uses words like density, inertia, surfaces, planes and so on. These are words that bring us closer to the physicality of the condition of destitution and forms of attachment. But these are also words which prepare the ground to breach the distance between the literal and the figural. To begin with, Jaaware tries to rigorously define touch by negating three possibilities of considering matter. First, the empirical stimulus response interactions, which can only lead to behaviourism. Second, and this follows empiricism: residually phenomenological possibilities of touch which can only deepen one's vertical attachment to the world. Third, there cannot be any transcendental-eidetic reduction of the tactile senses of our interactions. To have interest in the nature of sociality of touch means to have an abiding sense of the materiality and the reality of *touch itself*, like in this statement: "While talking and feeling of the wind on the skin, we talked of the rate at which particles strike the skin being proportionate to the least density that is touchable" (Jaaware, 2019). Here is where the real touch and the question of the sensory density reach the zone of the fictive. The *fiction is real* since scientific words like density can be made fictive once the contact point between the wind and the skin actually turn into a miraculous possibility, which is where the real and the fictive merge.

Touch is also a space which is to rigorously do with the surface of things. Inside means touching a memory or something at some phenomenological depth, which shall cancel the power and stench of the moments of intensity. That is not his objective. Indeed an inside can be reached only through *a cut*—cutting the plane of the surface. This means one has to be attentive to *touch itself*, the warmth or the lack of it, which is the fore most and only condition of destitution.

Destitution is the caressment of distancing from the surface. Destitution is such a form of ostracism.

The literal meaning of touch is evident: we touch something in order to touch that thing. But the figural meanings of touch could be felt through such devices as metonymy, allegory and metaphor. These are contents of touch, not form. This is where the realm of the material and the realm of language and rhetoric coalesce. The form common to all these is: contact. For instance, to touch the feet of elders or the idol of a god is a case in allegory (although objects touched—feet, are cases in synecdoche). You are touching the realm of the *sacred*. Similarly, to refrain from touching a person's dress or shoes or shadow are cases in bringing the figural relationship of allegory into the realm of banishment and exile. This form of creating the condition of destitution is an everyday happening—like keeping a deliberate distance from the waiter, the garbage collector, the taxi driver and the doorkeeper. These are forms of immediate ostracism, happening normally and viscerally, but have allegorical possibility in taking us to the zone of *disposability*. Metonymic and metaphorical touches are deployed in order to figuratively apprehend certain kinds of fetishism perhaps, like foot or hair or leather.

The fundamental position of the condition of the destitution of the touching animal is to consider the *just-born*. The neonate is also an automaton—a creature in the exact sense of the term. It is a blob of matter until it experiences touch itself and gets a sense about touch by means of primary interactions with the mother and other close ones. The lifting of the baby is the first step towards disciplining the body, stopping its free movement. It is only gradually that the neonate transforms itself into a unitary *body-with-parts* and turns into a child. The next stages of disciplining then begin: of deportment and strictures and limits over touching oneself and certain other bodies. This is the process of *bildung*. The point about the *right kind of contact* gradually makes itself manifest in our dealings. Touch becomes an instrument of sociability. The attitude of the body now changes, Jaaware concludes, and at an allegorical level, a *will* develops about oneself and other bodies too.

These stages lead to a juncture when the being is able to manipulate distance (by means of calibrating intimacy) from other beings and bodies. It is also a state of helplessness that begins from a realization of the separation from the mother and then traverses to other objects and people. A *territory* is created whereby touch and intimacy become places to be defended. There happens a zone of possession and another radically outside of it: "That which we touch repeatedly becomes our possession, imparting a synecdochic bit of our self to that object or person" (Jaaware, 2019). Hence, toys, clothes, lovers, wallets, private property—we are *enveloped* by these our possessions. Beyond this territory lies the other, the one who cannot be touched. There is the field of regulation, the extension of which is caste or such-like forms of the other, who is the destitute. The distancing act in time and space from another body or a group of bodies thus turns hierarchical, discriminating and social. This distancing act is that of envelopment, mediated through an ontological sense of distrust and disgust. This is at the root of destitution: to get into the chronotope of revulsion about an object or a group of people whose very shadow cannot be touched. This is where the allegory of touching and not-touching begins and then the territories and certain time-space travel with us.

The Thrown Project and Liberty-Beyond-Death

Are we doomed to remain destitute, especially those who are chosen by modes of sociality to be marked and ostracized? This is a strand that is a consistent and constant reminder in Jaaware's framework. This comes from an acute realization of not trying to skirt the issue of touching which is direct and immediate. The framework takes the full account of the complexity and figurative expanse of such a simple gesture, which is what the domain of the rhetorical limns. But we started this chapter by suggesting that there is a tremendous sense of hope about the idea of our common material existence too in the framework—that is to say, once we level with the real issue of what it means to actually practice caste, we would really notice how circuitous and jejune this project is, how very limiting its politics of imitating its own identity looks like.

Jaaware painstakingly unfolds to us the condition of the cast out and the abandoned. There is no skirting the immediacy and the power of the skin and its traces that determine relationships. One wonders about the political condition of the visceral nature of the destitute, once we realize the finitude of our existence? After the knowledge of our thrown condition and realizing the process of *bildung*, through which we learn to give in and participate in the condition of creating the destitute, what are the possibilities of the *just us*? In fact, one of the startling prospects that Jaaware shows to us is that all of us live in *potential destitution*—not only by endlessly and helplessly creating the conditions of distancing and abandonment, but also by being caught in the net of such exclusion ourselves. This is why he finds the state of the Brahmin to be so infinitely pitiable: caught in the web of excluding the untouchable, the Brahmin has to live a life within little boundaries and small strictures. The largeness and heterogeneity of life eludes him; the very joys and risks of touching the other being beyond him. Hence, he is doomed to live within a condition of small sociality: "All human beings are dalits, but not all human beings have, in society, the function of dalits" (Jaaware, 2019). Our functions are of a different order than our conditions of destitution. Functions can be ossified into identities, but the condition of touching or not touching is a trait that is of a material and fictive order that speaks to our common living.

The dual notions of the *elsewhere* and the *promiscuous*, which we had stressed earlier, could have opened other vistas and horizons. But how does one achieve such a mode of generosity if one is constantly and simultaneously aware of the creaturely thrown condition on one hand and our institutionalizing freedom into a future project of social parity on the other? What lies beyond the spiral of acceptance of finitude and the ever-receding idea of progress,for the destitute being? Jaaware's response is that there cannot be any solution unless we give in to our inner altruism and openness. No other project can diminish our limited sense of replicating identity unless we are munificent and embracing of life itself. He has thoroughly refuted any notion of seeking humanity, but has joyfully embraced an animality that only kills for food. There is a constant sense of the corporeal, and therefore, the limits of the corporeal. The final condition depends on what we do with ourselves—a condition that is not yet born. There is immense utopia in Jaaware's thinking, though he debunks any kind of social blueprint for the future. In fact, this utopian hope is what forecloses all speculation about immediate projects of realizable justice in the book. This is an attitude, a kind of pulsation that leads to a sense of transgressing all limits of our finite small existence around social conditioning, especially since we are aware of the finitude of our material ties.

It is important to note that Jaaware never makes destitution synonymous with abjection or misery. In this sense, he has kept himself outside of the kind of work done on abjection by Julia Kristeva (though the dynamism or pulsation is there in him, like Kristeva) or Judith Butler. He takes the body/object elsewhere. The jettisoned object, the radically excluded, is not a victim ever, but rather is thoroughly nonchalant since he is a real object working on this earth and deeply materialized as such. This is because in Jaaware's scheme of things, the other is *never infected,* and therefore, there is no scope for the casteist person to ever feel vindicated in his project. The casteist is himself in a condition of stasis as long as he accepts and continues to mark the limits of touch ablity. The coupling of the outcaste and the casteist persona will remain forever in a locked state of combat unless each realizes that destitution is the condition of living and can be transcended only by embracing radical difference, which is also our common destiny and hope. His destitute rather makes a mockery of the exclusionary matrix by voiding its concerns.

Certain strands of thought have tried to disturb the inside and outside of our bodies, taking a cue from deconstruction. Kristeva is the obvious instance. Steven Shaviro, following such a line of thinking, while discussing David Cronenberg's visceral films, points to the body's capacity to disturb certain categories of inside and outside and take flight:

> The polymorphousness of living tissue has the capacity to traverse all boundaries, to undo the rigidities of organic function and symbolic articulation. New arrangements of the flesh break down traditional binary oppositions between mind and matter, image and object, self and other, inside and outside, male and female, nature and culture, human and inhuman, organic and mechanical. (Shaviro, 1993).

Indeed, the living tissue can traverse, but the binaries are quite rigid and they decide the condition of exclusion in Jaaware. Therefore, he actually refrains from breaking the binaries by highlighting *aporia* and instability. Instead, right from the outset, he creates a serious binary of the outwardly/materially tactile and the inner points of bodies that can be only reached through orifices, cuts and through the heart. But he keeps away from the innards and the inward movements of our soul. This is because his materialism is severe and exact. His investment is in the real and the literal—and then the transferring of the real into the fictive takes place. This, one suspects, happens because there is an urge to bring two kinds of real together in Jaaware's conceptualization of the untouchable: the lived and the material. He does not splice open binaries, so that one can affirm instability, but works with the binaries by creating possibilities of a dialectic clash in other zones: between the animal and the human, the object and the being, touch and rhetoric, the literal and the figural and finally between finitude and freedom. Consequently, the text is taut, with open-ended possibilities, until in the final pages of the book he knowingly gives way to free flowing and joyous exhortations in and through language, thereby affirming utopian possibilities of our common living. He sets us free from all pressures of sociability.

Life lives in things—in and through sizes, figures and motion. Densely. But life is also not a conjunction of, and confrontation with, inert mass. *Lived experience* itself is perhaps the flow of an abstraction of the *real life*. That is the realm of the lifeworld, where the forms of matter and the senses are engendered into a rhythm of becoming. Friedrich Engels said that

> The material world that is perceivable through the senses and to which we ourselves belong, is the only reality: and our consciousness and thinking, however suprasensuous they may seem, are only the product of a material bodily organ—the brain. Matter is not a product of mind, but mind itself is merely the highest product of matter. (Engels, 1886/2005).

The sensible never resides in abstraction. There is always a material content of sensible and sensuous life. At the heart of Jaaware's method is the philosophy of thing, but *a throbbing philosophy of thing*, a kind of investment in the concreteness of living. He has mediated the material content of our living through touch, so that we do not wander into the spiral of sensible relativism by delving into the vertical depth of any phenomenological abstraction. Hence, his repeated insistence on the *surface* and the *real* conditions of destitution. But how can such concrete consciousness be thematized and extended?

Trân Duc Thao has tried to bring forth a productive encounter between Husserlian phenomenology and dialectical thinking by rigorously building up a philosophy of thing. It is not a coincidence that Jaaware refers to his work more than once in his book. The question about our animal existence and conscious use of human labour and processes of production (including production of the social) is brought into a confrontation with each other in Trân Duc Thao. With Descartes it was possible to dissociate sharply between body and soul, between mechanistic materialism and transcendental idealism. Scientific thought established itself over this dissociation. However, what positive investigation cannot meaningfully take up is the query: "how could *objects* take on meaning for human life and how could man himself emerge as an *objective reality*?" (Duc Thao, 1951/1971).

The disjunction between object and subject made it conversely clear that far from being a mechanical development in space, nature was a continuing process of great becoming which elevated all matter to life itself. Every form appears as a historical formation in a universal process. All living forms become more and more differentiated as the process of division of the cells keep happening through the interchange of matter. What is stressed in this line of thought is the material content of all sensuous experience, a route that straightaway takes us away from all mysticism (pure and regressive interior feeling) and gross empiricism (pure scientism) at the same time. The processes of formation, deformation and reformation of all matter are also a traffic and passage between the physical and the chemical, which implies at the same time identity and difference/non-identity. This is very crucial to understanding the notion of the futility of practising identity at a second order (social) level later, since all matter also forms and reforms through non-identity. The very phenomenon of life is dialectical. Therefore, forms are both living and non-living since all living forms develop through physio-chemical processes in element and matter, which is nothing but substance in circulation. In the words of Trân Duc Thao, "In as much as life *transcends* matter, it *suppresses* matter by *preserving* it—the negation resulting necessarily from preservation, and the preservation being implied in the negation" (Duc Thao, 1951/1971). The argument does not superimpose nature over matter, but describes the real process that constitutes life in and through the movements and motions of matter. Nature is a necessity through which matter finds freedom. Consciousness itself is nothing but the oculomotor determinations: "Life constitutes in *real* absorption of environmental matters. All consciousness is the consciousness of the self and the object at the same time" (Duc Thao, 1951/1971). The exterior becomes the interior.

This dialectical process between matter and nature and between consciousness and objective reality is of paramount importance for appreciating the location from where Jaaware is initiating his dual critique of the futility (and the stubborn nature) of caste practice, and the sociological and progressive processes of institutionalizing the very promiscuity of destitution. If physio-chemical processes determine the fundamental dialectic between being and becoming, between matter and life, then all other categories of destitution and exclusion are mere human ways of trying to discipline what is fundamentally promiscuous and variegated: which we also know by the name of life. Every act leaves a trace that gets repeated and newness develops. Fresh dispositions thus happen till such dispositions get ossified, and the process starts again. Ways of attraction and repulsion begin very early on. Nervous pulsations accumulate and we anticipate, grope, act, repress and start again. This is how all forms develop, die and return anew. We start touching and then repress the very process right at the outset of childhood, often helped by our parents. Attractive or repulsive sensibilities are retained as sensations that constitute lived experience. That mode of disciplining is carried over to caste practice eventually. The enduring of pulsating touch or non-touch thus turns self-identical, penetrates into the immanent past and is projected onto the infinite future. Anteriority, that endures, is projected. The disciplining of freedom through the practising of destitution is effected in the outer world through manipulation and detour of various kinds. The external effects make matter potent and punishing, but the anteriorizing of forms starts early on, as the cells multiply and its effects are retained through life-practices. Unless we realize this fundamental dialectical process, nothing can erase traces and differences of destitution (through matter and memory and fiction, traces shall travel). Not even death. Especially not death. We shall continue to practice the ways of abandoning others and alienating ourselves.

Given this our thrown condition, we are now in a position to return to the possibility of freedom. It is quite evident that freedom from the condition of destitution can take place from within the bowels of such thrownness that is essentially material, immediate and tactile. So, an exit can happen by taking a full measure of finitude, and not by some overhauling that is hastened and mediated through a project of futurity. That sort of hastening or institutionalizing of destitute condition, in fact, can only give rise to and perpetuate forms of complementary or competitive *schismogenesis*—which Gregory Bateson had described as "a process of differentiation in the norms of individual behaviour resulting from cumulative interaction between individuals" (Bateson, 1936). Schismogenetic conditions create a radical split in mutually aggravating ways among groups or individuals to the point of no return. The processes of such identity formation is akin to an arms race, whereby each group keeps revving up its primal thrown condition until the conflict among groups escalates to an absolutely ontological plane, where there remains no scope of any further manoeuvre. Instead of correcting the conditions of the natural givens by any sociological fix, one way is to keep tracking the dialectical processes and realizing that any escape from destitution can only happen collectively and at the level of bare life.

Therefore, Jaaware concludes his exploration with destitution itself as the condition of liberation:

First, a quotation from Emily Dickinson: "I'm Nobody! Who are you?/Are you-Nobody-too?/Then there's a pair of us!/Don't tell! they'd advertise—you know!" (Jaaware, 2019).

Advertising means getting busy with trying to make somebody out of nobodies and, in the process manufacture, new nobodies. It is only when you and I realize that each one of us are destitute-nobodies, in every which way right from the beginning, that our very attempts to create such distancing based on touch shall make no sense.

And then another quotation from W.H. Auden: "And always the loud angry crowd,/Very angry and very loud,/Law is We,/And always the soft idiot softly Me" (Jaaware, 2019).

Any notion of traversing to *elsewhere* means first confronting the here and now and then taking a collective leap to some unknown horizon. To consider elsewhere is to realize *we* are alive and talking. That is a good point to initiate change—foremost within parts of us, by embracing our inner invisibility. Elsewhere is to do something. Elsewhere means learning Korean and Chechnya Russian and Magyar and going somewhere, anywhere. Elsewhere is district nine and the alien ship. Elsewhere is thinking together like animals, since you are I are both nobodies. With an oracular voice, Jaaware ends his exhortations: "We are to help us, without god/s. We the People?" Elsewhere is *We the People* with an interrogation mark.

References

Bateson, Gregory. 1936. *Naven: A Survey of the Problems Suggested by a Composite Picture of the Culture of a New Guinea Tribe Drawn from Three Points of View.* Cambridge: Cambridge University Press.

Butler, Judith. 1993. *Bodies That Matter: On the Discursive Limits of 'Sex'*. New York: Routledge.

Duc Thao, Trân. 1951/1971. *Phenomenology and Dialectical Materialism.* Dordrecht: D. Reidel Publishing Company.

Engels, Friedrich. 1886/2005. *Ludwig Feuerbach and the End of Classical German Philosophy*. University Press of the Pacific.

Heidegger, Martin. 1971. *Poetry, Language, Thought.* Translated by A. Hofstadter. New York: Harper and Row.

Jaaware, Aniket. 2019. *Practicing Caste, On Touching and Not Touching.* Hyderabad: Orient Blackswan.

Kohler, Wolfgang. 1956. *The Mentality of Apes.* London: Routledge and Kegan Paul.

Kristeva, Julia. 1982. *Powers of Horror: An Essay on Abjection.* New York: Columbia University Press.

Schilder, Paul. 1978. *The Image and Appearance of the Human Body: Studies in the Constructive Energies of the Psyche.* New York: International University Press.

Shaviro, Steven. 1993. *The Cinematic Body.* Minneapolis: University of Minnesota Press.

The Creature in Action

Reckoning, Purgation and Civic Friction in Niccolo Machiavelli

In his major writings, especially in the *Discourses on Livy* and in *Florentine Histories*, Niccolo Machiavelli addresses a fundamental conflict in the very use and necessity of the idea of conflict itself: on one hand, he firmly believes that conflicts are inevitable to civic existence and flourishing. Deferral of conflict is not a choice given to us. In fact, periodic tumults can do some good in affirming certain lost democratic principles in the *civitas* by bringing the corrupt and the wayward aristocracy within the ambit of a certain popular reckoning. On the other hand, he seriously worries about the deepest wound and harm that existential modes of conflict might lead to, preventing cities and states from achieving stability and advancement in their wake.

Most of the time, in Machiavelli, such conflicts have a class nature to them: conflicts arise between the grandi/ottomati/*popolo grasso*—patricians and oligarchs, as senators and consuls on one side and plebeians/*popolo minuto*—with their opinions, calumnies and accusations and their own executive bodies like the tribunes and the popular assemblies on the other. But Machiavelli himself revises such binary formulations of conflicts in his later works: at certain conjunctures of history, tumults and distrust cut across classes, spreading laterally and taking more ominous contours. Internecine struggles lead to groupings now referred to as the 'ancient nobility,' 'popular nobles' and 'the plebs.' Ambition becomes the prime motivating factor and aspirations turn rogue. In such cases, groupuscules further narrow down their identities and turn into random collection of dissociated individuals, each equally struggling for power. The space of collective negotiation and bargaining begins to shrink as each identity, including the mercantile class of the new economy and the plebs, desire to safeguard and pursue their private interests.

Are violent conflicts another mode of negotiation? Are conflicts the initial signposts for asserting collective rights which might eventually lead to legal changes and fresh civic formulations, thus making a whole people more democratic? Or do real conflicts inevitably devolve into personal skirmishes, lynching and bloodletting? As such, are all serious conflicts finally existential and violent in nature with blood feud, factional politics and civil strife written all over them? Are such modes forms of periodic and necessary purgation in creaturely life or do these lead to running cycles of vendetta extraction and as such, have little to do with any genuine transformation of collective life? In between all this, Machiavelli tries to trace the realities of active citizenship—quite an advanced idea of political collective.

Post-Medieval Mass Politics and the Ambiguity of Power

Does Machiavelli's politics arise out of the 'discovery of the masses', as Sheldon Wolin had observed or is it that the Roman nobility, having recognized the power and force of the masses, gave popular discontent a conscious direction in order to maintain order and conduct a politics of imperial expansion, as Benedet to Fontana has claimed? Indeed, the "opinion of the people—its formation, organization, development, direction, and deployment" (Wolin, 1960) has been decisive in the shaping of modern politics.

It is Claude Lefort who has most penetratingly calculated the mathematics of modern mass politics with reference to Machiavelli. Lefort looked into the oeuvre of Machiavelli and tried to draw our attention to the inner motor of the political process that takes place between the subjects and the ruler. The stability of any regime depends on the dynamic relationship of adversarial and conflictual politics between the prince and the people. The two are existential adversaries to each other and yet there is a cat and mouse game that constantly characterizes the relationship. The dialectical principle between the two classes is left open and tensed. This game of formal distancing can break down into chaos if any of the sides decide to uncover fangs and turn violent. In such a case, the prince turns into a tyrant and the people, into a fascistic mob. *The Prince* and the *Discorsi* essentially deal with two sides of the same motor, calibrating the ever-dynamic relationship between the people and the nobility. The formal shifts in the sphere of regime that each side develops take place according to the alignment of historical conjunctures.

Machiavelli's concern, therefore, is in "the permanence of power and the repetition of accidents". It is a force-field of conflict that he delineates. The nature of each competing social group: "abstract agents, potential allies or the adversaries of the Prince" (Lefort, 2012) depends on the nature, mode and timings of the dangerous game being played. From within the belly of such radical finitude and contingency, where "only the constellation of events is meaningful" (Lefort, 2012), sometimes the order or custom shifts gear with the order of innovation and new modes of the political appear. In other times, conflict goes haywire and the system crashes. In fact, much of the Machiavelli's oeuvre consists of the depiction of the failed instances of political conflict. In such a scenario, actual violence in conflictual situations could actually be counterproductive; but the violent nature of the aggressive creaturely war-games must be constantly felt by all sides. Force needs to be husbanded. Deriving from relations of power, some must be cajoled while others killed, some honoured while others exiled. This calibrating and husbanding of force is the key to conflict. It is for this reason that in Machiavelli, a Prince 'more loved' always means one who is 'less hated'—for power is unstable, and history conjectural.

Since Machiavelli is not warm to the idea of natural law, the idea of governance in the *Discorsi*, where the question of class appears front and centre, is once again based on a speculation about human nature and its fundamental conflictual tendencies. The perversity of human nature is most apparent in the appetites of the *grandi* and the idea of people's power and its negotiation with such appetites is a warfare that hovers around institutions, which arise out of political tumult. The tribunal is one such restraining institutional apparatus, which was designed to put limits to the insolence of the *grandi*. The class struggle, as Lefort saw it, of course, could also be delimited by the Prince who could rein in the *grandi* if necessary. But the nature of struggle is positive in the first few chapters in the *Discorsi*. Not any legal framework or good education—but disjunction and disunity between the plebs and the senate bring prosperity and flourishing to Rome. Tumults are not noises; they are the cause for engendering freedom. Class divisions and social conflicts need not be masked; the productive tensions within the divisions must rather be explored. The power of such a free state fostered by disunity appears to be the regime of law itself. The tribune plays the role of the intermediary. Division of humours of the body politic fosters freedom. And therefore, the democratic crux of the argument appears to be simple: desire of people is the basis of all law and freedom. Within class struggle, law is established, it would appear. Law *happens* in Rome by giving full vent to people's appetite and ambitions. Hence, Lefort concludes: "It is the operation of desire that keeps the question of the unity of the state open, and, in exposing it, forces those who direct it to put its destiny back into play" (Lefort, 2012). This indeed appears to be the beginning of radical democracy which Lefort to Negri, Laclau to Castoriadis, have championed, with variations. But do creaturely motivations bedevil the claims of such democracy?

The issue about democratic radicalism becomes complicated once we reach *Discorsi* I.8, when Machiavelli begins to bring more forcefully the idea of humour into the scenario and, thereby, creates a platform to project internal divisions within popular politics. He makes a precise modern political distinction between the populist and the popular. The distinction is ingenious: that between indictments and calumnies. Indictments are run through an objective process, which is based on manifest evidence and judicial deliberation. Calumnies, by contrast, are spread in public squares and beneath arcades, which implicate people via rumour-mongering and hearsay. Calumny is venting of humour in a private and subjective manner with little objectivity. Lefort draws a different conclusion: "But we must not, on reading the text, be led to believe that beneath the necessity of judgment the effects of aggression are wiped away from the truth. Machiavelli does not authorize this conclusion" (Lefort, 2012). And the truth: the *grandi* existence is defined in terms of wrongful appetite and appropriation, while people gossiping and charging the *grandi* in anonymous ways and places is rightful intervention authorized by people's desire which ought to flow freely. People, caught between law and authority, try to be just and are never responsible for the downfall of the republic.

Lefort's conclusions about the nature of conflict in Machiavelli, albeit with occasional reservations, are rehearsed most powerfully in recent times by John McCormick. He argues that Machiavelli primarily relies on people's superior judgement and therefore, provides two provisions for them in order to wrest the initiative from the optimates (*ottimati*): "arm the people militarily with weapons and training; and arm them constitutionally with tribunes and assemblies" (McCormick, 2011). Sometimes, people are innovative (including dismembering the aristocrats), and in some other times, restorative. McCormick tells us that in contrast to Guicciardini's elite controlled notion of *governo stretto*, Machiavelli had proposed *governo largo*—an inclusive and democratic republic. There is also a hint of moral degeneracy of the republic in McCormick's evaluation. The *grandi* are sly. People, by comparison, are more decent and arrive as a moral force, in order to discipline the city-state. Machiavelli accuses powerful citizens who "sin in any manner against a free regime" (*Discorsi* I.7). Besides, new laws are enacted with people's intervention. These attributes bring back the republic to its first principles. But right in the Introduction to his influential book, *Machiavellian Democracy*, McCormick makes two telling points that colours his own thesis with a certain scepticism. One, an emphasis on elite accountability could threaten to overwhelm wider forms of citizen participation, which would otherwise be self-initiated and ground-up kind of activism. Second, since elite accountability is always imperfectly secured through electoral and representative political forms, common citizens, within structures of popular government, "have no choice in many circumstances, but to act in a 'reactive' way" (McCormick, 2011).

McCormick begins by assessing the two sides of the dialectical pole that keep the balance between the classes extremely taut. On one hand, with respect to the inclusive republican model, he feels that Machiavelli exhorts the *grandi* to be more accountable to an armed and politically conscious citizenry. So, educating the *grandi* about their responsibilities in the republic is one aspect of the scheme of his *paedeia*. McCormick takes a positive view of the idea of 'disunity leading to freedom' formulation and thinks that people serve as the regime's 'guard of liberty'. As to the ways by which the people serve guardians that prevent the *grandi* from seizing liberty, they do so "through an ensemble of pleb-enabling and noble constraining institutions" (McCormick, 2011)—collective plebeian action, the institution of tribunes, deliberative and legislative assemblies, standing for noble-dominated magistracies and so forth. This method is largely legal in nature. The ambit of law is only augmented, since the plebs are shackled by erstwhile laws. Good governance seems to be the objective. All these lead eventually to a deeper question—that of equitable distribution of property between the nobles and the ignoble, as proposed in *Discorsi* I.30. This is a far trickier domain, as we shall soon see.

The animosity is however, not just between two historically antagonistic classes, but between two existential conditions. Indeterminacy increases manifold in such a situation. From the side of the plebs, the key is to badger the *grandi*. From the side of the *grandi*, the essential element is to maintain the esoteric and secret ways to govern just that: secret. And at this point, another side of populist fomentation brews: that of accusations, calumnies and public trails. McCormick detects a regulatory mechanism in accusations that goes beyond deterrence and punishment—"an outlet for venting of social 'humours' that are generated by class antagonism" (McCormick, 2011). This is about public trails, which actually often overlap with word-of-mouth opinion mongering. This acceptance of reactionary nature of venting bile and animus, which are projected as progressive measures of class antagonism, is crucial to realizing the existential nature of populism in general. In *Discorsi* I.8, as mentioned earlier, Machiavelli has uncategorically differentiated between calumnies/unsubstantiated charges carried on in the murky dens and backrooms and public accusations, and has shown why the former is divisive and detrimental to all democratic and inclusive politics. Demagogic and factional excesses are counterproductive to democracy—since there are 'very many judges' under the category of people. The danger in slandering without investigating is the following: "And when the matter is not well arranged, there always follow great disorders, because slanders irritate but do not punish the citizens. And those who are irritated think of avenging themselves, rather hating than fearing the things that are said against them" (Machiavelli, 1965). Machiavelli, therefore, prescribes severe punishment for the slanderer. McCormick, however, argues that Machiavelli had changed position in the later chapters, in which he takes the violent route of prescribing death penalty—'memorable executions' for whom people think are the usurpers of liberty. In other words, to identify, isolate and lynch scapegoats would be a kosher method in order to proclaim exemplary punishment to what the plebs would consider errant behaviour on the part of the *grandi*. The implications for such a primal social order are obvious and it would have been brave of McCormick to go all the way with his argument, save that he worries about such an anarchic possibility with Machiavelli's prescriptions and distances himself from populist reigns of terror: "Political trials that actually enlist the entire people's judgment will rarely if ever execute citizens as do Sullan proscriptions, Stalinist purges, or Robespierrian terror campaigns. Coriolanus and Appius Claudius represent exceptional cases" (McCormick, 2011). One wishes that once the floodgates are opened, one is in the position to distinguish between ordinary and exceptional cases. The whole of the *socius* turns exceptional, until that becomes the new norm of a terrified, depressed and acutely insecure culture, civilizationally speaking. We are in the creaturely universe.

Ambition, Public Remedy and Procrastination: The Case of the Gracchi

The votaries of the republican notion of liberty emphasize certain key modes of political operation and practice: sociopolitical equality, subordination of the military to the political will of the people and a culture of political participation that cuts across classes. The public space is ideally defined in terms of a free and fair domain of expression, negotiation and political decision-making. Tribunes are a key to realizing such an ideal, as Machiavelli claims many times in the *Discorsi*. But there is a gap between idealizing Rome for practising such a politics where tumults lead to stability and in confronting actual instances of conflict. The case of the Gracchi brothers is a copybook, one that elucidates the processes of tumult and their implications.

As tribunes of the Roman state, the Brothers Gracchus tried to resolve the economic and civic hardships by reviving the Agrarian Laws of 133 BCE. The laws had two major components: one, the laws would limit the amount of publicly available land-holdings for any citizen, and second, those would allow lands seized from vanquished enemies to be freely distributed to the plebs. Often, nobles with patience and ingenuity would delay the Agrarian Laws to come to effect. So, sometimes an army was laid out or there were back and forth between tribunes in order to implement the laws. Sometimes, distant lands were colonized so that such laws could not reach on those lands. The re-enactment and implementation of the Agrarian Laws created animosity among the senators who coveted more land. Eventually, a cycle of retribution and 'private remedies' (the murder of Tiberius Gracchus by senators, to begin with) started, which led to the complete collapse of the republic. With the scandal of the Agrarian Laws, the nobles gradually took charge and began to place one of their own as the figurehead of absolutist power. It started with Sulla's dictatorship, which was the beginning of a pattern that would only come to conclusion with Caesarism. The Senate lost all power and the people lost their liberty. The *arcanum imperii* was laid bare and the army took charge. Rome became enchained.

In the *Discorsi*, Machiavelli begins the discussion on Agrarian Laws by making a general observation: "Whenever men cease fighting through necessity, they go to fighting through ambition, which is so powerful in human breasts that, whatever high rank men climb to, never does ambition abandon them" (Machiavelli, 1965). The first thing to note is the inevitability of the cycle of necessity and ambition: one attribute must necessarily lead to the other. The word fighting is significant in its usage—neither as any struggle of the underprivileged nor with any godly sense of contentment or fulfilment. Only through the means of necessity or ambition, man continues to fight. There is an element of individual power play and finality about fighting one's way through life. The creature is in action. Action, the fundamental trait of the universe, itself manifests as creatures. Ambition does not abandon you when you grow in economic or social stature—that is to say, it rather foments insatiable lust and greed. But the opposite is not true—nowhere does Machiavelli say that the *popolo* or the *plebs* is not ambitious or greedy. The larger category of man, the creature is constant; ambition transcends class or status.

In this context, John McCormick, perhaps the most vociferous and energetic supporter of Machiavelli's democratic and popular politics, accepts that Machiavelli is 'extremely cautious' in his appraisal and discussion of the Gracchi (McCormick, 2011). He further says that as Machiavelli indicts Brothers Gracchus (Tiberius and Gaius) for initiating and setting into motion the republic's decline, he also blames the ambition and avarice of the *grandi* for the same and concludes somewhat half-heartedly, "He may reproach their method there, but he does not besmirch the Gracchan cause" (McCormick, 2011). Were the Brothers Gracchus populist tyrants as was the verdict of the Senators or were they martyrs to the democratic cause? Could it be that the cycles of democratic deepening must lead to populism until a new cycle begins?

The larger point Machiavelli makes in the chapter is quite fatalistic. He starts despondently by declaring that all the bloodshed that ensued was beyond all 'lawful habits and customs'. He clearly values customary laws and habits rather than any ill-begotten way of destroying freedom, brought in the name of radical transformation. In fact, his support here is more for prudence than for initiative: while the intention of the Gracchi Brothers and their plebeian supporters ought to be praised, but not their prudence. It is a badly considered plan to invoke the past in order to promote equality in the current situation. This is no true innovation, he avers. Rather, irregularity in institutions and transactions increases. The whole Gracchi fracas also shows that fundamentally, the creaturely motive for acquiring property is stronger than claiming honour. Honour and position can still be shared among classes, but redistribution of property stirs a hornet's nest. The point about not harming women and usurping property are fundamental points about security in Machiavelli (Chapter 17 of *The Prince*). One remembers that after the return of his family to Florence in 1512, Giovanni de Medici was advised by Machiavelli about the recovery of property lost by the former's family in 1494: "Men feel more sorrow for a farm taken away from them than for a brother or a father put to death, because sometimes death is forgotten, but property never" (Fontana, 2017). Therefore, the socioeconomic aspects of a conflict rather than the purely political ones are to be dealt with more care and caution lest the conflict turns into a misadventure. In the final instance, civic liberty and individual security must be honoured.

The nobility cannot be stopped from their pursuits if the fomenters take a route that is slow and negotiatory in nature. Either the *plebs* procrastinate in taking on the *grandi* or plans a swift and violent means to eliminate them. The point about swift violence is not made explicitly in *Discorsi* I.37 and yet, Pedulla seems to hint at such a possibility:

> Cleomenes reappears in *Disc.* I.18 in regard to the need to 'come to extraordinary modes' (*venire allo straordinario*) and to use 'violence and arms' to reform a corrupted city, following the general principle that, 'when the ordinary modes (*modi ordinari*) are bad, respecting the ordinary limits (*termini ordinari*) is not enough.' These passages are not without consequence for our reading of *Disc.* I.37. Is Machiavelli suggesting that, faced with the impasse of the second century BCE, the Gracchi should have gone down the route of violence so as to win an opposition that could not be subdued with the traditional legislative tools and bloodless tumults of the early period? (Pedulla, 2018)

The hint could be there, but prudence allows only limited options and directs Machiavelli to consider finitude. Machiavelli's oft made disapproval of the futility of half-way measures is once again iterated in I.37, but the thrust of the argument is towards consideration and wisdom, rather than falling into the gyre of factional and private politics of vendetta.

In this context, Benedetto Fontana rightly reminds us of the cautionary lines from *The Prince,* Chapter 6: "There is nothing more difficult to plan or uncertain of success or more dangerous to carry out than an attempt to introduce new institutions, because the introducer has as his enemies all those who profit from the old institutions, and has as lukewarm defenders all those who will profit from the new institutions" (Fontana, 2017). Imprudent and half-baked challenge shall ultimately pave way for a violent backlash. The *grandi* can at best be delayed in their chosen pursuits of ambition and acquisition. In that manner, either evil comes later, or with time it disappears of itself. The timing and tempo of a conflict are significant factors in wresting initiatives. The pace needs to be calibrated.

But the point about conservation goes beyond the issue of power struggle. Right in the middle of this chapter, Machiavelli attributes material and military disbalance to natural causes—because men's cravings are always greater than their power to attain. The disbalance leads to enmity and war. The naturalistic explanation takes us towards explaining tumults in terms of humours and body fluids. This point is also made by Gabriele Pedulla: he refers to this as Machiavelli's 'anthropological turn.' Referring to Anthony Parel's pioneering work on Machiavelli's cosmological universe, Pedulla goes on to frame the issue in and through Hippocratic ideas of humour which make certain decisions and their effects as natural elements of political life:

> According to Renaissance science, diseases were not believed to result from an attack on the body by external pathogens. Rather, they originated from an imbalance (*dyscrasia*) in the four basic components of the organism: black bile (corresponding to the earth, and rooted in the spleen); yellow bile (fire, rooted in the liver); phlegm (water, rooted in the head); and blood (air, rooted in the heart). The predomination of any one of these fluids could trigger any number of pathologies that required prompt correction in accordance with the principle of *contrarium agens in contrarium*. (Pedulla, 2018)

These subjective aspects of political decisions are key elements in Machiavelli's assessment of and judgement on political conflict.

Discorsi I.37 is a perfect instance that shows the effects of the plummeting of a worthwhile and progressive political conflict to factionalism, especially if the turn is allowed to burn slow—via scandals, half-truths and a steady bloodshed. Extra institutional solutions require a mode that takes us into uncharted waters and the risk, if not worked out properly, could be devastating. Degeneration of political processes leads to a political dead-end. What started as having revolutionary potential for social change becomes an instrument for conserving power and privilege among struggling factions. Conflict, instead of helping the city-state thrive as was the hope in *Discorsi* I.4, ends up as a zero sum proposition. We are left with the fragility of human hope.

The Rhetoric of History: How Democratic Was the Ciompi Uprising?

Given that Machiavelli is a die-hard adversary of the natural law tradition, his readers come across a remarkable passage in Book III of *Florentine Histories* that attests to equality in purely organic and natural terms:

> Do not let their antiquity of blood … dismay you: for all men, having had the same beginning, are equally ancient and have been made by nature in one mode. Strip all of us naked, you will see that we are

> alike; dress us in their clothes and them in ours, and without a doubt, we shall appear noble and they ignoble, for only poverty and riches make us unequal. (Machiavelli, 1965)

The aforementioned passage is not historical, but is part of a longer speech ventriloquized by Machiavelli, impersonating as an anonymous wool carder of Florence during the Ciompi revolt in 1378. *Florentine Histories*, and especially the places where Machiavelli describes the Ciompi, is an important vector to understand the question of his democratic politics as well as his rhetorical strategies as a unique humanist historian. For a brief few months, beginning in the summer of 1378, Florence was ruled by the artisans and manual workers—*popolo minuto* (the little people). The revolt thoroughly disturbed both the emerging and entrenched political economy of Florence and its sociopolitical order. This was an insurgent government, which removed the wealthy nobles and their guilds altogether and within the scope a few months, passed through several phases until it was crushed by factions within and by the oligarchs from outside.

Delving deeper though, even the most democratic of Machiavelli scholars have noticed two crucial underlying markers of the revolt. One, a historical fact: that, in spite of the radicalism, the Ciompi's demands and aims were modest and can hardly be called transformative. Yves Winter, who has championed consistently this particular trait in Machiavelli, for instance, notes that at best,

> the artisans and small traders of Florence wanted the right to form a guild and demanded production increases for the wool industry to abate unemployment. On the whole, their petition remained well within the framework of the medieval corporatist system. It did not attempt to change or overthrow the regime nor to institute a more egalitarian order. Yet the new Ciompi government was weak and timid and remained deferential to the political and economic elites. (Winter, 2012)

The second aspect is Machiavelli's dual voice; we know that in all his tracts, he could place an argument on both sides of an issue (in *utramque partem*), much like we have noticed in the case of the Gracchi crisis. In no uncertain terms does he charge the mob and the lowest plebs (*infima plebe*). He blames the essential qualities of fear and hatred that runs the motor of the plebeian spirit. He unbraids them for ingratitude, arrogance and extraordinary insolence. He heaps praises on Michele di Lando, who though initially the wool carders' leader, was instrumental in crushing the revolt. And yet, Machiavelli attributes a rousing speech to the anonymous artisan that effectively tears down the oligarchic political and economic order.

If we leave aside the cynical hypothesis of a conspiratorial and ironical voice in the ventriloquized speech, one can reach only one conclusion: violence, both private and public, as a necessary means to conduct democratic politics by means of exploding the will of the people. In order to live with more *satisfaction* in their lives, the workers must take up arms and seize what is rightfully theirs. The strategy is pithy by the anonymous voice: 'It is to our advantage, therefore, as it appears to me, if we wish that our old errors be forgiven us, to make new ones, redoubling the evils, multiplying the arson and robbery—and to contrive to have many companions in this, because when many err, no one is punished, and though small faults are punished, great and grave ones are rewarded; and when many suffer, few seek for revenge, because universal injuries are borne with greater patience than particular.' The idea of conscience by the *popolo minuto* has to be jettisoned forthwith just like the Prince does. There is no turning back once the path of violence is undertaken. Instead, insurgents must double down—redouble evils, multiply arson and robbery. We realize that we return to fundamental and primal drives: the plebeians attempt to convert envy and fear into hatred. Winter has noted the use of the phrase 'violent satisfaction' by the artisan orator. It is a purgative and cathartic metaphor. Winter feels that this is a 'fantasmatic response to social conditions' and all oppression has psycho-social consequences. It is noteworthy that the votaries of the democratic turn in Machiavelli scholarship owns up to its anarchist core.

Dismembering and arson are to be redoubled—this is at the heart of conflicts, not institutional remedy; but long knives and private purging is the way to resolve economic and political differences. Is it then possible to say as the likes of McCormick claim, that the idea of radical democracy is not coterminous with reigns of terror? Isn't sublime terror an essential ingredient in apocalyptic, forthright and righteous action? Winter rightly notices a counter-strategy in this other strain:

> since the workers have already taken up arms they are liable to be prosecuted unless they are victorious. The Ciompi thus must pursue a double-pronged strategy: the emancipatory struggle for more freedom and more satisfaction must combined with the immediate tactical need to avoid punishment. This double aim is best attained not by retreat but by a multiplication of violence. (Winter, 2012)

Paradoxically, is swift action the most prudent arrow then in arsenal of the political actor? One may not channel disquiet and anger to the democratic institutions, after all. Anger is purged as hatred. Does this truth bring together Machiavelli's oeuvre as Lefort had suggested? Is Machiavelli then also a Schmittian *decisionist*? Does everything depend on how the will of the people is formed? Or is there scope for tarrying in conflict?

It is from such a realization that Filippo Del Lucchese would comment: "The various elements are blended and it is no longer possible to separate and precisely distinguish the 'humours', physiological element of any republic, from the 'parties', pathological element of Florentine politics" (Del Lucchese, 2009). Florence is built with a pattern of conflict that is more authentic—where physiology is perfectly congruent with pathology—than what is undertaken in Rome or Sparta. The absolute nature of conflict, 'absolute will to power and domination' is the staple of Machiavelli's later writings. Has not that always been a tendency in his thought? The guilds and *gonfaloniers* come and go as violence erupts periodically in Florence. And the Florentine particularity is the human universal. When both parties are placed at the same level, inevitable struggle happens, which further develops into factional politics. The city is entrapped in divisions, as it were. Such is the degenerate anatomy of conflict that we seem to "pass to the tragic and profound definition of Florence as a 'naturally partisan' city. From humours counter posed to parties, we pass to the 'humours of the parties'" (Del Lucchese, 2009). Relations of production are affected. In Rome, partisan conflicts led to ruination. In Florence, does existential bloodletting the other route: to a wonderful equity that would open up new possibilities? Del Lucchese arrives at this conclusion from his reading of *Florentine Histories*.

"There is no reality in history apart from wealth and servitude, domination and exploitation" (Del Lucchese, 2009).

The Wonderful Equality of Conflict

The political is autonomous in Machiavelli. This principle binds all his works. With the implosion of violence and partisan conflict in nurturing a certain kind of direct democratic set up, the question of sovereign hegemony must arise—as the original instituting moment of society. Antonio Negri describes democracy in terms of constituent power—as a system of absolute government. And absolutism means acceleration.

The constituent power, which for Negri, is a "force that bursts apart, breaks, interrupts, unhinges any preexisting equilibrium and any possible continuity. Constituent power is tied to the notion of democracy as absolute power. Thus, as a violent and expansive force, constituent power is a concept connected to the social preconstitution of the democratic totality" (Negri, 1999). In Machiavelli, constituent power arrives as the ongoing mutation and precariousness of history. Mutation 'establishes the logic of time on an ontological horizon of dense, multidirectional and changing materiality'. Time turns polyvalent. But mutation means whatever is a fatal and natural turn into history. And such a mutation is given direction by the political actors through a combination of judgement/prudence and arms. The subject intervenes in action as will and concentration. The other side to historical time is anthropological time. The constituent power must always reach such a radical level that all acts turn creative. For Negri, this constitutive principle is a heroic one in a world without divinity. Acts must create possibilities of strength. And yet *The Prince* is a book of conflicts based on antagonism and is tendential. Time is 'overburdened and unconcluded'. The dreams of the Prince are negations of movements that are originally affirmations, as a monarch or a myth; he goes beyond the limits and closes down possibilities and cuts short his trajectory. The *political* is left unresolved.

By contrast, Negri describes the disunion principle initiated in *Discorsi* I.4 as the 'hammer blow' to mixed government and to the theories of the Polybian cycle (Negri, 1999). But the real movement and theoretical innovation he traces to *Discorsi* I.17, where corruption of customs and degradation of laws within the city are put to question by Machiavelli. Here is the shift from structure to substance, from mixed governance to democratized anthropology. If people institute themselves through the exercise of constituent power, for Negri, the sole constitution of the Prince is democracy. Disunion now "embodies a motor of the continual reopening of history" (Negri, 1999). Insurrection and confrontation is defined by Negri at this stage with absolute reciprocity—moulding a creative and fighting model of governance:

> The constitutional process has become a play of productive subjects. The mixed constitution fades and disappears in front of this productive strength of the princes and of the subjects. The government by now is almost exclusively that which the new Prince had made of it—fury and order, impetus of virtue, creative capacity. The government is a fighting body. (Negri, 1999)

For Negri, the influence of the Prince intervenes in the *Discorsi*; such is power of absolutism in direct democracy. Negri argues for an existential synthesis between the Prince's decision and the will of the multitude: this productive tussle is the genesis of the constitution. The cautious, one-sided and progressive model of democracy, laid down by McCormick receives a revelatory dimension by passing the terror-filled actions of the plebs through the creative passage of classical dictatorship in Negri. Democracy is armed as the dictatorship for freedom blows its trumpet. Direct democracy is also righteous and constantly signals collective virtue (a dimension Negri christens as 'living labour') in order to fulfil its dream of common good. A combination of virtue and arms leads to absolute democracy: 'democracy is real Princedom'. And the rediscovery of inhuman freedom is the condition of strength for Negri, in contrast to power: "We are completely inside matter, inside passions, but we can stir up all this in a direction of freedom. With effort. Through actuality" (Negri, 1999). It can only come through a fight to death, realized though frenzied passion.

But in the *Florentine Histories*, the whole framework collapses: rupture seems more real than synthesis and the constituent power emerges only sporadically, like curls in a vortex. It never materializes. Fortune now rules over virtue and all mutation of history, inverts themselves into a tragic precariousness. Negri finds this radical predicament of conflict: bitterness turned into precariousness to be comical and grotesque, and pleasure, the only outlet and means to reconstruct the retreat of democracy.

This is the reason Althusser deduces, and Negri confirms, that Machiavelli "is the theoretician of the absence of all the conditions of a principle and a democracy; and it is from this absence, from this void, that Machiavelli, literally, wrenches away the desire for a subject and constitutes it into a program" (Negri, 1999). Constituent ontology becomes an aspect of absolute mutation. This point has been put across with lucidity by Sofia Näsström as she considers legitimacy and contestation in times of absolute contingency and eventual deluge. Not constituted power, but everything depends on what shape does the will of the people take at a particular conjecture, where the combined weight of 'unexamined prejudices, ancient battles, historical injustices, and sheer administrative fiat' are played out anterior to substantive democratic norms (Näsström, 2007).The mystery and the violence behind the working of the common will cannot be resolved. In order to get around the paradox of politics, Näsström makes people the object, rather than the source of legitimacy. But the problem is far more complex with Machiavelli, as we have seen.

In these circumstances, a unique response comes from Miguel Vatter, who looks carefully at the form of conflict in the Machiavellian universe. He too wonders about this spasmodic rhythm that turns rogue and inconclusive eventually. Taking a cue from Hannah Arendt, Vatter proposes a notion of no-rule that the plebs advance by means of which they at once distinguish themselves from the *populus* and create conditions for themselves to act as a constituent power to make equal law. But Vatter realizes that a certain rot begins to emerge in such a set-up, since articulation of grievance cannot be the basis of democracy. Redressing of grievance turns into a matter of pathos-filled private *consternation* and does not in itself advance democracy. In fact, politics of grievance redressal must degenerate into pastoral care and the savage plebs soon turn into an obedient army in support of a demagogic and charismatic military tyrant. People would like to be ordered, governed and ultimately saved. Guardianship returns into the *polis* instead of democracy. In this context, Vatter incisively cites Eric Voegelin's idea that in order to stem articulation from 'above', which becomes a kind of *mafia* politics of the mob, people must select their democratic representative from 'below', from among themselves. He overturns the principle of democratic representation, so that effective constituent power of the people can actually turn into constituted power, having enduring value in setting up a truly egalitarian political regime. Conflict would then be truly given a positive direction; and absence—a form. The wonderful equality of conflict would then be transferred from primal bloodletting and hate-mongering to the possibility of the equality of existence. In order to reach such a stage, instead of giving in to any 'metaphysics of the plebs' we must seek 'freedom of law' by constantly demanding equal law derived from the constituent power of the people. Equal law always stands athwart the order of the state and the ruthless tyranny of the mob.

References

Del Lucchese, Filippo. 2009. "Crisis and Power: Economics, Politics and Conflict in Machiavelli's Political Thought." In *History of Political Thought*. Vol. 30.1, Spring: 75–96.

Fontana, Benedetto. 2017. "Machiavelli and the Gracchi: Republican Liberty and Class Conflict." In David Johnston, Nadia Urbinati and Camila Vergara (eds.), *Machiavelli on Liberty and Conflict*. Chicago: University of Chicago Press.

Lefort, Claude. 2012. *Machiavelli in Making*. Translated by Michael B. Smith. Evanston: Northwestern University Press.

Litvin, Boris. 2019. "Mapping Rule and Subversion: Perspective and Democratic Turn in Machiavelli Scholarship." In *European Journal of Political Theory*. Vol. 18.1: 3–25.

Machiavelli, Niccolo. 1965. *Machiavelli, The Chief Works and Others*, 3 vols. Ed. Allan Gilbert. Durham, NC: Duke University Press.

McCormick, John P. 2011. *Machiavellian Democracy*. Cambridge: Cambridge University Press.

Näsström, Sofia. 2007. "The Legitimacy of the People." *Political Theory*. Vol. 35.5, October: 624–658.

Negri, Antonio. 1999. *Insurgencies, Constituent Power and the Modern State*. Minneapolis and London: University of Minnesota Press.

Pedulla, Gabriele. 2018. *Machiavelli in Tumult: The Discourses on Livy and the Origins of Political Conflictualism*. Cambridge: Cambridge University Press.

Vatter, Miguel. 2012. "The Quarrel between Populism and Republicanism: Machiavelli and the Antinomies of Plebeian Politics." In *Contemporary Political Theory.* Vol. 11: 242–263.

Voegelin, Eric. 1989–2008. *The Collected Works*, Vols. 1–34. Columbia, MO: University of Missouri Press.

Winter, Yves. 2012. "Plebeian Politics: Machiavelli and the Ciompi Uprising." In *Political Theory*. Vol. 40.6, December: 736–766.

Wolin, Sheldon S. 1960. *Politics and Vision: Continuity and Innovation in Western Political Thought.* Boston: Little, Brown and Company.

BOOK II

The Observant Creature

Raymond Geuss's World without Why

The luminous universe of Raymond Geuss is made up of a remarkable blend of generic forms (treatise, essays, poetry) and subject matter (philosophy, politics, art and literature), and a range of innovative methods—from no-nonsense realism to memorialization to a very high order of imaginative leap. The capacious spectrum of his world is captured wonderfully in the title of one of his later works—*A World without Why*. Through a series of deftly sketched essays, Geuss entrusts us with an ever-expanding vista of the humanities in general and philosophy in particular, even as we dive deep along with him into each thread and motif that he puts forth in this late work. The tapestry is actually woven around a particular way of looking into the myriad conjunctures of living itself: espousing and celebrating *unfamiliarity* and *puzzlement* in and with life's many encounters.

Very early on, in this particular work, Geuss makes a sharp observation: "The pursuit of clarity is in general a good thing, but the indiscriminate pursuit of clarity is a vice and a serious obstacle to the proper understanding of large parts of human life" (Geuss, 2014). He follows this insight to its limits. Much in our existence and in our interactions shall remain unexplained and that is how it is. What is the point in knowing more than what is required to live? There is nothing to despair about not solving every riddle, nothing bewildering about each turn of grating behaviour that we may sometimes receive from our fellow beings. In fact, much good comes of contrariety and unpredictability. Besides, have we truly come to terms with our own contradictions and inconsistencies? From what vantage do we pronounce quick judgement on people, events and issues? Once we acknowledge such finitude, other horizons open up.

Geuss's accommodative-ruminative canvas brings to us the concerns of a mind that is open to the many creaturely caprices and oddities, a keen awareness and acknowledgement of whatever is at once lofty and crooked within the timbre of humanity. With an understated humility,

Geuss puts aside the hubris of autonomy that marks the horizon of the modern, and the submission to the stars and providential hope that marks the mindscape of the antiquarian. Instead, he takes the difficult path of placing humans as one more species in this world, buffeted by uncertainties and relentless negotiations. I shall try to trace three of the themes that constitute his quest:

(a) To consider the role of obscurity as a definitive phenomenon in creaturely dealings.
(b) To look and reject the notion of 'constructive criticism' as a gainful endeavour in matters of judgement.
(c) To reflect upon the nature and role of untruth in human interactions.

Obscurity

Geuss begins with a simple question: why is lack of clarity considered a defect and a deficiency? He wonders instead whether hankering for clarity could not only turn out to be a wild goose chase, but also become a liability of sorts to those who do so. What if we put the subject under a different lens and inquire about the circumstances in which obscurity may acquire a gainful and positive value? What do we exactly mean when we say that something or some object or some observation is inherently obscure? Does the caveat arise when we consider the receptor's perspective—that the observer/decoder may misconstrue or get perplexed by the content (too many thoughts condensed into each phrase—that was Cicero's complaint against Thucydides style of expression) which the original obscure object or observation wishes to *hide*? Or does it mean that there indeed could be inherent obscurity (hidden/secret/esoteric) in some matter or style, but there could not be any 'inherent clarity' (the latter expression sounds strange to Geuss and rightly so)? Also, do words like clarity and obscurity rather operate within the contexts of our expectations, aims and wishes? Can there be absolute clarity in this mysterious cosmos?

From an aesthetic perspective, any idea of absolute clarity is incoherent, a failure of judgement to remain reflective and be conscious to the context. Geuss extends his argument by means of retelling a story from history as a case study:

The story pertains to the Pyrrhus of Epirus and his costly triumph against the Romans in the Battle of Asculum is 279 BCE. In his epic poem about ancient Roman history, Ennius makes Apollo bequeath the oracle to King Pyrrhus. The oracle could mean either that Pyrrhus would be able to vanquish the Romans or it could mean the opposite, namely, that the Romans would be able to conquer Pyrrhus. Who does the oracle favour? This is a deliberate form of ambiguity that Pyrrhus has to deal with; he takes seriously the first meaning only to discover the truth about the second much later. We are not sure as to what query of Pyrrhus the oracle responded. Was his original question not the right one? But we get a sense about the conclusion that he draws. Indeed, Pyrrhus heard what he wanted to hear—which makes human reception and interpretation subjective and context specific. His confidence about interpreting the message perhaps proves to be his weakness. At this time, Geuss ushers in the possibility of a third interpretation of the oracle: that it is indeterminate as to which side will be victorious; either Pyrrhus could defeat the Romans or it could be that the Romans would come out victorious.

Pyrrhus did not look for ambiguity in the oracle, which would have been otherwise a quite commonsensical thing to do. Perhaps, he was too self-absorbed or over-confident? Or was he dimwitted? But the real question about oracles is this (which pertains to the question of clarity/obscurity): if oracles are so notoriously ambiguous, why consult them in the first place? The first weakness of Pyrrhus is self-centeredness—the oracular response becomes an excuse for his own action. Human agency begins to consider itself superior to fate. Autonomy, that ever-receding hope of the humans, is a key weakness in all ventures, actions and endeavours. The quest for absolute autonomy could lead to singularity of purpose and identity—a condition that could prove to be liability to the very cause over which such singular focus is rested. Further, the ardour to seek limitless clarity in order to fortify one's autonomous status would mean asking too many mindless and half-hazard questions eventually. Is such an inquirer fit to receive any genuine response? The second weakness is the obverse: the recognition that since larger powers decide all creaturely course of action, it is wiser to be resigned and rely on the predictions of the gods. Such a form of determinism can either lead to having faith in some total order or an absolute resignation to chaos. A deterministic warrior begins to rely upon assurances and gives in to the calls of security or submits himself to the vagaries of fortune. He does not remain heroic anymore. Does such a despondent and insecure person use the oracle as a deterministic crutch for erecting an illusion of certainty? But there is no determinate answer 'hidden' in the oracle that can be excavated and deciphered. Indeed, it lies too much at the surface, ambiguous in the very nature of the rhetorical play. Fate smiles wryly as we turn confident about our agency or give it away to fate's arbitrary machinations.

The more complicated fallout of the oracle hinges upon the very nature of Pyrrhus' actual plan of action in the battle field. Did the oracle want him to finish off the enemy in a single battle, or did it suggest that he be more strategic or that he subjugates the enemy? Here, Geuss begins to actually delve into the roots of the phrase *Pyrrhic victory*. The more Pyrrhus starts to win battles against the Romans, the more his position becomes weak as he loses valuable men whom he is unable to replace. Is victory in the short run (tactical) a choice one makes in battles as against more strategic and long term policy decisions about the nature of action in a war? What exactly is permanent victory, if at all such a state is possible to achieve?

Geuss rightly says that the oracle is supposed to be a riddle, and therefore, the ambiguity of each oracular pronouncement comes from its essential nature. In fact, oracles are even more obscure than riddles. Riddles can be solved. Oracles are often left indeterminate, so that they are 'fulfilled' once the *event is over*. Everyone concerned realizes the nature of their prophecy only much later, as the fallout of human action takes its toll in absolutely creaturely terms. Even after its fulfilment, oracular ambiguity may still persist and interpretations can still vary. Geuss asks once again a simple counter-question: why don't gods initially tell things with enough clarity so that the implications are immediately understood? The non-believer's response is that there are indeed no gods. The priests feign oracular wisdom and the whole exercise is a hoax. The Epicurean response is that gods are actually uninterested in trivial human activities and, therefore, do not provide any useful response through oracles. Gods merely play games in which humans are deployed as "tokens on a cosmological board" (Geuss, 2014). Were the gods themselves muddled under the influence of ambrosia? Perhaps, there will always be a lag between divine language and the language of the humans?

So, what could be a gainful evaluation of obscurity under such circumstances? One answer is that the order or incalculability is never fully worked out. Gods must have their own logic and larger purpose in maintaining some kind of necessary ambiguity in intent and communication. Geuss avers: "One does not, however, necessarily improve people by telling them clearly, directly, and in a form they can easily and correctly assimilate what they (think they) want to know" (Geuss, 2014). Perhaps, larger forces try to push and motivate us to seek our own truths? As we try to prove our mettle through experience, no path of determined wisdom or full autonomy is sufficient. By failing, we realize the nature and scope of our ignorance. And become mindful of finitude. This does not mean we stop acting and stop taking decisions. But oracles make us realize the nature and difficulty in taking decisions, given the variables in every action. We pursue action or truth by accepting the cognitive limitations of our understanding. The idea of the oracle is to create puzzlement and by encountering such productive puzzlements, we motivate ourselves to pursue right action and necessary decision—knowing full well that such actions may in turn produce further complications. It is a wager. This strategy does not work for Pyrrhus, because he is not puzzled when he should have been. For a great commander, he is far too confident and impetuous. Besides, as history tells us, he was also probably mercurial and failed to focus adequately in war and diplomacy. Not instruction, but the oracular ambiguity tells us that we learn better about life through suffering.

There is yet another level to the narrative, even as such historical stories are recounted and transmitted through generations: the story tellers/poets (*vates*) themselves. The *vates* does not know what the gods are thinking. So, he cannot possibly enter into the minds of the gods to assess their pedagogic purpose in oracular pronouncements. Only one thing is clear: gods did not require or felt it would defeat the purpose of education if there is absolute clarity in our transactions. It is not a question of whether or not there should be clarity. The point is that there isn't and we learn to deal with life's contradictions in a considered manner, by and by. Each confrontation is a contingent test. Oracles and stories are real and, in this sense, these may help shift people's attitudes by removing rigidity and impetuousness from the horizon of our expectations. To confront obscurity is also to realize "that our society, mode of life, forms of imagination, and language are interconnected" (Geuss, 2014). Our perception and more importantly, imagining of the world becomes different if we are to regularly encounter ambiguity of life's various challenges. More than immediate and active intervention the oracular stirs us to think, wish and take leaps of fantasy. This is the third positive aspect of dealing in obscurity.

Appreciating the oracular mode brings us closer to the utter chaos of everyday living and perhaps helps improve our tempered, yet decisive, response to such chaos. Confronting obscurity makes us agile and tempered at the same time. On the other hand, unless our societies are totally free, generative and truly generous, demands for absolute clarity can be seen as fostering conformity and repressive ideological structures, though the claims may be democratic. To demand clarity of this kind is to foster anti-intellectualism. The capacity to unknot a riddle is at once a factor of our instinct and intelligence. We may fail or succeed to read it, but that is of little consequence. Valuable obscurity is never obscurity for the sake of it. It is rather a by-product of what the *vates* takes us through—indirectly, through digressions and ambiguities. By fully understanding a work of art or a poem, just like living itself, we may have already relinquished the most valuable aspects of such gifts.

Substitution

What do we do in the act of criticism? This is the first question that Geuss asks as he tries to grapple with a corollary: why do people often ask the critics to come up with some constructive suggestions about the subject or arrangement being critiqued and not 'merely' denigrate or run down some action, problem, person or issue? What exactly is so haloed and universal about constructive criticism? Where does the responsibility of the critic lie? Does the idea of constructive criticism arise out of moral (rather than cognitive) fear of some kind of anarchic ceding of onus on the part of the critic?

Geuss feels that criticism lies at the intersection of four essential coordinates—which he names as structural, evaluative, argumentative and performative, respectively. The first dimension concerns the differentiation and accounting of the constituent elements of the problem, issue or the subject critiqued. This element can have some value-based input or description involved in it even as the structures are differentiated. But it does not offer direct judgemental parameters. It rather illuminates and/or augments the features, motives and associations of the subject or the problem. This dimension could also flesh out, propose measures and predict the consequences or implications of certain acts. The second, or the evaluative dimension of criticism, is judgemental in nature. It affirms the fact that to have a critical attitude is to be discriminating. Approving a work of art or a brave act is not designated as a critique. The capacity to and the position from which such a judgement is pronounced puts the beholder in a position superior to the object critiqued. There is negativity involved in acts of evaluative demolition. The structural-analytical and the evaluative dimensions of criticism sometimes come together. To put reasons in order to support the critic's claims brings us to the third coordinate: the argumentative. The values, on the basis of which the criticism is mounted, is defended now by various means—deploying logic and passion, taken forward through examples and illustrations. The final and the performative aspect of criticism has to do with acting upon the earlier three coordinates and publicly indict or vote down the object critiqued.

All these dimensions can be brought to bear upon any matter when our individual mental states and choices are deliberated first within and then in interaction with others, socially. The intermeshing gives the whole thing a formal and institutional shape. But the integration of ideas, our intentions and the expression given to those ideas, are ever contingent and evolving. The speech act that comes out in the public as 'voice' or 'critical position' might in fact deviate significantly from the internal psychic state in which the matter had first germinated and pickled. Given such an overlaying, what exactly would constructive criticism mean?

The underlying assumption behind the idea of constructive criticism arises out of a liberal reformist hope: that all criticism should help improve the lack which the critic finds in the art object, with a problem at hand or with some social arrangement. It hopes action would be taken towards greater perfectibility, once the critical process is completed.

There is a further assumption of a target agent or audience, which will act after going through the criticism, so as to improve upon the original entangled issue, deficiencies or the thing itself which is being analyzed and dissected. The target audience is almost held in ransom to a demand to be fulfilled in future: the improvement of the state of affairs. The constructive critic demands remedial and concrete steps, those that would go beyond analysis and judgement.

The fundamental difficulty in such an expectation is that there can be divergences between the critic's hope and expectations about the issues that he raises and those on the side of receiving or implanting such constructive ideas. The very baseline notion of what constitutes constructive might be different to various parties. How is the critic supposed to know what is reasonable for the parties who would take heed to his suggestions? Does human interaction work through perfect communicative reason? To have a perfect match between both parties, each side has to speak and understand the internal scheme of things. That would be truly constructive. Most of the time, the mismatch happens, since the critic tries to smuggle in an external element to pass judgement over the subject and the receiver/reader/receptor brings yet another set of criteria to decide whether or not it is worth following and implementing the suggestions proposed in the act of criticism. Now, this gap could be constructive in itself in the sense that through disagreements, the process and business of criticism evolves towards betterment and refinement. But it could also mean a cycle of conversation, where the process remains forever open-ended and a certain radical incommensurability lurks beneath what is apparent. Such incommensurability expands until it erupts at certain contingent conjunctures.

Once Geuss delineates the obstacles that may beset the very notion of constructive criticism, he puts forth his central argument: *that it is wiser to think of criticism in terms of providing alternatives and possibilities than as acts that bequeath us with a fixed list of constructive remedies.* For true remedies in life are none. Characteristically, Geuss wonders about the many contradictions and the malleable nature of humanity itself and the knotty possibilities that such contradiction inevitably brings forth. Irresolvable problems are rife. At best, the critics can suggest some substitutes as possibilities to tackle the issues at hand.

A mature and elemental idea of constructive criticism would then look like a method by which substitutes are proposed to the world about the subject at hand. But to rely on substitutes is often a narrow way of atomistically dealing with problems. Such criticism merely offers us the best from two or more finite choices. Besides, substitutability may not work in the context of larger frameworks. Substitutability has its own limits: say, dealing with death or surpassing forms of ecstasy, neither of which can be truly substituted. Constructive criticism based on providing alternatives shall never come close to uniqueness. Substitutes also do not allow us to appreciate genuine interconnectedness between subjects or their finitude. Besides, there cannot be any true mode of transformation or leap with substitution or with such a reformist notion of constructive criticism. Pure negative judgement and reformist patterns of substitutes are non-choices in criticism, for neither realizes the contradictions and *aporia* involved in each encounter, system or thought process that humans actually go through at the creaturely level. Are befuddled creatures perennially caught in a progressive-regressive bind as conscious agentic beings in this planet—between authoritative, activist and solution-based criticism and relativizing to criticism to the extent of suggesting limited patterns, archetypes or substitutes? Are critics doomed to reframe the *anthropocene debate* from time to time in newer ways without reaching any consensus? Who gets to decide the exact lines and contours between nature and society, between memory and history, history and geology, geology and cosmology?

Lying

Why does lying get such bad press? This is Geuss's third significant question about the human condition and its evaluation by humanity. Does this evaluation happen from an expectation of celebrating an apparent higher human capacity: speaking truth? On such a scale, lying seems to be a corruption and a perversion. But is lying an absolute depravity? Geuss puts forth some counterfactuals. What if in some context the alterative choice is violence and use of force? Or: what if the liar is unaware of the purport of his utterances? What about a situation in which the liar is himself taken in by the lie as truth before spreading it, in contrast to someone who plainly tells untruth?

The sharp distinction between truth and untruth as moral categories is a relatively modern phenomenon. It is also culture specific. That falling for a lie can have painful implications is a far more universal condition as opposed to imputing moral wrongfulness to the act of lying. Odysseus was a habitual swearer of oaths and a dissembler. In *Nicomachean Ethics*, Aristotle views the opposite of truthfulness (in only two instances, Geuss informs us) more as a failure in the way of living. The person who dissembles or lies is found short in his own merits in the sense that he makes overly elaborate claims or is being too self-deprecating in stating certain facts. Similarly, in Plato, the philosopher-kings can indulge in noble lies, so that the good state of the city is maintained. The problem is not with lies, but with appearances which keeps us away from truth. However, there was a concept to truth telling/free speech (*parrhesia*) in ancient Greece—one that Geuss transliterates as 'outspokenness'. This is truth spoken to power—an act of courage, the opposite of discretion and pusillanimity, not lying. The idea of *parrhesia* shows that both truth and lie could turn into political acts, depending on the context. It shows that to be politically involved does not always mean indulging in needless guile and subterfuge. There is nothing inherently higher or lower about these choices. The usage of truth or lie could depend rather on the effect it makes on the given situation and on the actors involved at that time.

One of the underlying assumptions about the moral distinction made between truth and falsehood relies on the fact that truth is closer to reality and is, therefore, simpler and more pristine. To this, Geuss says: "I would contend that what is 'out there' is usually a farrago of truths, half-truths, misperceptions, indifferent appearance, and illusion that needs to be seriously processed before one can accept any of it as 'real'" (Geuss, 2014). Are we talking here about post-truth or something even beyond relativism? Not at all. It is rather that truth has to be carefully gleaned and that there are various facets to the real. And that we must be ready to search deep within the welter of numerous shades and processes, until we come up with an accepted notion of truth. Once we realize the tortuous nature of truth, the question of acceptance or rejection arises. That is entirely a subjective or a cultural decision, which may have other motivations. If we leave aside such extraneous factors, at the least, it requires a kind of involved asceticism to look at the world *as it is*: directly, with no blinkers, but with sufficient self-reflection.

There are various forms of deception, duplicity being just one of the possibilities. So also with truth—'truthfulness' as a moral category is of a rather recent vintage. If one is obsessed with straightforward speech/comportment and with immaculately virtuous beings, one is also dogged about lying as a case in duplicity. The two attitudes are complementary to each other. The overall framework turns virtuous and a *sincere* belief is affirmed. Such a person is seeking some anchorage within flux. But having such a belief does not alter our messy, stuttering creaturely predicament. In this context, Geuss asks: can we indict an opportunist fantast? Naïve moralizing, in fact, is likely to take us away from any recoverable truth. It is far more fruitful to seek truth within the pathologies of human foibles and error-prone interactions, what Geuss wonderfully calls "a series of differentially structured complex conjunctions of cognitive, psychological, moral, and political failures of a different kind, conscious deception, insouciance, unconscious self-deception, wishful thinking, lack of attention, lethargy, distraction, suppression of dissent, and inertia" (Geuss, 2014). To heed such complexity is to historicize enmeshed beings caught up in the welter of the times.

Invitation

We are now in a position to trace a certain triangulation in Geuss's mind that speaks a common language. By doing so, we may be able to follow a distinct pattern in his thought process. What might be the source of these threefold concerns: of acknowledging and celebrating obscurity, questioning the banality of substituting one alternative for another and imploring us to be more attentive before we make quick moral binaries of truth/lie? On the face of it, one conjecture could be that Geuss rejects functionality and refuses to give any strict purpose to life, art and philosophy. He shuns one and every kind of totalizing tunnel-vision. Just like he titles his last book: *Who Needs a Worldview?* By purpose and worldview, one means juridical or communicative legitimacy, any endogenous generating of moral normativity, movement towards a rigid telos or a combination thereof. Instead, the very flow of life with its many entanglements is far more important to appreciate.

The other, more positive inference is that he accepts with humility the truth that reason and clarity are radically inaccessible to human beings. So, there is no use trying to hanker for such *unachievables*. Is he trying to evade the stubborn habits of universal ratiocination or the requirement of some higher normative framework in our daily dealings? That would be a deterministic or a nihilistic conclusion. Or is it a classical sceptical move of placing radical emptiness against essentialized habit? It is evident that Geuss is deeply involved in life's processes and its myriad hues, rather than giving up. His is an affirmative sceptical voice. All that he suggests is to be wary of the common urge to get to the bottom of an event, deed or subject. The urge to 'know more' forestalls appreciation of living forces. The 'why-game' is foredoomed and yet, thinkers and reformers have tried to provide all kinds of speculative solutions to this universal conundrum. Systematic and generalized solutions may not work for the intricate contingencies that life throws at us at every turn. Yet, speculative philosophers have tried to play the 'why-game', so that they can provide living creatures with some *solace*. Some have tried to reconcile the manifold crisscross of motives, desires and actions into a totalizing system—say, like Martin Heidegger or G.W.F. Hegel—coming from opposite sides, in addressing the vicissitudes of modernity. The alternative course requires us to stop contemplating about happenings and wondering about motives in creaturely acts. The criterion has to be altered altogether. The best course is to dive into action. Just live. Deeds and facts would then replace the labyrinth in which thought mires itself needlessly. The public consequences of such action will have to be borne by the actor, of course. But by means of being deeply involved with the times that one lives and being simultaneously aware of creaturely finitude, each individual actor might just be able to orient his or her selfhood in a more resolute manner when contingency strikes, as it must.

Here, Geuss posits a third alternative. This he calls *invitation*—to look at, observe or consider something—an event, a disposition, a variation in mood, acts and pronouncements. Just that much. One puts two or more alternatives juxtaposed against each other and invites oneself or others to consider and keenly look at the alternatives without necessarily trying to answer the question 'why'. Such an invitation refrains from indulging in concepts and 'lines or argument'. An invitation makes no claims or demands: "An invitation has neither the direct constructive or coercive power of action nor the indirect coercive power of ratiocination" (Geuss, 2014). Yet, accepting an invitation to consider a painting or facets of a political issue will have an effect upon us. Joining the question as an invitee could perhaps mean we now give more importance to a dimension previously overlooked or taken for granted?

This openness to possibilities—the expansive invitation that Geuss proffers, affirms the point about the centrality of conflict and disagreement in our temporal dealings. Normative principles with ideological moorings do not help in life, which is peppered with surprises, ambiguities and contingent situations at every turn. It is for this reason that he thinks innate or substantive natural rights (pure autonomy) prior to any political process of contestation to be some kind of 'puffery' or 'white magic' (Geuss and Hamilton, 2013). By contrast, Geuss acknowledges *thrownness* of our existence, but does not provide any resolution to it. *Thrownness* for Geuss is not a fatalistic given unlike many earth and soil phenomenologists. It is rather a zone where the obscure nature of riddles and claims are explored, and alternatives are posited. The realization of our thrown condition in fact makes him look for deeper entanglements in life's mysteries and jump into those possibilities, rather than foreshorten those in favour of some simplified, universal panacea. Hence, the *invitation* to consider multiple prospects to any given problem, so that a realistic stock-taking can happen. This stock-taking, however, does not and cannot predict contingencies, crises and miracles.

In order to make his point clearer, Geuss has elsewhere given us a vivid image:

> Three persons struggling to stay afloat on a plank that will only bear the weight of one have no common good or, at any rate, no practically feasible common good, although, of course, one can say that it would be better for all concerned if the situation were different from what it is, and one can fantasize about what their common good would be if they were not in the situation they are in. (Geuss, 2003)

There is no scope for any liberal humanist normative fantasy here that might afford the luxury of belief in human rights or in any common good. For Geuss, those are fertile imaginings that vital creatures can ill afford:

> One can, of course, say and imagine various things about a 'common' or 'public' good.... This is a bit like saying of the three people clinging to the plank that the public good would require that they be in a lifeboat or that each of them have a flotation vest; true enough, and if each were a fish, they could all swim happily away. (Geuss, 2003)

These options are incoherent, because they fantastically hope for some sweet exit by bypassing hard bargaining, without paying the necessary price that all crisis and contestation demand. There are no transcendental standpoints from which we can pass judgement on living and feel smug about it. Indeed, to that extent, humans wish they were fish—for in pure contingency only the survival instinct of the astute fish might take one to freedom. Living is a thread that relates one contingent moment to another; rarely with some breathing space in between.

In his works, therefore, Geuss has tried to constantly distinguish real freedom from happiness or morality: "If 'freedom' is not the same as 'happiness' it is not the same as 'morality' either. So, if one wants to make progress in the right direction in understanding freedom as an ethical ideal one has to thread one's way through the minefield" (Geuss and Hollis, 1995). Indeed, there is no evading the minefield, filled with the many contradictions and ambiguities that life throws at us. Humanity as such is bound to come up with older social experiments in newer forms that shall disturb the liberal consensus and juridical legitimacy. That is the reason, for instance, we witness such a polarized world at this time after a relatively affirmative second half of the 20th century. To be aware of this minefield means being mindful both to the historical conditions of the issue one is investigating and to the processes of investigation itself. It means to be aware of diverse cognitive and affective interests that drive us—which Geuss has elsewhere designated as the "labile constellation of different forms of valuation which are continually shifting in an equally unstable institutional environment or set of environments" (Geuss, 2008).

One of the cornerstones of creaturely dealings, and therefore of proper intellectual history of the colourful and mysterious species called *homo sapiens* (not *homo liberalis*), is the appreciation of the fact that speakers and actors of the species end up saying or doing more or less than what they intend. And the nature of the cleft between intention and expression and our reception of valence depends on the context and contingency of the moment, not on any set chronology or pattern. Perish the idea of perfect cognitive communication. Geuss reminds us elsewhere how Willard Quine had asserted that even our innermost thoughts must be constantly translated since the dialogue inside is never rational or finished: "in the inner dialogue my soul conducts with itself, I encounter a speaker who uses a language that is utterly alien and completely opaque to me" (Geuss, 2020). I am contingent to my own being.

The external manifestations of radical contingency are often more dramatic. The contingent moment remains shrouded in the mysterious history of civilization, until eruptions happen at appointed hours—following cycles and counter-cycles—*corsi e ricorsi*, as Vico has put it. During such hours/events creaturely desires, demands and rearrangements in power gradient become blindingly apparent, as if a film is removed from the mission of civilization itself. Indeed, the underside of civilization is always about the stirrings of the lurking, instinctive creature. The creaturely predicament makes the civilizing mission more perilous, robust and adventurous. Therefore, above everything else, sceptical realism celebrates the force of vital powers, a constant presence and mingling of sorrow and joy, of wonder and dejection. The cult of accessibility is denied any power over us. That is how we embrace living—the very *service of life*, more vigorously and ethically.

References

Damon, Cynthia and Joseph Farrell (eds.). 2020. *Ennius' Annals: Poetry and History*. Cambridge: Cambridge University Press.

Geuss, Raymond. 2003. *Public Goods, Private Goods*. Princeton and Oxford: Princeton University Press.

———.2014. *A World without Why*. Princeton and Oxford: Princeton University Press.

———. 2020. *Who Needs a Worldview?* Cambridge, MA and London: Harvard University Press.

Geuss, Raymond. 2019. "Republic of Discussion: Habermas at Ninety." In *The Point*. 18 June. https://thepointmag.com/politics/a-republic-of-discussion-habermas-at-ninety/. Accession date: 11 August 2020.

———. 2008. "Culture as Ideal and as Boundary." In *Arion: A Journal of Humanities and the Classics*. Third Series. Vol. 16.1, Spring–Summer: 133–154. https://www.jstor.org/stable/29737382. Accession date: 17 April 2020.

Geuss, Raymond and Martin Hollis. 1995. "Freedom as an Ideal." In *Proceedings of the Aristotelian Society*, Supplementary Volumes. Vol. 69: 87–112 Published by Oxford University Press on behalf of The Aristotelian Society. https://www.jstor.org/stable/4107073. Accession date: 17 April 2020.

Geuss, Raymond and Lawrence Hamilton. 2013. "Human Rights: A Very Bad Idea." In *Theoria: A Journal of Social and Political Theory*. Vol. 60.135, June: 83–103. https://www.jstor.org/stable/42705258. Accession date: 16 April 2020.

The Generous Creature

Boredom, Debauchery and Salvation in Oxana Timofeeva

> It's not easy to decide what would be more humanist: to charge a pig that bit a child with a criminal assault and behead it in the main square, or to defend it by saying that a pig cannot be condemned, because it lacks intelligence, morality, and, therefore, is outside the law. Here lies the paradox: from our perspective, medieval animal trials look simply preposterous, while the position of their humanist advocates is easier to understand. But isn't it that precisely within the logic of the latter the culture of slaughterhouse becomes possible…? (Timofeeva, 2018)

These words come from Oxana Timofeeva, whose book *The History of Animals: A Philosophy* alters the way we look into the metaphor and reality of animals. Do we hunt down animals and other creatures through open and public trails or save and slaughter them by kindness, by means of attributing some primal authenticity to their being? In this domain, we begin to ask from our vantage: can they suffer?

Indeed, both politics of inclusion and that of exclusion unleash violence by establishing a certain order of things. The discourse of inclusion presupposes harmony and accord among all categories and levels of creatures. Within the inclusive set up, the animals have now become part of the slaughterhouses, pet shops and luxury safaris. In this sense, we have advanced from displaying animals in zoos and circuses as they began for the first time to disappear from daily life. This fact is true for much of the advanced world. In certain other parts of the world, like in the Indian subcontinent, the case for the inclusion of certain domestic animals is made in the name of religion and community values. Exclusion, on the other hand, insists on the creaturely superiority of human beings—ethically and ontologically, even prior to delving into the question of consciousness.

Quite early on in her book Timofeeva refers to Akira Mizuta's astute observation that animals never entirely vanish from the human horizon, but exist in a state of *perpetual vanishing*. Animals linger. And pray, who are we? (Those able to name the term 'animal' collectively for all other living creatures and ask either 'Can they suffer?' or 'Can they be allowed to defile our precincts?') Are some of us marked and picked up as animals too by others who claim to be divine? As Timofeeva takes up these questions, she carries us along with her through a powerful genealogical journey. Along with her ingenious hypothesis on animal genealogy, she also leaves us with two other corollaries—a critique of the idea of nature as a lost paradise or as a site to practice organic authenticity and a revision of our understanding of the nature-culture divide, for animals stand firmly within the social in Timofeeva's universe.

Two Paradigms

In spite of all the attempts to attract animal attention and concern, the animals themselves remain free and indifferent to human projects that hope to deal with and engage with them. Here, Timofeeva relates man's apparent superiority with a remarkable form of inward battle—summoning of envy and jealousy at the projected realization that animals must be taking pleasure in things and living a freer and better life than the humans. Man cannot hold on to a greater period onto the lofty idea of human dignity and begin to worry about the outlaw nature of animals that he himself cannot achieve. The human being sees himself in the mirror as an animal, but has to play the game of being a human. Hence, a schism takes root within. His life and existence turns into a matter of misrecognizing the animal. Jacques Derrida puts this situation in most stark and lucid terms when he imagines the image of a naked human figure and a cat looking at and considering each other in their apocalyptic naiveté:

> The impropriety [*malséance*] of a certain animal nude before the other animal, from that point on one might call it a kind of *animalséance*: the single, incomparable and original experience of the impropriety that would come from appearing in truth naked, in front of the insistent gaze of the animal, a benevolent or pitiless gaze,

> surprised or cognizant. The gaze of a seer, visionary, or extra-lucid blind person. It is as if I were ashamed, therefore, naked in front of this cat, but also ashamed for being. A reflected shame, the mirror of a shame ashamed of itself, a shame that is at the same time specular, unjustifiable, and unable to be admitted to. At the optical center of this reflection would appear this thing-and in my eyes the focus of this incomparable experience—that is called nudity. And about which it is believed that it is proper to man, that is to say foreign to animals, naked as they are, or so it is thought, without the slightest inkling of being so. (Derrida and Wills, 2002)

Animals cannot be ever naked. But man must be so; by means of mediating nudity through shame. Hence, clothing must be *discovered*. Without shame, there is no sense of good and evil, and hence, man must summon prudence by invoking moral disgust in order to restore the cosmic hierarchy of beings. Man jealously guards his humanity as he enviously disavows himself from his own *animiséance*. But this summoning of shame and nudity and this game with the cat, this serious encounter is that of *fort/da*—gone/there. The animal-other must be seen and forgotten continuously. The encounter with the bare cat is a continuum: the 'incomparable experience'. Neither does shame go away (so that he wishes to dress himself and chase himself out of the room) nor does the power of the encounter leave the human for he wishes the cat to appear again and again before him in its full starkness and its insistent laser gaze—such is the enchainment and the desire to be 'compressed' with it, to be alongside it. The animal comes before me, says Derrida, and I keep on following it after me. Derrida wishes to see this encounter in and through different registers, simultaneously innocent and cruel: "the passion of the animal, my passion of the animal, my passion of the animal other" (Derrida and Wills, 2002). In these registers, at once free and under surveillance, man *announces himself to himself*. In fact, such an announcement is also filled with a certain melancholic muteness. The lamentation happens since the loss of the schism within the encounter ensures "a death to come in the surviving of a ghost", as one realizes the price incurred as one pays off the ever-necessary debt to human dignity (Derrida and Wills, 2002).

Aristotle, on the other hand, is invested in cosmic order and in the principle of life which is prudential. Each animal knows its place in that order. Each creature follows a mimetic pattern of habit; this provides "continuity and succession of all living beings" (Timofeeva, 2018). In order to drive home her point, Timofeeva tells us two stories from the XLVII chapter of *The Nicomachean Ethics*. Both the stories pertain to incest. In the first one, a camel keeper forced the colt to have intercourse with his mother after putting a wrap over her. But after he completed the act, the colt bit the keeper to death. In the second story, a Scythian king brought the colt of a high quality mare to mate with her. She was concealed under a wrap, but once the mating was over and the mare's face was uncovered, the colt ran away and threw itself down the cliffs. This second story is a clear equivalent of the Oedipus myth. Inhibitions, therefore, is made to seem natural to the animals rather than being a culturally developed fact as claimed by a certain anthropological view, which deals in taboos and community rules. However, we are aware of polygamy and inbreeding among animals. So why stress naturalism as a moral category? Aristotle's point is that animals follow a natural law—but the underlying moral fear is that of destabilizing some cosmic order by being degenerate and imprudent. Animals are animal (from plural they turn into to a homogenous category, an attribute) by nature as are the slaves or the untouchables—all aware of their status in the scheme of things. Hence, all follow a certain order. The animals follow the cosmic laws without consciously knowing those laws. In this context, Timofeeva reminds us that Georges Bataille had pointed out that in the human imagination the horse resembles whatever is formally perfect and dignified in creation. The horse corresponds to the idea of classical proportion and arrogance, unlike the spider or the hippopotamus, which rather resembles the demented, ugly and immoral barbarians. Horses are closest to humans, imagined to cement the idea of a buffer against the fragility of the cosmos. Horses are included within the prudential and the dignified scheme of things. Those who are foreign and ape like, by contrast, are aliens. They are suspect and a source of danger. Such monsters must be excluded and exorcised since they represent the *inhuman*.

So, the binary is created—either one argues for continuity and affinity of the animals with the humans or one vigorously distinguishes the two on the basis of certain anthropological traits. Both the perspectives, in their own ways, begin by imposing moral laws over animals as if they are natural laws. And since the lines between the two are sometimes blurred, often humans do not know whether to banish or welcome the animals back in their midst. Hence, the melancholy and the lament. This happens, as we have already pointed out, owing to a primitive form of envy, creating a divided selfhood among those who consider themselves to have domesticated and conquered their creaturely attributes my means of practice and sensitization.

Gilbert Simondon bequeaths us another kind of speculation: that there are psychical, vital and psychosocial modes and potentialities which unify all creatures. Life is all about being individuated, with repeated attempts to cope with contingency through internal structures and vital mechanisms. The sensory regime is transferred to the psychic. And the psychic is also not the intellectual regime. Individuation concerns "a certain habit, a habit which enables (the most differentiated) animals to learn, and by acquisition of experience, they acquire a certain capacity to foresee what is presented and to palliate the different inconveniences of possible events" (Simondon, 2011). It is a combination of prediction and prudence. In this context, Timofeeva recalls Kafka's absurdist animals—those events are escape routes for animals who are least interested in imitating human beings. Animals are actually bored by human beings, but they are wary of the latter's craft—and about the game of exclusion/inclusion. Apes converted to humans since they had no choice, in order to break out their individuated struggling lives. The apes began to imitate humans, so that they can act freely. In Kafka's world, therefore, dogs commit hunger strike, mice form collectives of music lovers and horses turn into lawyers.

The Hovering Undead

Between the pole of domestication (Aristotle) and that of destitution (Derrida), Timofeeva steers her genealogical boat. To begin with, a contemporary mode to conceptually consider and be with animals has been to attribute divine and sovereign status to them. Georges Bataille, for instance, considers the archaic-totemic nature of the kinship tie between the humans and animals in terms of the awestruck mortals and the sacred-sacrificial icons. Animals, in such a world, had less to do with power and more with freedom, since animals did not labour in order to live. This projection of authenticity and immanence to the animals, and by extension, the romanticization of the primitive community living that goes with it, has been questioned by the likes of Jean-Luc Nancy. But Timofeeva's issue is not with this projection (for Nancy himself is projecting his own ideas onto Bataille), but that Bataille does not consider the nature of contemporary sacredness in which the animal does not have any sacrificial and sovereign place in the society (it is thoroughly domesticated). Sacredness has been transferred to other domains (to capitalism or to sports for instance) as it has been disenchanted from its earlier immanent status. Step by step, the Western imagination has moved from the archaic-sacred to conceiving animals with a godlike or a human face (in medieval and early modern bestiaries, for instance), eventually facilitating and paving the way for animal trails and executions, carried through religious or secular tribunals. The process of anthropomorphizing animals and then excluding them from the *socius*, has been steady, long and arduous, until with modernity animals would be once again reinstated among us on the basis of their rights (and not divinity or intellect). Animals are also juridical legal things now. We welcome them back, by mediating through a patronizing process with little moral or creaturely impetus in it. The rights argument is paradoxically an offshoot of the same humanist impulse which brought animals down from the totemic to the manageable in the first place.

The other paradigm relates animals to innocence. St. Francis of Assisi would speak with animals just as Rousseau would do with plants. The medieval innocence of the animals was gradually sanctified as they were made to pass through a process of purification. This is the Christian utopia of poverty and charity. Bareness of nudity becomes an enriching power. Timofeeva notices a similar impulse in the writings of Georgio Agamben and Antonio Negri, who often go back to St. Francis in order to attest love, simplicity and innocence in living beings. After the mechanical revolution, however, things changed and animals were largely viewed as automatons with no feelings, mind or soul. It was felt that they did not desire or suffer. The process of exclusion started. But as marked earlier, the more one tries to exorcise the projections of naiveté, innocence and insanity, the more they take root. The hyperbolic moment of insanity and animality is domesticated, but never fully gotten rid of. With Freud, we know that even the unconscious subject thinks. Nothing is erased truly and all the traces are never covered up.

The crucial line of enquiry that Timofeeva follows through concerns a certain conceptual turn that has taken place in modernity by means of which the animals are simultaneously accepted and rejected by the reasonable and empathetic human beings. In G.W.F. Hegel's scheme of things, for instance, animal life is at once the summit of natural beauty and yet restricted, since the needs for such a life are narrow: fulfilling sex and nourishment. The interior of the animals remain concealed and the exterior is not as beautiful as the humans. Human relationship with nature is abstract and theoretical whereas the animal scales and feathers, underdeveloped skin and protruding mouths, are a measure of a certain spiritual and intellectual absence. The explosive impulses of the animal, which Bataille had related to sacredness, are converted into a lack by Hegel. The truly soothing and sculptural animal to Hegel is the Greek man's profile. The otherization of the animals almost takes a racist turn. For Hegel, the crucial move is to consciously self-negate and overcome the animal existence. Most crucially for Hegel, animals do not have a sense of death and finitude and, therefore, they do not own their life. The animal is thus included within the metaphysical system and put in its rightful place. Besides, the animal appears as subjectivity in Hegel rather than as a thing, unlike what we encounter in the mechanical tradition. In the Hegelian scheme, "any substance should thus be an opportunity for the subject—in a negative movement, which is at the same time a totality of spirit, having to pass through alienation and rupture, and to face finitude in order to overcome it" (Timofeeva, 2018). Nature should be confronted with as a source that fosters alienation, and spirit should recognize itself in that mirror and move towards unity by overcoming its enticement. The universal must overcome the particular in Hegel. The hierarchy and fixity of creatures in Hegel is as strong as in Aristotle.

The problem arises since Hegel also claims transformation of the spirit. He is neither warm to the idea of evolution in the Darwinian scheme, nor is he a historicist like Marx, and in that sense, he is an idealist. And yet is he a prophet of change? Looking closely, we shall find that while a conceptual evolution does take place in Hegel, no real one happens. Rather, the totality to truth beckons him. The dialectic of the spirit constantly moves by accepting the inner unity of truth. There is no proper mixing of singularities (between levels of animality and then between animal and man), but the individuation of beings in their singularities are maintained—quite the obverse scheme to Simondon's suggestions. That is the reason the Hegelian animal has voice, but no sense. It also has no language, which is the crucial anthropomorphic distinction imbued within such unfolding of the universal spirit of history.

The Hegelian system thus removes the human animal from its animality and naturalizes it within a certain fixity. This is the state of being *undead*. The real complication for Timofeeva is that as soon as we suppress, remove and banish the human-animal from our midst the human too dies along with the animal. Man watches himself "ceasing to be" (Timofeeva, 2018). The sacrificer dies along with the animal. The sacrificer turns itself into an animal. This is the zone of internalized death. According to Timofeeva, it is here that we enter the zone of the repressed: the unconscious. Man, by banishing man-animal, turns unhappy and insecure. Will cannot fully suppress drive and things begin to hover within a space of an unhappy limbo. The indeterminate straying nature of man comes to the fore. He begins to isolate himself the more he tries to negate the unconscious. We turn into insecure and anxious Hegelian animals. Given such conditions for the Hegelian modernity to kick in, we could truly turn survivalist and beastly at this juncture and look forward to an end of history as the spirit approaches the absolute truth. Paradoxically but logically, this would mean reverting to the state of nature and to the instinct of survivalism. This is the Kojevian inference derived out of Hegel's insights.

The other option is to accept creaturely life in its full bareness and accept rest and detachment. Agamben works towards such a possibility—which was most starkly put to test during the first year (2020) of the Corona virus pandemic, when he opted to become unpopular in arguing for such ascetic sangfroid at a time when the Hobbes/Kojeve survivalist instinct seemed to loom large over humanity.

The third alternative is the realist one: to persist with utter indeterminacy of the 'open wound' and 'unemployed negativity', of our living. Humanity would seem to have hardly come out of the cycles of desire in this third scheme. Bataille would vote for the last one—in which it is not the human, but the desperate animal which negates itself by secretly retaining its sovereignty. It begins to mediate animality and the 'open wound' by means of engaging in eroticism, art, laughter and play.

The Generous Animal and Toska

Timofeeva's hero is undoubtedly Andrei Platonov, the Russian writer, philosopher, playwright and poet. In his writings, she discovers a profound identification with a particular subjective dispensation that can only come from living a *poor life*. It is in response to such an existence that she aligns communism with animality. The essential attribute of Platonov's writings can be described by the enigmatic and untranslatable word *toska*. The word at once connotes melancholy, longing, torment and depression. Pining, mental throes and restlessness come under its ambit. But *toska* is not a passive existential quality. Since *toska* is a condition of unbearable pressure, it can also turn interruptive. It has little to do with nostalgia and much more with breaking free. Boredom and freedom speak to each other through *toska*. Timofeeva develops a politico-ontological perspective, through which she dives into Platonov's world of plants and animals. This, she gives the name of *poor life*. In Platonov's world, human beings come out of microbes and worms and matter is incandescent. There are a few characteristics of such a poor life. Foremost is diligence. Since Platonov's creatures live impoverished lives, they cannot afford to be rash and 'cool'. All the animals, including humans, work in order to maintain their lives. In this sense, they are steady, focused and relaxed at the same time. His animals are naïve and mature. In this sense, Platonov's animals come close to Kafka's who search a way out for freedom, but are aware of their finitude. Diligence is another name for creating a kind of distance from the world and to observe it closely. It is a rigorous method to consider our own precarious animal status. Diligence is an act of deepening one's self-relation. It is an intuitive kind of prudence.

The second quality of the creatures that belong to poor life is their generosity. Animals wish to give and share. Their world is the obverse of the Kojevian/Hobbesian universe. Their misery and lack paradoxically make them giving. They are close to being sacrificial though not in a primitive-sacred way, but rather in a way that comes out of *toska*;

the deepest of realizations that comes only with poverty. Instead of existentially going inward or turning violent and greedy, Platonov's animals begin to give: Here is an instance from the story called *Cow*:

> We had a cow. While she lived, my mother, my father and I all ate milk from her. Then she had a son—a calf—and he drank from her too. There were three of us and he made four, and there was enough milk for us all. The cow also ploughed and carried loads. Then her son was sold for meat, he was killed and eaten. The cow was very unhappy, but she soon died from a train. And she was eaten too, because she was beef. Now there is nothing. The cow gave us everything, that is her milk, her son, her meat, her skin, her innards and her bones, she was kind. (Platonov, 1999)

This givingness marks the soul which eats flesh and which feeds the body in turn. The soul is material—*anima*, a moving force, matter of body that circulates among all bodies—animals to humans, from fishes and planktons to plants. Eating and sexual intimacy make each of us devour the other and the energy of diligence and generosity flows from body to body. Hard work for us, all animals, means we are welcoming and participating in sexual activities—this is Timofeeva's inference. *Toska* converts boredom into excitement and intense action. Joy and expenditure of living in animals are unlimited. Vulnerability and destiny of the working class, the animals of this world, find respite in loving satisfaction and in death. Platonov's animals intensely suffer. After diligence and generosity, suffering is the third common attribute that binds all poor animals of the world.

And yet poor life refuses to give up on its hard-earned joys. Animal passion is unlimited. It draws from the dialectics of nature—cruelty, ferocity and adherence to death. There is a remarkable narration of a sheep circle in Platonov's story *Soul*: "sheep are wandering across the desert in search of some grass, people are pursuing the sheep and predators and dogs are going after other people, eating those who die" (Platonov, 1999). But within the tragic always lurks hope, since animals and humans are interchangeable—a dog was a former human, or a camel sits like a human, "propped up on his front legs in a drift of sand" (Timofeeva, 2018). Platonov's animals are humans in disguise, imprisoned in his natural body and tormented by his intellect. But they are all potential disruptors, which is the effect of the essential insanity developing out of *toska*.

The utopia of transformation stands on the hope to be liberated from the creaturely reliance on necessity and to be preserved from the vagaries of contingency. The fusion of the animal and the human, the social and the natural orders is essential. And one need not be nice and civil about such encounters, for they are visceral and cut-throat. This desire for emancipation and egalitarianism arises out of deep boredom and unendurable suffering that fosters in the existing conditions. *Toska* pushes all animals to follow their destiny, which is the only alternative other than extinction and death. Poor life produces humour as well as pain. Humour and diligence arise out of the equity of pain. Creatures show immense resilience and generosity within the finitude of *poor life*.

Timofeeva calls Platonov's communists the revolutionary animals. The energy expended by such communist animals is, however, nothing to do with sublation of sexual desire or natural needs: "Quite the opposite—it is a kind of debauchery" (Timofeeva, 2018). If revolution means transformation at the planetary plane—freedom from the creaturely condition itself, that change is already inscribed in the unconscious animal nature. Such an inscription awaits and anticipates salvation from those who value equity of the species-being and call themselves communists. Such a powerful and materialist salvific move is the very obverse of the emptiness of internalized oblivion. It exceeds ennui. Without the absurd gesture of taking with our animal and forgotten, repressed side, there is no creaturely emancipation. The revolutionary must always be aware of the catastrophe and the misery of the animal. Otherwise, man would be left alone only with mourning rather than any emancipation. And mourning has to do only with suffering, not destitution.

Are we *attuned* to what we have no knowledge of, but that which suffuses the creaturely predicament? Are we not mutually implicated, ungainly creatures suffused from head to toe in *toska,* if we care to give in to the liberating surplus of consciousness? In the final instance, Oxana Timofeeva holds on to the liberation of a giving generosity in creaturely exchange. Freedom lies hidden within boredom and oblivion. To the debauched and the diligent, sometimes deliverance arrives as a miracle that only poor life can bring forth. But the spirit needs unlocking.

Animals, joyous and despairing, stunned and energetic, forgotten and erotic, are the only hope for the anticipatory human. To put that insight in Timofeeva's oracular voice: the animal is the only real outlaw.

References

Agamben, Giorgio. 2004. *The Open: Man and Animal.* Translated by Kevin Attell. Stanford: Stanford University Press.

Collarco, Matthew. 2008. *Zoographies.* New York: Columbia University Press.

Derrida, Jacques and David Wills. 2002. "The Animal That Therefore I Am (More to Follow)." In *Critical Inquiry*. Vol. 28.2, Winter: 369–418.

Platonov, Andrei. 1999. *Soul.* New York: New York Review Books.

Simondon, Gilbert. 2011. *Two Lessons on Animal and Man.* Minneapolis: Univocal.

Timofeeva, Oxana. 2018. *The History of Animals: A Philosophy*. London and New York: Bloomsbury.

———. 2016. "Living in Parasite: Marx, Serres, Platonov, and the Animal Kingdom." In *Rethinking Marxism*. Vol. 28.1: 91–107.

Timofeeva, Oxana and M. Buna. 2018. "Why Still Look at Animals: A Conversation with Oxana Timofeeva." In *LA Review of Books.* 27 October. https://lareviewofbooks.org/article/why-still-look-at-animals-a-conversation-with-oxana-timofeeva/. Accession date: 10 May 2021.

Wolfe, Carey. 2008. *Philosophy and Animal Life*. New York: Columbia University Press.

Uexküll, Jakob von. 2010. *A Foray into the Worlds of Animals and Humans.* Translated by Joseph D. O'Neill. Minneapolis: University of Minnesota Press.

The Creature as the Spirit-Wrestler

Lev Shestov and Caprice Incarnate

Nicolas Berdyaev's capacious 1948 work, *The Russian Idea*, begins by placing two contradictory principles that reside at the heart of the Russian soul: one, an elemental paganism and the other, a form of ascetic monasticism. On one hand, cruelty and a disposition to violence, and the other, kindliness, gentleness and humanity,

> a belief in rites and ceremonies, but also a quest for truth: individualism, a heightened consciousness of personality, together with an impersonal collectivism: nationalism, laudation of self; and universalism, the ideal of the universal man: an eschatological messianic spirit of religion, and a devotion which finds its expression in externals: a search for God, and a militant godlessness: humility and arrogance: slavery and revolt. (Berdyaev, 1948)

In the same book, Berdyaev acknowledges that the figure of L. Shestov, the one who saw 'the tree of life' to be the opposite of 'the tree of the knowledge of good and evil', to be most essential in order to understand *the multiform Russian Renaissance* of the beginning of the 20th century.

Athens and Jerusalem, published in 1937, is Lev Shestov's (born: Lev Issakovich Schwarzman) mature work, written after he had left Russia and settled in Paris. Berdyaev's reflections, especially on the question of despair and sublimation, singularly and explosively come true in this work. The work is a profoundly interruptive gesture in creaturely explorations. From the realm of the humdrum, he takes us to a realm that lies beyond the tragic. Shestov is more known as someone who had spent a lifetime, saturated in and with unadulterated despair, propelled by, what has been called, a 'personal avalanche' in his life. Louis Shein, for instance, describes this sense of being devastated, and hence, illuminated by an avalanche by recounting the following lines from *In Job's Balances*, written by Shestov himself:

> when he comes for a soul, sees that he has come too soon, so he does not take the soul away, but leaves the man one of the innumerable pairs of eyes with which his body is covered. And then the man sees strange and new things, more than other men see and more than he himself sees with his natural eyes. But since all our other organs of sense, and even our reason, agree with our ordinary sight … the new vision seems to be outside the law, ridiculous … it seems only a step short of madness … not poetic madness … but the madness for which men are pent in cells. (Shestov, 1928–1937/1966).

But despair is only the penultimate stage that buffets living creatures. Czeslaw Milosz specifically marks Shestov's daring and insolence instead. Shestov would have little to do with abstraction and universal claims, for he was suffused with dogged madness and divine stupidity.

Much like Kierkegaard, for Shestov, abstractions are fruits of human cowardice, and like Kierkegaard, he would feel that "human cowardice cannot bear what death and insanity has to tell us" (Shestov, 1928–1937/1966). In the elaborations of *Athens and Jerusalem*, Shestov dives headlong into *de profundis* even as he takes apart speculative philosophy—which is otherwise his singular preoccupation. In his later works, we see clearly what the stakes are. Can we think of creatures outside of contradictions and totalized truth claims? Are we scandalized to even consider submitting to a wrathful, contingently active God? Does our fear take us to streamlining the basic stimuli of Old Testament (OT) with gnosis, speculation and eventually with reason and thus constrain the original impulse of Judaism? What hubris makes us think we can explain accidents and events through workable paradoxes? Is not paradox the greatest of dogmas? What is clarity, what distinctness is reached by *solving* riddles? Shestov responds to the suffering and horror of living by invoking the blinding capriciousness and incomprehensibility of Jehovah, the god of the OT. In his final work, he provides us with a 'faithful' understanding of revelation, as opposed to the immutable laws of speculation—the ones in which the creature is able to play with Necessity.

But Shestov's real investment is in life and with life's contingency and finitude. In contrast to Spinoza, who asks us not to laugh, weep or hate, but to understand, Shestov's whole endeavour is directed towards the minutest of our responses to the stimuli that surrounds us and makes us what we are. It revolts Shestov whenever the abstract is placed before the creature. Abstractions are deliverances of consciousness; universal judgements that are never open to the demands of the spirit. One cannot mould or transform any *doxa*. Right at the outset of this work, Shestov makes it apparent that in actual terms what goes by the name of critical philosophy (post Kantian) is actually not very different from forms of dogmatism. One is assimilated into the other. Leibniz believed in two fundamental tenets: the principle of contradiction and the principle of sufficient reason. Descartes merely refined the insight into a dualistic system. Cogito required no proof or demonstrability, once all doubts were systematically eviscerated. Besides, if Descartes would formally doubt the existence of God, his edifice would have collapsed. In real terms, no proof is required for indulging in speculation; it is geared to protect the vulnerability of the creature by seeking a justification for our existence and for the purposes of ethical decision-making. But what is this figment of autonomous ethics? Universal truths rather help us become indignant and righteous beings; speculation helps us get rid of generosity and expansiveness of the soul-force.

Why should reason be irritated every time we give in to our desires, hopes and dejections? Should it not be the other way round? In fact, reason constraints, and by constraining, it persuades us into making Manichean divisions: good and bad, true and false, logic and rhetoric. All constraints become persuasive to humans and that becomes that aim and effect of all knowledge. Shestov says that three major preoccupations—God, the immortality of the soul and freedom, are demonstrable to the critical thinker. So, the latter creates an elaborate web and sends faith, immortality and true freedom to the underground since their existence is impossible to prove. Only "when it is a question of the existence of objects outside ourselves, then faith does not suffice, then it is absolutely necessary to have proof" (Shestov, 1928–1937/1966). But that postulated object outside us or as an object of faith (ritual, colour, song, relic) cannot be endured. Therefore, Shestov asks the radical question:

> Is it not just the opposite which should have happened? The 'scandal' of philosophy, one would think, consists in the impossibility of proving the existence of God; but it does not happen because man is horrified to depend on the unknowable and the finitude of existence.

> It threatens his very sense of secure and stable self. (Shestov, 1928–1937/1966)

So, that nebulous region is given a name in speculative philosophy: *supra-sensible*. Only we are able to hear echoes from that zone and are forced to be confounded by reason and reason's deputy—universal ethics. We are bound forever to the cogs of dreary indifference.

The ways to conceive and believe in any supreme being and its interventions in our midst is also given a name: working of the *deus ex machina,* which is the greatest absurdity of our existence. Instead of falling into the hands of a living God, it is important to create necessity and wonder about its hide and seek with the agency of the creature. That is mitigating: universal truth spreads over our wounds like an invisible balm. It even rejoices. We orient ourselves according to the necessity of fixed stars—astral fate or reason's dicta. Since truths of our experience surprise and irritate us, the immutability of constraining universal theories persuade and calm us—the *deus ex machina* being one such explanatory category. The self feels contended by espousing some kind of resolution. Understanding means acceptance. In distress, we seek the crutch of speculative philosophy. Such an abstract notion of feeling goodwill that bypasses life, Shestov rejects. We have trained ourselves to forget the encounters of the vulnerable creature with the distant, blind and omnipotent giver of laws. One can prolong security, but cannot avoid absolute wreckage and eventual death. The idea of finitude: that everything that has a beginning must come to an end—this, the man of the Bible is not willing to accept. For the man of the Bible, the drudgery of autonomous ethics means nothing. He sees and feels the God who reveals himself to the prophet on Mount Sinai. The man of the Bible is not moved by any duty to perform the laws of the being. True contemplation (which constrains and persuades the man of speculation) means nothing to him. For grace and benediction, he waits.

The Psalmist, says Shestov, takes us to *what is* and to what one can feel in the guts and sees by means of the eye of the mind. His truths are not determined by what is given. He does not rejoice after *finding* the truth. His *searchings* do not constitute in seeking facts and distinguishing truth from falsehood. Shestov perceptively says: "The fact that on earth righteous men are poisoned like mad dogs does not at all trouble the philosophers, for they believe it in no way threatens philosophy" (Shestov, 1928–1937/1966). Speculative philosophy is purely interested in rationalizing living, even if that happens by means of highlighting irrationality or chance or joy. The open truth of revelation confronts our deepest fears and hopes—therefore, it irritates man. It reminds him of his helplessness as a creature trying to forge some rudimentary legal framework and social norms even as destruction and devastation lurks and then falls upon him. Shestov grapples with what he calls the 'pure arbitrary', where human beings have no place to lean upon anything. And within the ambit of the pure arbitrary lie all our anxieties and hopes, joys and sorrows. Understanding exploits the hiatus between creatures and contradictions. Therefore, we must begin from being and not from knowledge.

Shestov shuns all habits of thought, all categories in which we have become habituated to think: the tree of learning must not choke the tree of life, he feels. Soulless knowledge and speculation does not confront the bare creature. The fear of the fantastic (and the horrors of the history of human beings) makes a triumphant return in faith—it abandons itself joyously to the disposition of the Creator. This confrontation with our inmost self is the route to freedom. The material fuses in and with divine innocence. The original ideas of shame, humiliation and enslavement are banished from existence. The power of the Biblical revelation, instead, lies in its being at once *incomparably miraculous* and *monstrously absurd*. The power goes beyond all comprehension. Nothing is anymore impossible, for it is neither reflection of the world, nor any false promise to 'exhausted humanity'. The unlimited will of the Creator reigns. There is no split between ruinous evil and ineffectual good.

Cry Halt before Necessity

The mystery of creation and its consequences for humans who roam about and work hard in this oblong planet only grows with time. Premonitions and disquiet create and uncreate creaturely interactions as we grapple with our bare, sorrowful chores in the sub-lunar region of our existence. What superhuman efforts we require as organisms in the planet in order to justify our deeds and desires! Are beings constrained to follow this phenomenon as universal fate and truth? How is it that the beings have no power over such truth which crushes them and truth has all the power to crush and destroy them? Indeed, someone *can say* such things but *cannot think* about such possibilities as curiosities. Did the totalizers and the fatalists, like Hamlet "lack the gall to make oppression bitter?" (Shestov, 1928–1937/1966). Therefore, pain and bitterness, things that constrain, become part of ineluctable Necessity. "Cry halt before Necessity" says Aristotle in his *Ethics* and *Metaphysics*. But since injustice is no longer listened to, first it protests and then turns silent. But Necessity does not listen to oaths and prayers too. Cries reverberate in wilderness. Only the Psalmist is not bound by Necessity. He cannot forget Jerusalem. A great and final battle he takes up against Necessity. He dares, defying all shame. Shestov says that "nothing can justify this boundless audacity; it is the extreme expression of shamelessness" (Shestov, 1928–1937/1966). Aristotle seeks a mean and castigates as depravity and vice everything that dares defy this middle zone of being. He is the arche scientist who passes judgements on matter and its motion and affirms Necessity. The Psalmist defies this middle existence of acceptance and determinism.

You can either be shameless; you can turn away from the real to the fantastic or may submit to the invincible limits of Necessity. Such is the truth that constrains creatures. Parmenides, Heraclitus and Anaxagoras carried out their work constrained by such an oppressive truth—which was postulated by their times and more forcefully later, by Socrates and his interlocutors. And the beauty of such a virtuous world view is that it needs man's blessing and man shall wilfully bless such universal explanations. This: since fear of the unknown and the accidental reigns in man's heart. Man shall therefore go on singing *hosannas* to strange and indifferent stones.

All established science (though paradigms may shift) recognizes the Necessity of matter as primordial and original with no beginning and end. One exception is David Hume. Hume came to the conclusion that Necessity is nothing, but only bonds established by humans—phenomena that are only connected by *relationships of fact*. But Shestov feels that Hume did not take his own sceptical arguments to their logical conclusion. And this provided Immanuel Kant an opportunity to restore Necessity through his categorical imperatives and the critical moral framework. For Hume, reality exists only in dreams and hence, he began by taking contingency and fantasy seriously. Hume came close to taking us outside of synthetic judgements. He made us see why interactions are truly and completely inaccessible since there were no necessary bonds between phenomena. And if anything could flow from anything, the principle of contradiction would take a beating. You cannot justify existence through paradoxes that can be unified. Or seek reconciliation of opposites by deploying forms of dialectical thinking. Being and thought turn into spectres. But Hume's doubt was brushed aside by the joint power of Aristotle and Kant—who sowed the necessary formulas of incantation and virtue amidst a harmonious and rational universe. Doubt is never academic in Shestov. It is a creative force that permeates living. Sceptical denial is put to affirm the vehemence of life.

In forms of rationalization, all creatures and even God is subordinate to Necessity. God commanded once and we all obey since, including He himself to the laws of the cosmos. Why has his terrible and mighty nature of the command and the revelation to his Creations—all take a back seat? Why no intimacy anymore with the mysteries of his command and their relationship to the created beings? This happened, Shestov explains,

> because the mysterious and inconceivable moment of command (*jubere*) was pushed back into the eternity of the past and declared unique (*semel jussit*), while for ordinary usage men chose obedience, the *parere*, which seems to be the comprehensible, natural, and normal fate not only of the creature but also of the Creator Himself. (Shestov, 1928–1937/1966)

All things arbitrary, puzzling, fantastic and inconceivable were brushed aside. Everything was converted into 'dear and natural'. The task of philosophy was to strengthen such a necessity through incantations and reasoning. Therefore, the stoics submitted to fate. And the cynics put all their confidence into reflective human reason. The stoics and the cynics are castigated by critical modernity, not for turning around and squaring with truth, but because they dared to call nakedness as nakedness. They gave the phenomenon of turning around its right name. To Shestov: that is an unpardonable crime.

Others are blessed since they look around and are silent. Why? Hence, Shestov says: "No one can answer. It seems that everyman, like Socrates, has at his side a demon who, indecisive moments, demands of him judgments and acts whose meaning remains incomprehensible to him and forever hidden" (Shestov, 1928–1937/1966). All mysteries are thus stifled. All are happy that a power should finally be found, a power that binds and decides on our behalf, which delivers us from the freedom of will and makes us realize that we must stop and 'Cry Halt before Necessity'. Destiny reigns. Habit must rule.

Has being ever found any adequate expression outside of thought? Especially if it dares to turn around. Turning around and looking backward actually paralyzes man. He cannot afford to see what already exists. That petrifies him. He wants to forget fear, apprehension and anxiety. Only turning indifferent by giving in to necessity can save him. The principle of contradiction must be peppered with threats. Creatures must be persuaded by the laws of necessity. It affixes the seal of eternity to the event and freezes the seeker's will. One cannot dare or doubt, struggle or resist once necessity intervenes. Most of all—one cannot allow caprice into the scheme of things, especially within the folds of the critique of reason.

We have handed over our destiny to obedience (by following principles of contradiction and identity) rather than to command. When righteous men are put to death, the explanation is silence following universal obedience. Contradiction makes all propositions move towards a larger unity and hence makes those contradictions non-existent. Such principles merely become *executive instruments*. The revelatory powers of the oracle are slowly turned into solvable riddles. And here Shestov asks a powerful question: *But what if we do not ask anything of anyone?* Can we bring necessity, identity and contradiction under our command? We can hardly give such power to God himself. We can at best seek light under the yoke of obedience, since we fear all accidents and scurry day and night under the yoke of the most inevitable of accidents, which is also most certain: death. The threat of the accident is the threat of metaphysical truth. Spinoza can at best say that the laws of thought are laws of stones endowed with intensity.

But that is not preordained. We are all stones when we turn backwards and begin to inquire and reflect—that is what Spinoza and Bergson shall affirm. There we halt. But there is no Crying Halt before necessity if you know that the fantastic lurks and lies everywhere. To be with the fantastic is the only way to get rid of all crushing exhortations of philosophy. We turn into *what is* through pure *will.*

There is no contentment ever. Only ceaseless irritation. Relentless encounters with the purgatorial in this living existence are the only wisdom possible. Contentment with oneself is the highest form of hoax. Sacrifice more so. Only the flow of force and preordained power of the command resounds. All clarity and distinctness in Western metaphysics is about good and evil. Only the God of Genesis is ruthless and distant. He plays with us. Necessity will not budge. It will not confront caprice ever. But God would. He shows how inane is the very idea of a face-off between agency and necessity. With the capricious God does the possibility of encountering eternal mystery arises.

Those Overwhelming Lines

All pleasure is shadow-like—unreal—this is the cornerstone of the Platonic way of looking into the world. With pleasure you are nailed. In order to affirm this truth, he even turns away from the Demiurge. According to Shestov, therefore Plato wishes to flee from the cave but cannot, since: "it is necessary that our corporeal eyes forget how to see when it is given us to penetrate into the region where the gods live with their limitless freedom and without our knowledge, without even the perfect knowledge that we call omniscience" (Shestov, 1928–1937/1966). The illusory is the primordial right of necessity. Celebrating illusion becomes a constraint—only to be viewed through the spiritual eyes. Outside of the cave, there is neither being nor thought.

Aristotle places imitative power against the creative. He brings ideas into matter. Philosophy begins to further limit God's creative activity. Even Nicholas of Cusa to Dun Scotus, everyone seeks something outside and beyond God—*intelligence,* or some other higher power. They did not need to be reminded that God created humans out of dust. No one dared to give God the limitless sovereignty that the OT had assigned. And yet, there are insurmountables to which even such sovereign power must bow, even God who "cannot save man against his will, and that He cannot make what has been not to have been" (Shestov, 1928–1937/1966). Groping outside is of no help. If one reads Hegel's *Essence of Christianity*, for instance, one would see that he wants Christianity to be transformed through reason and conscience. He reads it through Aristotelian necessity. Faith is finite in Hegel and he abhors miracles. The OT is not interested in the immortality of the soul. It seeks faith in stones and in signs written over the thunder. Faith is knowledge to Hegel and therefore the marriage at Cana or the resurrection of Lazarus are only meaningless inventions to him. To him miracles are a violation of natural relationships. It does not occur to him, Shestov says, that the natural relationship of things is the violation of the spirit!

Shestov is convinced that Hegel merely completes what Kant had initiated. The latter's practical reason already contains Hegel's metaphysics. For Hegel, the individual must forget himself and be unified with the object of reverence. The thinking consciousness decides on the object of truth, which is to recognize the sensible. This aspect becomes freedom. Metaphysical and positive knowledge comes together. Hegel deploys *geist* (that works inwardly and spiritually in us) instead of practical reason in order to suppress fantasy. As a counter, Shestov (1928–1937/1966) gives an example from Pushkin in order to show the power of fantasy, anguish and repentance:

> The long scroll of my memories unrolls before me;
> And in reading my life with disgust,
> I tremble and curse.
> I moan bitterly and bitterly weep,
> But I cannot blot out these overwhelming lines.

No practical reason can alley what Pushkin's soul longs for. The trembling of the creature needs no verification. No contradiction can keep things open-ended anymore. Miracles (of the *Bible* or of the *Arabian Nights*) do not rely upon the testimony of the spirit or upon any pre-existent harmony. Here, one recalls Shestov's lifelong interest in literature and Milosz's perceptive speculation that the former's spiritual crisis developed from a deep desire to possess the lyrical genius. So there were two options left to him: either to express himself conceptually about Shakespeare, Tolstoy or Pushkin or "at a given moment ... fall(s) silent and leave(s) much unsaid because the border of communicable has been crossed" (Milosz, 1979). He realized that unlike the idealists, the best of the artists met the inconsistencies, scandals and meaninglessness of life head on. In Fichte and Schelling, by contrast, science is replaced by the 'mechanism of free spirit'. How can any 'mechanism' of freedom help us, as the idealists demand? Philosophy and thinking does not care about the unforeseen, the original and the power of creative action. The terror and miracle of creation and rupture can happen only in the deliverance of living creatures.

Immanuel Kant's famous phrase in *Critique of Practical Reason*—"The starry sky above me and the moral law within me," Shestov feels can only be bested by the lyrical digression in the third chapter of the same work:

> Duty! Thou sublime and mighty name that dost embrace nothing charming or insinuating but requirest submission and yet seekest not to move the will by threatening aught that would arouse natural aversion or terror, but only holdest forth a law which of itself finds entrance into the mind and yet gains reluctant reverence (though not always obedience)—a law before which all inclinations are dumb even though they secretly work against it: what origin is there worthy of thee, and where is to be found the root of thy noble descent which proudly rejects all kinship with the inclinations and from which to be descended is the indispensable condition of the only worth which men can give themselves? (Kant, 1788/2002)

This is the basis of Kant's 'ethical formalism'. Duty is the adoration of truth—the foundation and condition of autonomous morality. Reason and the sanctity of moral law must guide man. Is Hegel's 'spirit' any different from Kant's 'duty', Shestov asks?

Looking backwards irritates critical philosophy. Pleasing reason allays the suffering humanity. Practical reason is not indignant and it does not betray. And on the other side of the fulcrum are the metaphysical consolations. They permit man to go without any metaphysics. Only abstract generality can lead to contentment. God, the immortality of soul and free will does not exist. These are dreams and representations from which pure concepts must be salvaged. The creature must hide all truth from himself.

Man is free, in critical philosophy, to the extent that he can judge using reason and moral law. He lives since he ought to follow the categorical imperatives. Hence, Shestov says: "The practical reason leaves nature in peace, but its 'will to power' demands that men should submit to it" (Shestov, 1928–1937/1966). No one ever commanded and none cowered and saw the light. We are rather born to follow and obey universals. The man of desire (the 'voluptuary') shall be afraid of the gallows and the man of wonder shall be restrained by the dicta of moral laws. But who is this voluptuary whom Kant fears? Shestov replies: "The concept of the voluptuary is the Pushkin who wrote *The Egyptian Nights*; it is the Don Juan of Spanish legend; it is the Orpheus and Pygmalion of ancient mythology; it is also the immortal author of The Song of Songs" (Shestov, 1966). Why so? Since,

> Orpheus was not afraid to go down to Hades to seek out Eurydice; Pygmalion demanded of the gods a miracle; Don Juan pressed the hand of the statue that had come alive; in Pushkin a timid young man gives his life for a night with Cleopatra. And in *The Song of Songs* we read that love is strong as death. (Shestov, 1928–1937/1966)

Shestov seeks freedom in being daring, in wonder, in the miraculous, in moment's surrender, and in the gamble that love plays with death. All of these demand the impossible and since they do so—the impossible becomes possible. Such reckless acts are beyond men (humanists, moral pimps, motivators and managers of reconciliation) who conspire and persuade others to constrain. Kant has no other choice, but to clothe man with a shroud even before fate hits him. Kant makes man quiet and cautious. The hypnotic usurps the place of the miraculous.

Passions and desires must bow down to obligation and prohibition and we must rise above the contingent. Never embrace and give in to contingency's fierce and fatal power. Therefore, we invent synthetic *a priori* judgements and natural relationships. Constraint becomes happiness. Miracles and commands terrify and repel all and sundry. Hence Shestov: "The sight of a man who is ready and capable of directing his own destiny at his own risk and peril and following his own will poisons the existence of our reason. God Himself seems to us a monster if He refuses to obey" (Shestov, 1928–1937/1966). There is only one way to evade the combined power of the believers of Necessity: to dare everything and to accept the great and culminating struggle and go forward without foreknowing what awaits us. This is a readiness, a preparation that is born out of terminal anguish, an anguish that finally binds man in a comradeship with death. The foretaste of the sting of death frees the creature. This is the only way to defeat contemplation and contentment with oneself and arrive closer to primordial freedom.

The Paralyzed Ass

As philosophy advanced, the Manichean opposition between good and evil was elided by transferring those into two new and mitigating categories: pleasant and bad. But this was only a face-saver and the old moral categories erupt in times whenever humans turn openly into creatures again—like in our times. Why was this substitution necessary? Especially since now no one apparently confuses knowledge anymore with virtue. Why was the shift necessary if "the most limited mind realizes that one can know and at the same time be full of vice just as one can be ignorant and at the same time a saint" (Shestov, 1966). Aristotelians, Idealists and Kantians try to sell an ethically autonomous existence; for that to happen the shift was necessary. Spinoza stands at the other end. He seeks true philosophy rather than the best variant. To Shestov, Spinoza and Hegel were naturalists. Misfortune may strike anyone, and not just the impious. But still he did not sever virtue from knowledge. It was simply a different model of edification. Both ask man to rise above into materialist generalities. Endurance of fate is crucial in such a scheme of things: endurance that refuses the creature itself. *Endurance is the opposite of perdurance.* The former suffocates. The latter is diligent, childlike and generous.

Hegel would, therefore, simultaneously trust and distrust knowledge and set up a system that would take on Kant's critique of reason. A system would be developed which attests to distrust of distrust, though man would know that knowledge hides the terrible and the spiteful. Henceforth the European would follow the serpent but would seek radicalism within the clash between the serpent and God, between the master and the bondsman. We must pass through and test all experience with the dialectic. Shestov feels that all this is in keeping with the heritage of Socrates: of Athens, of the order of beings. And here he rightly takes us back to the debate between Socrates and the Sophists. When the Greeks in the second half of 5th century discovered that the Olympian Gods were the products of human imagination and that everything was conceived in order to constrain human beings, the Sophists reacted violently by asserting that if nothing was true, everything was allowed. Man was the final measure of things and since the dead will not rise, life could be dissipated in eating, drinking and rejoicing. This is a proto-Humean move. Stung by the Sophists, Socrates realized that there has to be a limit to questioning or that questioning itself needs to be framed within a system. To extol change and accept finitude of our existence was not acceptable to him. He refused to answer clearly whether God existed or not. He would rather speak of the immortality of the soul.

Shestov reminds us that Heraclites and the tragedians knew about the horrors of creation, that everything passes; they prepared us for the "terror the agonizing uncertainty of our transient and sorrowful existence" (Shestov, 1928–1937/1966). God has prepared us for something that surpasses all dreams and hopes. The tragedians gave us humility. They taught us that it is shameful to talk about death, about which we know nothing. Similarly, Heraclites and the men of Bible were not systemic thinkers. They were enthusiasts.

The forbidden fruit of the tree of knowledge became our universal instead. And the edification of philosophy would arrive via the serpent (for Socrates the serpent is the Delphic God). And to feed on the fruit of knowledge is to discourse daily on virtue. The best must be sought hereafter between the 'too much' and 'not enough'. This ground will be first taken by Aristotle and then by Hegel. Both play good against the evil and the collision between the two is left open-ended. They desire temporal goods that go beyond the Platonic virtue. Shestov comments that this kind of wisdom brings such happiness which is worse than the worst of misfortune that strikes the mortal creature. The serpent has only temporal power over the tree of knowledge. But how much influence does it have on life?

If Hegel is Aristotle reincarnated, Spinoza has the Socratic spirit engrafted in his thoughts. From intellect and experience, we travel to the realm of the senses. The Socratic spirit prepares us for catastrophes. The passing comes and goes and yet the moment of severance from the object of attachment and return to nothingness is acutely painful to the creature. Pain makes senses numb and man is transformed like an inanimate object where diverse forces clash. Man is hardly free. He is rather divided between an absurd assumption of the unreal and the reality of the nightmares. In waking, reason protects us by means of rationalizing absurdities through contradictions. Spinoza, like Cusanos before him, must accept reality. But can we pass from the nightmare of reality to the world of contradiction without realizing the bounds that God has assigned for us? Spinoza denies God in a purposeless universe but how do we know whether God has set Himself purposes? This is the question that Shestov asks.

The debate around free will is crucial here. Luther and Spinoza, in their different ways realize that freedom is but a chimera. We are bound to necessity and force, respectively. Freedom is a mystery to them; it hides contradictions within it. One can get rid of specific problems but not the contradictions. On the other hand, Erasmus and Leibniz come to the opposite conclusion: that it is possible to have free will within certain constraints. Human endeavors within creaturely constraint seem possible to the latter two while the other two are moved only by inward experience. In order to explain the deterministic conundrum within Spinozist thinking, Shestov gives the example of Buridan's ass:

> An ass placed at an equal distance between two bales of hay will die of hunger, he [Spinoza] says, but it will not turn towards the one or the other unless an external force intervenes. And man is in a similar situation: he goes to his ruin, he knows that death lies in wait for him, but even the consciousness of the greatest dangers will not draw him out of the lethargy to which he has been condemned by the 'order and connection of things' that has always existed and remains forever unchangeable just as the bird hypnotized by the serpent throws itself, on its own, into the monster's jaws. (Shestov, 1928–1937/1966)

Everything that man undertakes in order to be free seems futile and he is relegated to the prison house of vital forces that percolates in and pervades matter. Freedom is thus paralyzed. All his efforts lead to no deliverance. Man turns unhappy as he begins to 'think' and is unable to achieve any change. A certain past is forever lost when God used to direct everything to some definite end. The *irrevocability of the past* therefore torments us, the end point of the waning of all that used to be precious to us. There are no high and important purposes anymore to be realized in the universe. Knowledge has put an end to such ambition. Shestov sums up the predicament: "The will and the intellect of God as little resemble the will and the intellect of man as the constellation called the Dog resembles the dog, the barking animal" (Shestov, 1928–1937/1966). For Spinoza 'under the aspect of eternity' (*sub specie aeternitatis*) is coterminous with Necessity. But his eternity evades God; God is not the source and creator of all laws. And man stands outside good and evil but is not free. Man might well stay away from all purposes and instincts. The creature is yet again beyond all passions. But what about the mysterious enchanter who lurks? Besides, now we have arrived at the obverse of Mani's conclusions: if man cannot chose between good and evil, man "must be content with 'choosing' between the evil that is not subordinated to him and the good that is likewise no longer in his power" (Shestov, 1928–1937/1966). Man is hardly a thinking being but rather turns out to be the infamous and paralyzed ass.

Like a Cripple with Slack Arms and Legs

The idea of finality in Bible—that an omnipotent God created and blesses man—animates and paves a way of living that is alien to Athens. Rational thought (particularly Aristotelianism) intervened within Hebraism right from the middle ages. For the Scholastics and later for Spinoza, the God of thunder, lightning and sound of trumpets of OT merely tries to break the hardness of the Israelites in order to make them obedient rather than reveal to them the *absolute attributes of his essence*. When different orders of things strike up against each other we must therefore choose between Athens and Jerusalem. The nature of illumination is different.

That is the reason why in spite of their apparent realization of deterministic forces (that will is not free) in creaturely interactions, Luther and Spinoza live in two different worlds. Both might think that there is a law which like a hammer crushes rocks, a fire or wind, and that it also shakes and razes mountains but while Spinoza believes that the role of theology is mere piety, to Luther it is philosophy that makes us obedient and only faith (*sola fide*) that can save humanity. According to Shestov, the likes of Socrates and Spinoza wish to put a 'good face on a bad situation.' But why not prefer anxiety instead? And therefore be happy in eating and drinking. Here there is no difference between a prudent man, a reckless one or a dunce. All want to *conclude* speculation. *Everyone is stupid.*

What is common to Spinoza and Luther is a kind of mad terror. According to Shestov,

> Both of them experienced something akin to what a man buried alive feels: he feels that he is living, but he knows that he can do nothing to save himself, and that all that remains to him is to envy the dead who do not have to be concerned with saving themselves. (Shestov, 1928–1937/1966)

Terror and joy do not have to be proven. They are. They happen. Do arguments stupefy further our contemplative detachment in the face of such calamity? Man's supposed righteousness means nothing in proximity to immeasurable joy and terror. Man accepts and rejoices in the trumpet rolls of thunder and lightning in Spinoza, as natural forces collide. In Luther, it is man's faith that can only salvage him but that too if only the hidden God shows him sufficient grace—that is not guaranteed by good work in this world at all. Luther saw man's devastation at every corner. But man, who is faced by God on one side and fate on the other—would choose none. Such is the nature of edification.

Luther begins to struggle against necessity and free will at the same time. Most of all he revolts against the idea the man can morally perfect himself and remove the obstinate beast from within. The idea of virtuous man is a mirage. The enchained man is a direct result of original sin. The source of truth is not in law but in faith. Conscience is a modern existentialist construct. If the reason of conscience drives you towards righteous choice, ascend into utter darkness of faith. At the mountain top, there is no law for Moses. Only command. Luther, therefore, seeks grace only at some contingent moment—there cannot be any measurement of calamity, no possible adapting to circumstance, save waiting for the Omnipotent. The audacity of Luther is born of tears and despair. Luther is not a philosopher of the 'ought'.

Philosophers and moralists feel they fight against decadence. It merely changes shape. Decadence has a curious relationship with instinct. It wishes to bring happiness and instinct together. Instincts and the unconscious work in mysterious ways. Shestov says that although Nietzsche often mocks Luther, in the latter he finds the poetic form of the Bible. And to bring us close to such poesy, he quotes Luther's terrible words: "Man must distrust his own works and, like a cripple with slack arms and legs, implore grace as the effector of works" (Shestov, 1928–1937/1966). He refers to Kierkegaard's notion of the *thorn in the flesh* in order to buttress the point: "You wish to run faster than ever, but you feel that you cannot even lift your feet from the ground" (Shestov, 1928–1937/1966). We can only look straight into what lies before us, with hearts frozen. Luther still has some hope for grace to arrive. No such luxury in Nietzsche.

But there is a new revelation in both. Eternal return flashes past creatures at the verge of annihilation. A fallen man, Nietzsche begins to speak anew about will to power. In nothingness—omnipotence! What is the force in Nietzsche that defies the philosophy of contentment? Shestov quotes from *Dawn of Day*:

> madness, you inhabitants of the sky—madness, that I may finally believe in myself! Send me delirium and convulsions, sudden clarity and sudden darkness, throw me into icy cold and into heat more intense than any man has ever felt, terrify me with mysterious noises and phantoms, make me howl and groan and crawl like a beast—only that I may believe in myself! Doubt devours me. (Shestov, 1928–1937/1966)

Sola fide and madness—do these take us to the creature, lurking beneath what we call man?

The harsh and cruel God of Luther deserves our eternal hatred and in that detestation we confront ourselves. But could Luther actually touch the truth about the creaturely condition? Does he truly allow us to demand the impossible? Is he still bound to free and objective inquiry? What is the status of suffering and passion in Luther and Nietzsche? Experience is not sufficient. It only brings conviction and belief. Conviction (especially about a philosophical or an activist system) is the enemy of passion and raging desire. It is here that Shestov appears as truly radical.

Indeed, Luther thinks that God must crush and grind the self-confidence and the illusion of righteousness of his creation—man—by using is hammer so that the latter realizes his sinful and impure state. And responding to this realization centuries later Nietzsche says that in man twin impulses play: "there is matter, shred, excess, clay, mire, folly, chaos; but there is also the creator, the sculptor, the hardness of the hammer, the divinity of the spectator, and the seventh day: do you understand this contrast?" (Shestov, 1928–1937/1966). He has to be broken, forged and refined through suffering. All thinking must encounter the stunned gawkiness of the infamous ass in him.

But asks Shestov, does Nietzsche's devastating critique and his eventual turn to will to power and eternal return, invoked to reveal the world, sufficiently cognizant of human reckoning? Does he want to redeem the past after all by calling forth memory? Does the soul of man wish to proclaim its rights? All that has happened will not happen ever because not *memory*, but *will* makes past non-existent. There is no redemption anywhere for Nietzsche. A terrible power of the will that returns can only crush the monster of fate that rules human existence. There is no truth or falsehood—only nothingness. The will is his hammer. But could it break the power of reason and sanity? Is that the reason for highlighting *amor fati*—to love necessity? Does he seek truth elsewhere—in a flash and in the joyous accident of fate? How could he have traversed beyond good and evil in that case? Did he become ally to the monster that he wished to destroy? And what about will?

Luther, on the other hand, walks with the prophets and the apostles. God had sent his son to earth only to save men, not to propound any universal truth. More the human struggles, more he shall sink. Truth lies only in the power of the Omnipotent. God does not fear anything and so he can transfer all sins to his creatures and can abrogate those if necessary. In fact, Shestov reminds us that Luther had penned the following words about Christ: "All the prophets saw this in the spirit: that Christ would be the greatest robber, thief, defiler of the temple, murderer, adulterer, etc., such that no greater will ever be in the world" (Shestov, 1928–1937/1966). God himself then is the creator of all evil. Only giving away reason can make us see this terrible truth. It is important to note here that often Shestov operates through, what has been called 'metaparadoxes'. There is a periodic, but constant, justification of the vehemence of the spirit argued in a logical fashion.

The Shirt is Sewn in Tears

Hope, for Kierkegaard, is born out of an internal tension. Hope is fostered by consolation and edification. Inward soiling dons a different mask in Kierkegaard. He mocks philosophers of not living in the categories they dare to think. Such was his life of torment, Shestov writes, that Kierkegaard had nothing else left to sacrifice after a point. He knows that stones were at least content to be quiet, but men knew how to laugh and mock. But can he reject shame and sing like Orpheus about his predicament? Does he hide his nakedness when he says he has nothing more to sacrifice? It is not that he lacks courage to face infinite pain but that he succumbs to peace that is reached through resignation: "This resignation is that shirt of which an old folk-tale speaks; its thread is woven in tears, the shirt is sewn in tears.... The mystery of life consists in the fact that every man must sew for himself such a shirt" (Shestov, 1928–1937/1966). The right to weep and curse ends in resignation and in the absurd. Here lies calm and peace. Is this the way to suspend the ethical, even as he faces Abraham? Or is he torn between Socrates and Abraham? Did he not say that in the world of the spirit all are invited? Does he place despair and wonder side by side then?

Does Kierkegaard consider the tragic hero as the knight of faith who passes through the universal only to renounce it and turn to the solitary, particular and the unceremonious? He encounters no living soul. The knight of faith is hounded out of the universal which he had briefly espoused. There is no support even from the church and the temple. But Kierkegaard also argues for greatness in tragedy, something that Shestov finds an unnecessary detour to grandeur. Did he forget the blows of *malleus Dei*—the hammer of God? Shestov deduces from Kierkegaard's personal afflictions that although he did not explain the blows as being 'natural', he could not get rid of the nightmares. So in *Repetition*, he takes refuge in Job, a miserable man and a 'private thinker'. Kierkegaard enjoins himself to Job because he is a man who 'fights through the boundary disputes of faith' with passion and ferociousness. He passes through the diurnal tribunal of extreme torment but he does not accept his fate as natural, glossed by false consolations. He sees and experiences how freedom is paralyzed. His three friends irritate him as they try to seek explanations for his misfortune. He levels with wickedness rather than with piety. The deepest of suffering is to be able to see that nothing can be changed and yet be in love—to see that misery and despair repeats with vengeance in our living and yet feel wonder and miracle in the bones. Such is the suffering of divine love. Shestov says that indeed many things are impossible even to God: "God's situation is worse even than Kierkegaard's or Nietzsche's into whose soul has crept 'the most fearful, the blackest, the most terrifying'" (Shestov, 1928–1937/1966). Therefore, God does not know anything. He creates everything.

Shestov, however, questions the existential categories in Kierkegaard that the latter creates, which have no Biblical equivalents, and hence, are purely symbolic in nature. This, Shestov surmises, is done to evade his personal afflictions. What force paralyses his will? Does the Biblical serpent become a matter of coming to terms with personal experience but expressed in existentialist terms? How the disturbance of the struggle lead to nothingness—nothingness as an explanatory category? Nothingness produces anxiety but there is no such thing in the Bible. Anxiety is not fear in the sense that it is not a phenomenon arising out of any definite factor (say the fear that is aroused in children by terrifying fairy tales) and yet anxiety predates fall in Kierkegaard and becomes the possibility of the reality of freedom. Shame and anxiety are not the fallout of fall in him but possibilities—possibilities of gaining innocence. He brings himself ever so close to the abyss of immutability. Is this the intellectual love of God? Is that the reason that he refuses to acknowledge the actuality of the serpent in the fall narrative? Nothingness becomes something—this is the crux of Shestov's critique.

Shestov actually feels that the absurdist side of Kierkegaard is far more fatalistic and hence does not reckon with the conditions of the particular creature. Original sin is a matter of impotence and dizziness to him and the horror of the command existential. It is for this reason that Kierkegaard, sometime later in his life, became incensed when he heard that a mother who had lost her child being consoled by a pastor by recalling to her how God had tested Abraham and Job. Such edification was intolerable to the absurdist. The more creatures try to overcome finitude, the more they devolve into slumber and somnolence. We can try to be like God—knowing good and evil—in our horror. At best. But where lies the freedom of ignorance?

'I Believe because It Is Absurd'

God, 'with one blow and without the shadow of proof proclaims', is the essence of revelation. God creates and commands. The matter stands settled. God delivers his truths without justification. The truths are self-evident and therefore invincible. But how have we been acquiring it without giving in to another cache of self-evident truths—the one that Athens asserts?

The modern philosophers are indebted to the medieval scholastics who liked to believe that Greek philosophy is the second OT. Philosophy likes to believe that Judeo-Christian revelation is the religious source of its own origin. The amalgamation of Christianity and Greek philosophy seems to have been good for both the traditions. Self-evident truths discovered by natural reason could come together with revealed truth during the middle ages—that is the claim. By applying the method of analogy, medieval philosophy transfers empirical facts that the intelligence discovers by coming in contact with eternal verity that it gives the name of the metaphysical. And without medieval philosophy, which fuses Biblical revelation with thinking, there could not be modern philosophy. But then we know that revelation is founded on nothing and has never ever proved anything.

So, what were the means and methods by which the medieval man could express Biblical truths? One is by implying truths through allegories and thus 'raising up' Bible to the philosophic plane. Others affirm that knowledge (gnosis) is coterminous with eternal salvation and in fact gnosis could be in the higher plane. Shestov enquires: Were such philosophers looking for wisdom (founded on knowledge) or knowledge from Bible? This question becomes especially important in the light of the seminal event that takes place in the *Book of Genesis*: man is not just punished for disobeying God but for being greedy about knowledge, which hides death in itself. In *Genesis*, the metaphysics of knowledge is strictly bound to the metaphysics of being, concludes Shestov: "If God has spoken truly, knowledge leads to death; if the serpent has spoken truly, knowledge makes man like God. This was the question posed before the first man, and the one posed before us now" (Shestov, 1928–1937/1966). After that event, man is not just content with the fruit (that) but wanted to find out reasons (why). He wants revealed truth to turn self-evident. It is rare that philosophers like Heidegger emerge, who try to relate revelation with the Greek concept of *aletheia* (to bring forth truth).

Others like Anselm wants direct evidence of God—one that is based on contradiction. Faith suddenly becomes the opaque principle; intelligence the active and transparent one. Shestov reminds us that Duns Scotus never quit the 'irresistible desire' to know, although he was certain of God's total independence. And Boethius argues for wisdom in consolation. Such philosophers feel that faith must understand its own content. Faith engenders reason. Shestov ironically recalls that the first man must have been seduced exactly in this manner: thinking there is nothing wrong or condemnable in his desire to know. The issue for a certain strand of medieval Christianity was moral degradation right from the beginning. Not just a critique of knowledge. To St. Augustine, Adam's immoderate love and union with his partner is profligacy. Sin happened, it came into being. Moral evil is thus given direction by free will in the created cosmos by the act of indulging in pleasure. The prohibitions are commands to assign a free (and not dependent as claimed by reason) relationship between the Divine Father and man. The problem is that the medieval man believes in sin but he also hankers to know. Therefore, obedience to the universal returns via Aristotle and Plotinus, by means of extending OT in a certain direction. Gnosis is another metaphysics of knowledge, which helps the Christian philosophers distinguish between good and evil.

There are of course the Patristic fathers like Tertullian who oppose Jerusalem to Athens. Gospel is the way to salvation and not to knowledge, as St Paul would also suggests. It is Tertullian in *De carne Christi* (On the Flesh of Christ) who in a famous passage most powerfully gave shape to what can be called 'created truth': "The son of God was crucified: it does not shame because it is shameful; and the son of God died: it is absolutely credible because it is absurd; and having been buried, he rose from the dead; it is certain because it is impossible" (Shestov, 1928–1937/1966). Created truth rejects natural morality and brings us directly in contact with the creature in its reckoning with the absurd. The commands of devastation and wonder are certain, especially because they are impossible.

We know that at the end of the ancient age, Plotinus also wished to escape knowledge. He seeks ecstasy, soaring above logos. No foundation or support of knowledge is required either for the One or for man. Shestov brilliantly realizes that Plotinus is taking apart the idea that the end of freedom is in destruction or in comfort of the universal. Instead, he affirms the daring principle of rootlessness. Rootlessness removes all obligation—most importantly it makes the contradiction between the sacred and reason redundant. Similarly, by the end of the middle ages the project of amalgamation of contradiction is abandoned and truth is once again transported into the realm of *credibilia* (things to be believed) by the likes of Duns Scotus—what the Bible tells about God was the truth. God is the 'efficient cause,' immovable, unchangeable, and does not cease to exist after creating the world. Both Occam and Duns Scotus go further and attack the autonomy of morality, a cornerstone of Greek philosophy as propounded by Socrates. God is obliged to nothing and therefore the occurrence of what God wishes is right, said Occam—if God so wishes there would be wickedness and lawless arbitrariness. We are brought into a terrible and ecstatic zone of groundlessness where the creature dances in glee. The creator is also the destroyer and vice versa. In this context, one recalls Shestov illuminating comment in another context: "The first and essential condition of life is lawlessness. Laws are a refreshing sleep. Lawlessness is creative activity" (Shestov, 1905).

By contrast, the principle of contradiction works through an inner logic. In St. Athanasius words: "Just as opposed to desire is that which is reasonably chosen, so what exists by nature precedes and is superior to free choice" (Shestov, 1928–1937/1966). God's free will is aligned with the order of being by proposing the contradiction. Sometimes it is even admitted that certain contradictions do not follow under God's omnipotence. Most significantly, medieval philosophy find it difficult to square with the Biblical notion that all work of divine creation came about by instantaneous fiat. God does not feel exasperation or regret. The principle of contradiction could not dent revealed truth. Only the pre-Socratics and Homer could feel what revelation could be in a non-Christian sense—by forging fantasy with the senses. Revelation acknowledges will and desire. Revelation is not allegory. "I know that God is one" means something different from "I believe in one God", says Shestov. He is solely concerned with the decisive events and effects of the divine command in human living. And God is the name of an active, living, creative being.

Rootlessness and nomadism—those who do not know where they are going but still travel, is the bedrock principle of faith. And enthusiasm is the key to faith. But not righteous purification. It is neither catharsis nor gnosis that the creature encounters deep down. Nothingness is rather made into the impossible in faith. The poets lie and those who level with their predicament also lie since they are unable to rise higher—according to reason: "For verily I say unto you, if ye have faith as a grain of mustard seed, ye shall say to this mountain 'Remove hence to yonder place'; and it shall remove and nothing shall be impossible for you" (Matthew XVII, 20, Mark XI, 23 and Luke XVII, 6). This mysterious and creative power is unacceptable to Athens. It is a scandal to Athens—immoral and revolting. Revelation takes on all glory and superhuman efforts that we may strive for. This is the reason that Dostoevsky, who read the Bible thoroughly in prison, thought that impossibility is a stone wall. He knows that it is impossible to do without tortures. As Shestov puts it:

> It is not others that Dostoevsky mocks, it is not with others—with Socrates, Plato and Aristotle—that he argues; it is with himself that he enters into battle, in himself that he tries painfully to overcome the fallen man and that *cupiditas scientiae* which Adam, who tasted the fruits of the forbidden tree, transmitted to us. This is why he had to say—no, not to say, but to cry: 'I insist on my caprice and that it be guaranteed to me!' Or again: 'I wish to live according to my foolish will and not according to the rational will'. (Shestov, 1928–1937/1966)

And he can cry with the prophet: "Death, where is thy sting? Hell, where is thy victory?" This is the free domain of the base and innocent creature.

The penchant for reflecting on faith is a desperate one and in medieval Christian philosophy such a tendency is paradoxically claimed through a process of attesting nature—that grace cannot abolish nature. In this manner, God's ordered power is attested as opposed to his absolute power. Shestov cites from St. Thomas Aquinas: "Some say that the animals which are now wild and kill other animals were in that state (before the sin) tame, not only toward men but toward animals. But this is completely unreasonable. For the nature of animals was not changed through the sin of man so that those, for example lions and falcons, for whom it is now natural to eat the flesh of others then lived on plants" (Shestov, 1928–1937/1966). Indeed, it is unreasonable to think that the carnivores were grass eating creatures during pre-lapsarian times. But then we recall (Isaiah, LXV, 25): "the wolf and the lamb shall feed side by side and the lion will eat straw like the bullock." The impossible is real. St. Francis of Assisi called the wolf his brother. This could happen because like Isaiah, St. Francis did not hanker for knowledge about 'naturalness' nor did he wish to transform revelatory truths into self-evident metaphysical principles. Shestov says that it does not matter to the one who is chained to waiting for the divine command whether man is born of Adam or an ape. The issue is of no relevance to the creature.

Nothing mitigates the vehemence of living, but where does the slumber of spirit lead to? We serve by volition, but is our will bound by sin—the infernal tyrant? Or by love—the divine messenger? Or is this merely a scholastic quibble? The answer to this, Shestov again gives through Luther and the Prophets who saw in Christ,

> the greatest robber, thief, blasphemer, murderer, adulterer, etc., such that no greater would ever be in the world ... God sent his only begotten son into the world and threw upon him all the sins of all men, saying, 'Be thou Peter, that denier; Paul, that persecutor, blasphemer and violent man; David, that adulterer; that sinner who ate the apple in paradise; that robber on the cross—in short, be thou the man who committed the sins of all men.' (Shestov, 1928–1937/1966)

Such realization shows that God was indeed capable of effacing and abolishing the past sins of Peter, Paul and David and consider those in equity with the original sin, the sin of Adam, from which all the other sins emerged and show that none ever existed. Created truth is the state of innocence and ignorance—destroyer of presumptuousness. Such a state is the very obverse of anything that affirms the freedom to obey. To philosophy this will be an absolute absurdity. It would also be good to remember that some of the trenchant criticisms against Shestov's unorthodox reading of OT have come not from the philosophers but rather from the more orthodox Biblical scholars who found no scriptural justification of some of the most radical ideas of Shestov—like fall as a condition of constraint, absolute freedom of man, God as a genuine respondent to facticity of history and to our tragic condition and most importantly, release from moral law.

Silence or Query?

The higher dicta of metaphysical certainty remain beyond the limits of vulnerability. Humans, for instance, listen and ostensibly give their approval to universal generalities but act as if they heard nothing when the time comes. They keep on repeating platitudes of process and the mantras of correctness but act as they please. Shestov sums up the psychological moment in these words: "I see the better and approve of it, but I follow the worse" (Shestov, 1928–1937/1966). This happens because the answers to 'why?' or 'why me?' are not given ever to the creatures or the given answers are not the expected ones. Attempts to explain misfortunes further aggravate them. Nor do consolations help. The phrase 'insofar' as creatures can alleviate the pain of other creatures—this becomes unbearable to the ones in turmoil.

'Whence come evil?' is such a question to which there are no answers. Or consider a question such as the following: 'Why does that which *is* in no way correspond to that which we wish would be?' These are not appropriate questions to the theory of knowledge. Sometimes answers kill questions. Still man seeks tranquillity and fears the inevitability of impossibility. We know very little and what we do know is relative, says Shestov. The darkness is indeed impenetrable. Our attempts to relate our everyday ordeals to systems of knowledge makes us believe that only the possible shall happen, although that is belied every day. Events burst forth with an arbitrariness that leaves the creature dumbstruck and instead of confronting misfortune squarely it seeks answers in vain, or nurses its wounds hoping for better days.

On the other side stand certain soft spoken writers—who wish to say a few words but the idea of raising their voice and being voluble is repugnant to them. This means that they will rather suppress their inmost thoughts and/or give those thoughts some sweet direction. What started as being soft-spoken eventually makes them silent. Silence turns out to be a universal and autonomous virtue that might take on the might of the great questioning spirit. In this manner, neither side levels with living.

Actually, misfortune is only countered by miraculous metamorphosis—not with knowledge. Shestov gives an example. He asks why is it that "How does it happen that in the eye of our neighbor we see the smallest straw and that in our own we do not see even a beam?" (Shestov, 1928–1937/1966). The creaturely explanation: imperfection. But suppose the straw in the neighbour's eye remain a straw but somehow miraculously transform the beam in our eyes into something useful and mysterious. And conversely, the straw in our eye begins to grow and mutates into a stupendous beam. Such metamorphoses is impossible and hence, always a possibility. Such metamorphosis can happen only if we do not suspend our judgement and give in to free play of real transformation—if creatures would set up their own demands and express their will. Miracles and coherence do not go hand in hand.

The initiate—the *underground man*—does not *solve* the mystery. It is not a truth (what Shestov calls *the second sight*) to be possessed once and for all. When mystery fades away, the initiate realizes his lowly status in the scheme of things. The initiate is either a simpleton or a possessed or both. He is a miserable vagabond who travels without knowing where he is going. But he also trembles with the expectation of something great and miraculous to happen. The initiate in not unlike Lev Shestov himself—a philosopher-*dukho borec* (spirit-wrestler). And for such a variety of wrestler, truth is not despair—that would be rather the *penultimate expression*. It is in confronting struggle in its full glare, without seeking any explanation.

References

Beaumont, Matthew. 2020. *Lev Shestov: Philosopher of the Sleepless Night*. London and New York: Bloomsbury.

Berdyaev, Nicolas. 1948. *The Russian Idea*. New York: The Macmillan Company.

Bernard, Martin (ed.). 1970. *Great Twentieth Century Philosophers: Shestov, Rozenweig, Buber*. New York: Macmillan.

Copleston, Fredrick C. 1988. *Russian Religious Philosophy: Selected Aspects*. Search Press, Tunbridge Wells, UK and University of Notre Dame Press, Indiana.

———. 1986. *Philosophy in Russia: From Herzen to Lenin and Berdyaev*. Search Press, Tunbridge Wells, UK and University of Notre Dame Press, Indiana.

Edie, James, James Scanlan and Mary-Barbara Zeldin (Eds.). 1976. *Russian Philosophy*, 3 vols. Knoxville: University of Tennessee Press.

Kant, Immanuel. 1788/2002. *Critique of Practical Reason*. Indianapolis: Hackett Publishing Co, Inc.

Kleine, George. 2011. "Skepticism and Faith in Shestov's Early Critique of Rationalism." In *Studies in East European Thought*. Vol. 63.1: 15–29.

Milosz, Czslaw. 1977. "Shestov, or the Purity of Despair." In *Emperor of the Earth: Modes of Eccentric Thinking*. Berkeley: University of California Press. pp. 99–119.

Oppo, Andrea. 2020. *Lev Shestov: The Philosophy and Works of a Tragic Thinker*. Academic Studies Press.

Shein, Louis. 1967. "Lev Shestov: A Russian Existentialist." *The Russian Review*. Vol. 26.3, July: 278–285.

Shestov, Lev. 1928–1937/1966. *Athens and Jerusalem*. Athens, Ohio: Ohio University Press.

———. 1929/2016. *In Job's Balances*. Create Space Independent Publishing Platform.

———. 1905/2015. *All Things are Possible/Apotheosis for Groundlessness*. South Yarra, Victoria: Leopold Classic Library.

———. 1966. *Chekov and Other Essays*. Ann Arbor: University of Michigan Press.

BOOK III

The Plastic Creature

Reinventing Tragedy: Simon Critchley's Invitation

> [In Tragedy] through violence we are intimate with some characters onstage in an exorbitant way for a brief time
>
> —Anne Carson, *Grief Lessons*

Why does tragedy exist and why does it have to reappear with its devastating exactitude in and through time's gyres? In *Grief Lessons*, Anne Carson memorably responds by directly addressing the questioner:

> Because you are full of rage. Why are you full of rage? Because you are full of grief. Ask a headhunter why he cuts off human heads. He'll say that rage impels him and rage is born of grief. The act of severing and tossing away the victim's head enables him to throw away all of his bereavements.... Perhaps, you think this does not apply to you. Yet you recall the day your wife, driving you to your mother's funeral, turned left instead of right at the intersection and you had to scream at her so loud other drivers turned to look. When you tore off her head and threw it out the window they nodded, changed gears, drove away. (Carson, 2006)

How do we deal with the repetitive loop of violence, and silence, that follows violence? Shall we have a different perspective of life and living relationships, if we begin to acknowledge our complicity in the events that overtake us during wounded times? Are such tragic and wounded times, periods that are out of joint, not about us and them in the behavioural sense, but about a collective sojourn through a black hole of dense, viscous *conflictual matter*? How do we deal with our disavowed grief, once rage has taken its toll? Is it possible to give a better account of the complex tragic dialectics that time throws at us by keeping away both from inert and self regarding pacifism and from justifying violence as a universal *apriori*?

Simon Critchley, who says that he is not a classical scholar, has invited us to witness afresh the great democratic challenge of tragedy—by trying to weave the past with the contemporaneous, by marking the effects of affect in periodic popular upheavals and by underlining absurdity with action in *Tragedy, The Greeks and Us*. Critchley's wager is on a dynamic model of classical tragedy, which speaks to the present in the sense that it brings us face to face with disorientation and ambiguity. Confronted by genuine crisis, encountering tragedy helps us face the starkest of questions in life: What is to be done? To which there is never any readymade answer. Especially when at least two (if not more) equally valid truths collide in and bring about any tragic condition. Critchley's book (much in line with his other works on applied philosophy, ranging from the poetry of Wallace Stevens to his investments in the *avant garde*, religion, music, humour or football) is an invitation to define theory through action, keeping away ideas, especially the tyranny of philosophical ordering and explanatory principles. So, what exactly constitutes tragic consciousness?

Collisions

The first thing about tragedy is action. Theatre is action. Tragedy is not idle speculation; nor is it about *bios theoretikos*—contemplative life. It has also nothing to do with the cultivation of higher or divine life. It rather affirms materiality of living, life's contradictory flow and its moving action, often brought into sharp and confrontational relief by artificially dramatizing conflict and by shortening space and time over the theatrical arena. Tragedy is, therefore, conceived as *mimesis praxeos*, a difficult passing through the barricades and collisions of life's uncertainties. Tragedy is also political action—in the sense that it is neither about the downfall of the hero, nor merely about the cathartic reaction of the spectators. It has much to do with the rearrangement of the terrain of the city state—the polis, itself. The crucial question is whether such action is geared towards and is able to extend a democratic space as Critchley claims to be or is it that conflicts of two contrary truths must remain inconclusive, and therefore, true riddles be never properly solved. In other words, how can scepticism about creaturely conflict be aligned to democracy? There is a productive tension in

Critchley as he tries to align his modern and progressive definition of tragedy with his profound and capacious acceptance of the role fate and absurdity in human interactions and conflicts. Let us consider the stakes and in the process try to think afresh about the nature of tragic consciousness.

Critchley has rightly emphasized the telescoping of time in tragic circumstances. Tragedy celebrates partial knowledge and partial resolution. Time does not allow the actors engulfed within the tragic chain of events to come out with any finality or closure. The past intervenes in the lives of the characters who act in the present. But the past acts in a way so that the tragic protagonists are also aware of their doings and yet they wilfully rush towards their fate. Machiavelli, in a very different context, possibly got a sense of this interplay between fortuna and the downfall of the heroic brought about by necessity when he said:

> since the inclinations that make you act, so far as they conform with her doings, are the causes of your good and your ill … because while you are whirled about by the rim of a wheel that for the moment is lucky and good, she is wont to reverse its course in midcircle. (Machiavelli, 1989)

Certain features of tragic action work to bring about or foretell disasters—like prophecy, which leads to destruction of the one who acts knowing full well the consequences of certain actions. Inevitability is not brought about by fate but fate is corroborated by wilful human actions and hubris. Will and necessity are inextricably tied in tragedy. The force of what has gone before returns to demarcate what is to come. But all of that happens in the present, within the unity marked for space and time—theatrically speaking. The present is frenetic and out of joint. Critchley sums up the situation: "The past is not past, the future folds back upon itself, and the present is shot through with fluxions of past and future that destabilize it … [tragedy's] conjunction is disjunction" (Critchley, 2020). Tragedy stands at the margins of the old order that is about to give way and the new, which is still to arrive. Tragedy also slows down time by bringing into light whatever is flawed about us. It shows that human beings can at once be noble, foolish and deceptive. In and through this slowing down and relativizing of time, we realize whatever is perishable and vulnerable within us. Time is also intertwined in tragedy in yet another way. The time of gods invades the theatrical space and makes itself manifest within human temporality. In tragedy, the dead are not fully gone and the living not fully alive. Tragic action *converts into theory* this enmeshing where human autonomy arrives not as any clear progress but in the form of an acute attentive exercise in finitude and as an emergence. Human time belabours to understand cosmic movements and is only partially successful. Often this intertwining of the two temporal frames lead to irretrievable devastation in the human scheme of things.

This two aspects that frame tragedy, namely, collisions among the various temporal frames and the primacy of action rather than speculation, make it special. An appreciation of the two aspects provide those blessed with tragic consciousness with humility, by means of limiting the scope of knowability and by playing out a sense of foreboding, leading to the play of destiny that is in store for the creaturely. In Critchley's words: "The core contradiction of tragedy is that we both know and we don't know at one and the same time and are destroyed in the process" (Critchley, 2020). This disorientation fosters sceptical realism—of not knowing what to do. He gives several names to this state. One such name is *transcendental opacity.* The other is *ontological scepticism.* Elsewhere, he will talk about sophistry in the same vein. More about that anon.

What Tragedy Is Not

But first, Critchley clears the ground by telling us what tragedy is not. The initial step is to refute the thesis that tragedy arises out of primitive rituals, especially through the celebration of the Dionysian cult. The rituals themselves are not denied, but the thrust of the explanations are. This is a characteristic modern and political move on the part of Critchley. If Nietzsche argues for such an anarcho-religious origin of tragedy, from the other side Aristotle says that the beginning of tragedy involves the dithyramb. Further: that the members of the Chorus are followers of Dionysus. Thespis adds the first actor to such an arche form and action in the theatrical sense initiates. Judgement in *agon*, or tragic contest, is issued by the priest—that is the claim. Aristotle also adds that tragedy arose out of satyr plays but it acquires grandeur (*megethos*) only when it distinguishes itself from such piety and worshipping. The ideas of ritual, scapegoating or sacrifice give all action an anthropological and timeless dimension and nurtures cultural explanation of the tragic. E.R. Dodds' study of the irrational elements (what he calls 'psychic interventions' in the Homeric world, mediated through the notions of *ate*, *moira*, *menos* and *thumos*) among the Greeks has been crucial in pushing this approach. In order to counter such a claim of authenticity, Critchley secularizes the notion of the ritual itself and calls the whole act *metaritual*—that is to say, "it is the rational *reenactment* or *reappropriation* of the mythic ritual within the context of the aesthetic, institutional and political regime" (Critchley, 2020). Instead of the sacral, he would rather accept tragedy as an *inauthentic ritual*. The secondary point that Critchley makes in this context is to ask us to divert our preoccupation with the etiological habit of seeking origin narratives of tragedy. We are not to seek *the birth of tragedy*. That would be wild goose chase and would bear no fruitful result. Rather, we must renew our attention and bond with the *life and action of tragedy*.

Critchley's politics of secularization becomes further explicit, when he takes apart the second explanation: moral psychology. Moral psychology assumes a structure of the psyche and some corresponding sense of virtue in individuals. Morality and psyche are expressed in terms of unity and integration. A certain reasonableness, practicality or moral law must restrain desire, for instance. Or that virtue and happiness are to be related in contemplative life. Consequently, the outward manifestation of this integrative way of thinking often would mean relating justice to goodness, moral law and considering freedom in terms of social necessity and validity. Critchley's point is simple: one cannot find any such psychic integration in tragedy. The opposite seems to be true since the characters are in various states of battle within their psyche and with fate. The battle is even extended to the gods. Tragedies are more about psychic dissolution and adjournment. Intense passion played out in the present among the actors and the force of our doings in the past breaks down all connections between reason, morality and psyche. Humans are in profound contradiction in tragic circumstances. No integration in possible. Moral philosophy's delusion of relating rationality with freedom comes to naught. But this does mean we do away with both the questions of psyche and freedom; in fact those questions take centre stage and humans confront themselves and their creaturely interlocutors in full public gear and private vulnerability. The questions about desire and virtue, about the play of passions within a divided society are asked with a certain directness that only tragedy in action can raise.

This follows with a critique of theories about tragedy that pertains to its aesthetic idealization, primarily arising out of the Germanphone world. To such an imagination, according to Critchley, "the tragic becomes the name for that domain of experience in which an intellectual intuition of the whole is still possible" (Critchley, 2020). The idea is that since we do not have the knowledge of the absolute—God, soul or other forms of the whole, only exemplary forms of art can bring us close to such an absolute if we can tune in to the aesthetic content by way of experiencing its form. Torn between Kantian absolute categories and Spinozist materialism, Schelling, for instance, advanced a third option, that of the tragic: his claim is that experiencing tragedy takes us closer to the sublime thought. And such crossover happens through suffering. We suffer and accept fate since through repeated suffering we realize the finitude of our empirical existence and reach. Endurance developed out of suffering becomes the way to idealize tragedy. Art helps us in this highest goal. Again, Critchley's barb is both aesthetic and political since such idealization of the tragic mode not only universalizes Kantian ideas about aesthetics but also valourizes a certain Philhellenism. Such a sentimental romanticization of tragedy rejects modernity wholesale by suggesting that it lacks fate in its scheme of things. A canon within the canon is formed. Therefore, we cannot have traffic at all with the present and the past. The obvious example of such an approach is George Steiner's grand despair about the vanishing of the tragic craft and spirit.

But the greatest act of policing of the conditions of the tragic is done by Socrates and the Platonists. The fundamental drive is to assert a certain truth about society. Critchley calls this *logology.* The fundamental point about truth-hunting is to distance the measure from the creaturely to the divine. God manifests himself among humans sometimes in the form of pure knowledge. This is philosophy's highest ambition, to transcend corporeality, and try reaching closer to the gods.

Philosophy aims at blessedness; tragedy at human fallibility. Critchley shows such truth hunting can lead to moral absolutism and therefore turn anti-political. At certain points in his dialogues, Socrates actually begins to speak to himself. Such is his conviction. The result is an attestation of radical solitariness built upon righteousness. As long as one is invested in the immortality of the soul and in the rewards of virtue in the afterlife, he cannot inculcate tragic consciousness since "tragedy presents a conflictually constituted world defined by ambiguity, duplicity, uncertainty, and unknowability, a world that cannot be rendered rationally fully intelligible through some metaphysical first principles, axioms, tables of categories, or whatever" (Critchley, 2020).

At the very rhetorical and generic level, the Platonic dialogue stands at the other side of tragic conflict in action. The dialogue is an indirect pedagogical tool which seeks to displace direct action. Dialogues in such a form steadily take us away from confrontation of life's variegated experiences, by rooting for certainty and divinity. The wager is to highlight Socrates' death, which looms in the background—a price extracted for speaking truth to power, as opposed to the deaths of tragic protagonists, who are destroyed for human fallibility and fate's dictum. The city must therefore turn ordered and civic if it has to avoid anarchy. But what kind of a dialogue is such a monologous form of indirect communication? What has sincerity to do with life and art? In fact, rhetoric and style have a larger function. The question of justice in Socrates is the question of deciding about the nature of the city which will gradually be structured around truth rather than be democratically wagered upon. There shall henceforth be rules for poetry in the just *polis*. Poetry must guarantee courage and should be unafraid of death. Besides, excessive lamentation or laughter must be excised from art and literature in general. Lamentation and laugher are private matters. If wantonly deployed in public, these make us effeminate and slavish. This is regulation of affect in a most structured manner. Such promulgation not only marks the death knell for tragedy but for the comic imagination too. All this leads to the conclusion that there indeed is a moral economy of such a mimetic approach to living. Education becomes a different beast than what one would gain if one passes through the labyrinth of the tragic instead.

The good can be mimicked. That is the basis of this particular moral economy. For such goodness to happen and stay with us, the guardians must use a fusion of *diegesis* (in case of lyric—hymns to gods for instance, may be admitted to the city) and *mimesis* (for drama). One must not mimic the bad or speak in one's own voice. In fact, there is a litany of what mimicking badness means in *The Republic*—from imitating slaves to madmen, blacksmiths to the neighing of horses or the roaring of sea and thunder. Man in the just polis must above all inculcate prudence—such is the ferocity of the binding moral economy of the civic law in the Socratic universe. The advice is to restrain all excesses, since excesses foster licentiousness. Tragedy itself must be purged for it fosters democracy into anarchy and therefore pushes the polis into eventual tyranny: it "enslaves citizens and turns them into subjects of spectacle" (Critchley, 2020). Seduction of art must be exorcised at all cost. Like useless love, tragedy and poetry are not beneficial to the psyche or the city. Instead, one must concentrate on the nature of the analogy and relationship between the just soul and cosmos. This takes us closer to understanding the nature of the divine and the secrets of afterlife. Such are the rewards of philosophical life.

What Shall I Do?

Partial knowledge is the soul of tragedy. Partial knowledge creates ambiguity and a scope for deception. But all are implicated in such forms of ambiguity. Critchley cities a central passage from *Geogias* which says by means of legends and emotions, tragedy weaves a tapestry around deception where the deceiver is more honest than the non-deceiver and the deceived more prudent than the non-deceived.

Justice is conflict. And moral aims shall have no clear dénouement. It queers norms of hierarchy and gender. We deal with ontological finitude in tragedy. The tragic hero himself is the problem, who can neither be relinquished nor fully banished. Tragedy makes us stand stark and face to face with the protagonist, who is grappling with the singular riddle to which there is no clear solution: *What shall I do?*

The mode that is closest to tragedy can be called sophistry. Sophistry works with *antilogia*, or contradiction, as a critical method, Critchley reminds us. Tragedy opens up the space for dangerous passions to battle with each other. It also begins to take deception seriously. The first thing about sophists is to accept and celebrate that man is the measure of everything—that man is fallible, even the most virtuous one, especially the one who is exceptional otherwise. Therefore logic, argument, virtue and decision-making capacity—all can and must only be learnt in this living world, in and through action. There is nothing universal about living. There is no use hankering for afterlife—gods are after us and we are flies who traverse wilfully towards destruction. It is, therefore, far more exciting to cherish the limitedness of human intelligence and life's brevity. Besides, to every problem there are at least two responses, if not more. So, one has to be open to the use of double arguments for each crisis or problem that one confronts—and be trained in *dissoi logoi*, which means looking at both sides of a case. We must learn to play with arguments and crisis. Georgias, for instance, did not teach via dicta but through a method, a *hodas*, which steadfastly kept away from imparting values. This particular technique of pedagogy happens rather through *elankos* or refutation. Sophists realize that in a world of decayed democracy there is a profound ambiguity. Sophists inherently have a sense of the tragic. So, they exploit such contextual realism by employing *dissoi logoi*, where we see multiple sides of an issue and reserve our judgement and yet take certain decisions that can only give us a sense of partial closure.

From a tragic perspective, to uncover any underlying ontological truth is error and fancy. Here Critchley gets very close to nihilism, which is a clear thread in the book. Sophistry eventually undermines all philosophical talk about being. Georgias, in fact, believes that nothing exists. If at all anything does exist, it is unknowable for humans.If anything is not apprehensible, one cannot communicate with others at all. All these leads to a classic nihilistic conclusion about tragedy: the issue now settles down to 'on the not being', to the extent that the sophist may undermine his own being. The persuasive lie in tragedy is not ordinary deception at the level of mimesis anymore. The lie is about our very existence and the futility of confrontations among vulnerable, fallible and arrogant creatures. To the question 'What is to be done?' there will never be any satisfactory answer. Each significant truth cancels each other. This he calls the position of *ethical irresponsibility*. This particular nihilistic strain in Critchley's take however, comes with a price. The contradiction in his own thesis becomes sharper when we notice a powerful counter theme in his formulation of tragedy: "Ancient tragedy is not ancient. It is quintessentially modern" (Critchley, 2020).

The City Itself

Critchley's take on tragedy is resolutely modern. That is the reason he keeps away from primitive-ritualism, aesthetic idealism, moral psychology and Socratic policing. His notion of theatre is also spectatorial. Right at the outset he begins to connect the spectator—*theoros*, with theatre—*theatron* and theory—*theoria*. Theatre is always theoretical and theory is the other name of theatre, "where we are spectators on a drama that unfolds: our drama" (Critchley, 2020). Human action (*praxis*) is explored and put into a massive interrogation in and through the empty space of theatre. Theory is therefore action. Such an ingenious network of associations immediately makes possible two things: one, what is commonsensically often conceived in terms of idea/abstraction (theory) becomes an outcome and evolution of action. Philosophy cannot arise before or beyond life and life's vivid drama. And two, such an idea of theory in the final instance is decided by the spectators—collectively by the citizens who watch and imbibe the devastating unfolding and the personal and social consequences of tragic action. Theatre suddenly turns into a radically democratic space.

It is evident that Critchley's radical democratic but active spectators are also 'thinking public' in the modern sense of the term. This is a way to contemporanize tragedy. But that does not mean he dilutes action and contingency—the nerve-centres of classical tragic consciousness. Critchley's concerns are neither philological nor strictly historical-anthropological/ritualist. It is more in line with the works of Jean Pierre Vernant and Pierre Vidal-Naquet who bring together the aesthetic preoccupations of the tragic within the frameworks of history, social institutions and the practice of a certain culture of democracy. But the crucial leap that Critchley takes is that instead of harping on collective and personal responsibility, he concentrates on breakdown, chaos and contingency that must run all tragic action. Tragedy presupposes uncharted waters. So, Critchley begins to address the metaphysical and ontological questions that tragedy raises, without abandoning the democratic possibility of objective evaluation of the genre. Within the polis, he decentres tragic action in order to look beyond any conventional form of ethics. This dual tendency creates the productive tension in his formulations.

The hero in the Greek tragedy is not a solution to the problem but the problem itself. Notice Critchley has not used the term protagonist but hero, for grappling with gender is a major preoccupation in his book. The hero carries with him a deadly disease (some flaw) which must take the city state towards destruction. As stated, Critchley has been constantly trying to make a case for the democratic nature of tragedy. In such a scheme of things, the central point is the following: the clash between the characters or the progression of plot is of little value. What is of real significance is how the city space might receive an education that takes place simply by its citizens' witnessing of tragic action so that it might turn democratic in its politics, rather than through developing lofty and assured philosophical prudence.

Tragedy, in this sense, is forever contemporary. In our times, we are troubled by similar issues of narcissism as did the tragic actors. We see things but do not necessarily hear. We are equally tormented with the secular truisms of liberal democracy, just like the Greeks used to be with Platonism—each trying to grapple with and bring the vagaries of creaturely excesses, natural interventions and pure *fortuna* within the ambit of order. Finally, tragedy refuses to remain within a fixed traditional mores. It celebrates break, and wilfully manipulates the founding myths of the city, in order to hasten the break: "It is an ancient version of modernity, a deliberate aesthetic innovation or self-conscious modernization" (Critchley, 2020). The political project of Critchley's thesis is for everyone to see.

In tragedy, the city goes through a process of prolonged suicide, over a few generations. One way to think about democracy is to consider law. It is a common way to assert modernity to Attic drama by suggesting that such drama moves from a world of vengeance/vendetta to a world of legality (in Oresteia, for instance). We traverse from retributive to restorative justice—one that is now based on due process and compassion. This is what democratic progress ought to be. Sometimes law courts themselves are theatres within a theatre. But the picture gets tangled when Critchley realizes that this progression may not have been fully linear. Furthermore, a progression to complete institutionalization of law may in fact undercut democracy. In such cases the legal framework must be renewed and that can only happen through direct action and through a process of collision of several truths in the public sphere. The Greek society functioned within a certain common law ambience—which comprised of both divine law and community precedence and custom. *Dike* or justice comprised of the fundamental procedures which were worked out through pronouncements/decisions or cases/transactions. But sometimes (as we see in tragedy) *kratos* or power takes over institutes. In such situations law could turn severely violent and sovereign or it could prove to be radically democratic and truly new. In such times the normative idea of law gets unhinged. In fact, it could sometimes change into its opposite. In such a legal situation where nothing is fixed, tragic action takes over and we begin to debate about the fundamentals of law itself. *Dike* itself was not always about following fixed principles but more a matter of "negotiated settlement of rival claims" (Havelock, 1978). Consequently, norms of propriety and reckless, but fated acts (*hubris*) would sometimes collide. Frenzy takes over and the gods relish such tumult. It gives them the excuse to intervene in earthly affairs. The gap between the fixity of *norma* and the upheavals effected through fated act is mediated in tragedy. Sometimes, justice is worked out through compensatory acts, but often it is extracted as straight retribution. Justice is often ordained—creatures are caught in the web of continued crime and violence in tragic cycles. Is justice then simply *to be*? How is it then possible to bring together tragedy and democracy?

It will not be digressive to recall that Terry Eagleton in *Sweet Violence* has also tried to understand tragedy by placing the cut and thrust of historical conjunctures alongside the *longue duree* of the creaturely body and the ecological, what he calls "the permanent structures of our species-being" (Eagleton, 2003). It is as true that man hobbles and bellows in agony, as it is a fact that material conditions and social relations give rise to such conditions of tragic exploitation and degradation. There is something slow-moving in even those who are the harbingers of violent change. The common note is fragility. And irreparable loss. There lies the family resemblance. Eagleton is piqued by the indignities and the degradations of the deprived of the world and that he relates to tragedy. Unlike Critchley, however, Eagleton is often disconcerted by the immanence of tragedy, the spiritual waste of it rather than by pure conjunctural contingency. At the same time, Eagleton is aware of the pitfalls of romanticizing tragedy, if it is not considered in the context of the economic and social issues that give rise to the blood-soaked episodes of contemporary butchery of humanity.

But in their consideration of the contemporary mutations of tragedy, both Critchley and Eagleton are moved by destiny, not misfortune. Both are suspicious of the patrician rhetoric and the mandarin disdain for modernity prevalent among the classical theorists of tragedy. Therefore, both see the contemporary in tragic terms and try to conceive freedom and resistance to fate from within the perimeters of sober realism. But most significantly, both seem to long for and pursue the infinite within such finitude. They agree that tragedy occurs whenever there is a fundamental dispute around the question of justice as fate intervenes. So, the characters and the spectators are brought face to face with radical crisis. Philosophy wishes to alley such crisis and quickly brings it back within the regime of order. Tragedy exacerbates the same crisis and takes it in severely realistic but uncertain directions—outside of ordinary ways of delivering justice. Everything becomes bare and yet there is no clear solution about the very idea of justness. Crisis has to be lived as such, for it cannot be arrested. So, one way to look at tragedy, (the other thread in the book) is through its inbuilt polyphonic mechanisms. The play-festivals in themselves were boisterous civic activities. *Demokratia* was indeed *theatrokratia*. Plato thinks that in such situations, the dictatorship of the mass—the mimetic tribe, takes over. Critchley rightly points out that the stakes are about the aesthetic regime of the political. In theatre, the spectacle of politics considers its own predicament.

The democratic possibility in learning through tragic action is compounded by a factor that we have already stated though: how does one account for the logical extension of sophistry and sceptical realism into nihilism—that there cannot be any predictable answer in crisis, and therefore, the city eventually espouses a value-free system? If such a value-free radical anarchic world is the truth that tragedy affirms, how can one argue for social justice, especially gender justice, as Critchley does in his book? How does one debate from multiple sides in a given crisis and yet consider that society indeed does progress through such an argumentative space that emerges out of action rather than through the dicta of philosophy of moral psychology?

The nebulous realm where democracy ends and anarchy begins is a blurred one. Perhaps, such a state can be called radically democratic, one that emerges out of *antiogian* or *antinomian* tendencies? This tangled issue becomes starker when we realize gradually that in the scheme of things, Critchley's real hero is Euripedes, who never takes us to any closure through tragic crisis but rather leaves us bewildered, in a state of tragicomedy. Is this what the city wants? Suppose we agree with Critchley that indeed the Socratic dictum is built upon the premise that dramatic mimesis destroys the psychic economy of the city by first heightening conflict and then by playing out private grievance and their rabid manifestations. Can such dramatic action or poetic cry be democratic? Aristotle demurs. Such a form of democracy, in fact, is a malady to the city. Theatricalization turns into a regime of tyranny instead. To this view, Critchley offers the alternative: Euripedean tragedy. What is the nature of his reasoning?

The Euripedian universe affirms that violence is constitutive of living. Critchley suggests that nothing can ever be whole or sole; every interaction in tragedy is twisted and divided against itself. It is all a marriage of convenience or adaptation in our interactions—no heaven or benevolent nature there. Rather, every aspect of existence is mortgaged to the slaughterhouse of history. Freedom that democracy gives us in tragedy can also turn into a license to confuse public goods with private pleasures, envy and cruelty. It can turn into raw gratification. But this stage of real, deathly conflict and its effects could also be read as non-moral clarification of the citizens' emotional states. Does such a definition of catharsis—as clarification—also give rise to shame among the spectators? Sometimes, Critchley seems to suggest that shame is a democratic emotion. But one thing is clear: catharsis is certainly not purgation, purification or sublimation. In fact, clarification may deflate morality. In this context, Critchley and Anne Carson discuss that catharsis is a curious and devastating state of being—not at all purging leading to poise. This devastation happens in darkness—all action actually takes place offstage. Onstage, we have words and more words, which is just the cover. But tragedy does not universalize; it keeps things partial, even with the *metabole,* or change of fortune. Likewise, *hamartia* is not just error of judgement, but our vulnerability owing to the basic experience of *thrownness* (after rallying against Heidegger for the better part of his book, Critchley finally warms up to him through this borrowing). Protagonists are divided against themselves in Euripedes. The spectators witness the sheer bloodthirsty nature of brigandage in his plays. Not grandeur. It is a theatre of depravity and in that sense, it may be called democratic: "the uncontainable and vast dimension of life flickers and flares up, something that we would rather keep out of view, but that presses in upon us with an unbearable insistence. Such is the monstrous" (Critchley, 2020). This state he calls 'epistemic mist'. Here is the acknowledgement of monstrosity in the civic space, but not for purging its claims. Monstrosity is an ambience; it hovers. There is neither organic integration nor any clear dénouement. Can this realization happen as a corrective or through a process of advancement/progress as Critchley claims, especially for the slaves and the women? Where is the reconciliation in this absurdity? The unseemly and the paltry are surely democratic, but do not have much to do with quenching modern man's hope of equity. The gaping wound is tragicomic, open-ended and impassive.

Simon Critchley seeks a 'constitutive outside' in tragedy (in fact, he cites Ernesto Laclau in order to make this point), out of which the *polis* is built. But this outside-that-stays-dormant is ever threatening in its immediacy. His tragic democracy is, therefore, neither affirmative nor negative. It is layered with intrigues and intricacies. There is no escape from the curse of fate and radical conflicts that arise out of our decisions.

References

Aylen, Leo. 1964. *Greek Tragedy and the Modern World.* London: Methuen and Co.

Beistegui, Miguel de and Simon Sparks (eds.). 2000. *Philosophy and Tragedy.* London and New York: Routledge.

Carson, Anne. 2006. *Grief Lessons.* New York: New York Review of Books.

Critchley, Simon. 2020. *Tragedy, The Greeks and Us.* London: Profile Books.

Eagleton, Terry. 2003. *Sweet Violence: The Idea of the Tragic.* Malden, MA, Oxford and Victoria: Blackwell Publishing.

Else, Gerald F. 1965. *The Origin and Early Form of Greek Tragedy.* Cambridge, MA: Harvard University Press.

Hall, Edith. 2010. *Greek Tragedy: Suffering Under the Sun*. Oxford, UK: Oxford University Press.

Havelock, Eric A. 1978. *The Greek Concept of Justice.* Cambridge, MA and London: Harvard University Press.

Henn, Thomas Rice. 1956. *The Harvest of Tragedy.* London: Methuen and Co.

Kelly, Henry Ansgar. 1993. *Ideas and Forms of Tragedy from Aristotle to the Middle Ages.* Cambridge, UK: Cambridge University Press.

Kennedy, Rebecca F. 2009. *Athena's Justice: Athena, Athens and the Concept of Justice in GreekTragedy.* Bern: Peter Lang.

Krieger, Murray. 1960. *The Tragic Vision: Variations on a Theme in Literary Interpretations.* Chicago and London: Holt, Rinehart and Winston.

Krook, Dorothea. 1969. *Elements of Tragedy.* New Haven, CT and London: Yale University Press.

Machiavelli, Niccolo. 1989. *Machiavelli, the Chief Works and Others.* Vol II. Trans. Allan H Gilbert. Durham and London: Duke University Press.

Reiss, Timothy. 1980. *Tragedy and Truth.* New Haven, CT and London: Yale University Press.

Vernant, Jean-Pierre and Pierre Vidal-Naquet. 1990 (French original 1973). *Myth and Tragedy in Ancient Greece.* Translated by Janet Lloyd. Princeton: Princeton University Press.

The Creature as the Blasted Mortar

Sarah Kane's Search for the Remainder

> He was shameless and therefore mythical.
>
> —Howard Barker, *Arguments for a Theatre*

> Words halfway to intelligence. This possibility of thinking in reverse and of suddenly reviling one's thought. This dialogue in thought. The ingestion, the breaking off of everything. And all at once this trickle of water on a volcano, the thin, slow falling of the mind.
>
> —Antonin Artaud, *The Nerve Meter*

In the middle of the short film *Skin* (screenplay by Sarah Kane, her third work after the plays *Blasted* and *Phaedra's Love*), the disoriented and disgruntled skinhead protagonist, Billy, is hit by a club on his back by a black man during a racist attack at a black wedding party. As young Billy falls flat on his belly, he begins to bludgeon another fallen black man on the head with a heavy brick. Each blow of the brick, with a dull thud sound—is overlaid with the peals of the church bell, coming from afar. The moment inaugurates what follows: the young man's relationship with a powerful black woman from the neighbourhood, Marcia. The short and manic relationship ignites the truth about the question of intimacy between *black* and *white* skin. Sex follows, and Billy turns into a prattling captive of a creature to Marcia. He is tied to the bed post and fed dog meat by her. Fascist tattoos are scrubbed off from his skin with bleach. In this tumult—poison, pity and the erotic are inextricably bound together. As the rituals of eroticism reach a crescendo, the young skinhead seems to have discovered abjection in love. Marcia, however, eventually finds companionship and solace in her young white woman flatmate. Bereft and babbling, Billy tries an overdose of drugs, begins to retch and howls inconsolably, though he finds an empathetic black neighbour by his side at the end. As the film progresses, the sound of the thuds increase, take new contours. The sounds turn more lyrical within the frames, so to speak. And so do the peals of the church bell, within our mindscape. By turning themselves into blathering, defeated and annihilated creatures, beings come closer to the divine. Or do they? Does the 'froth of injured innocence' have a resting place ever? In the universe of Sarah Kane, terror and vision jostle.

If racial politics is the condition of confronting the viscerality that is skin colour, justice is bared—by the erotic, and then restored, by the partially consolatory in *Skin*. The film underscores the fact that the two pigments of the skin are inextricably tied to each other. At the same time, it affirms that the very idea of normative equality among humans has turned defunct and jaded. Didacticism of the left and coolness of the right have made living and art moribund. But the skin does not, cannot hide the 'cut'. It is too palpable—with intoxicating sweat glands, proliferating warts, hair rising to exigent stimuli. That is the reason in *Job's Body*, Deane Juhan has pointed out that

> Skin and brain develop from exactly the same primitive cells. Depending upon how you look at it, the skin is the outer surface of the brain, or the brain is the deepest layer of the skin. [...] The skin is no more separated from the brain than the surface of a lake is separate from its depths. [...] The brain is a single functional unit, from cortex to fingertips to toes. To touch the surface is to stir the depths. (Juhan, 2002)

There is only one option: to rediscover political life by calling forth the creaturely, which has the ability to radically redistribute social and psychic energy and take us to another form of equity and closeness, even if achieved provisionally.

Sarah Kane takes 'social cut' very seriously. She celebrates the fault lines of defeat in the flow of molten matter on the stage. Her works hit relentlessly at the nauseating cheerfulness (what Howard Barker calls 'carnival mania')—the fodder for running the show of public morale of equitable realism and/or the habits of memory and tradition. To the contemporary historian of the British theatre and performance of the current *fin-de siècle*, Kane has been the foremost proponent of New Brutalism or the Theatre of the Catastrophe. The phenomenon is more difficult to explain than to bring her plays under the banner of such rubrics. She has herself rejected New Brutalism as a useful label that may describe her work. In fact, looked closely, we shall see that Kane tries something altogether beyond and outside the pale of political economy—a truly majestic ambition, even as we realize that the characters and the locales of her works are all parts of the post-Fordist world of informal labour and service economy. Kane has simultaneously contemporanized and universalized the tragic condition of our living. Richard Halpern traces her lineage to Aeschylus, Marlowe, Shakespeare, Milton and Beckett (Halpern, 2017).

Complexities of pain cannot be uplifting. Howard Barker calls tragedy "the secret curse in the confines of an alien religion" (Barker, 1989). This definition goes well with Kane's work, as a whole. Indeed, the most destabilizing elements of the tragic are its secret eruption and ecstasy. And the locale in which the curse erupts is a terrain over which the protagonists have little control. The unharmonious jarring notes of the tragic—leading to a sense of 'losing the thread' on the part of the spectators—are at once the effect and the malfunctioning of demand and longing.

Contradictions and Limit Experiences

The artist's job is not to exhort and elucidate. Following this dictum, in Kane's universe, nothing is digestible. But to experience dissonance in art, one need not practice amorality/nihilism nor hope art to provide any channel for catharsis-as-cure. This truth becomes doubly relevant in the contemporary context, since it is completely irrelevant to seek resolutions in times of social and personal fragmentation. As Mel Kenyon, Kane's agent and co-manager of her literary estate, writes, "The Strong Right is full of certainties, certainties which are abhorrent. The Left was full of certainties, certainties which proved to be bogus" (Urban, 2001). One may add that the liberal centre cannot be considered to be a properly worked out and credible standpoint, owing to its insipid and thin speculative nature. It does not have the creative rigour, capaciousness and flight of old humanism. Dissonance, therefore, needs to be felt, but also steered dispassionately whereby the most intimate of relationalities can be laid bare and juxtaposed with both random and complex set of dramatic cruelties that take place across the world. Can the micro routines of intimate violence along with the fallout thereof and the large canvas of historical tragedies be brought together in art, so that at the end, we are left with a sense of creaturely stocktaking and are able to assess the futility of this deadly game?

Blasted (1995) indeed goes for the jugular in this very complicated sense; not merely to depict *in-yer-face* violence. The first thing to notice is a kind of deliberate baroque exaggeration in the gestures, intuitions and behaviour of the protagonists: the casual racism and exaggerated manliness that Ian flaunts and the stammering, hysterical and confused nature of Cate. She is prone to bouts of concussion. We have a premonition (that will be borne out later): that the relationship between power and pain could be inverted in a moment's notice. Hidden beneath proclaimed masculinity is abject surrender. Cate actually dares Ian very early on when he threatens her with hurting and shooting. She intuitively says that he will not be able to do all that since he 'is soft'. Later, he would admit that he is scared of dying. As far as Cate is concerned: stammer and hysteria hide a resolute sense of action, which erupts over the stage, with no prior notice. Besides, fate might intervene as new enforcers of force (the soldier) may arise out of nowhere and a new set of erotic-retributive relationship might ensure. Cycles of intimacy and violence begin to take new dimensions, but there is also a sense of déjà vu as we begin to reach a crescendo with violence and abjectness. Violence turns self-perpetuating, what is called 'wreak' in the revenge tragedy tradition. The moments of her fit are, therefore, described by Cate as when the world slows down and she gets stuck in. The moment of stasis is also the moment of ecstasy. Everything is blocked out, Cate tells Ian, who wants to make love in order to divert the exchange towards cheery normalcy. Ian, of course, shall have no normalcy hereafter. We are all torturers and victims alike. There are no bystanders in times of spiralling violence.

The crackle of Kane's scorching vision sears us, not because of its amorality and trance-like quality, but because she owes her sense of violence to a certain taut straining that lies between thinking and sensuality, between craft and intuition, making things strange in the process. One way to look at violence of this nature is to abandon all sense of the martyrlogical in her characters (to relate her last play *4:48 Psychosis* to her act of self-immolation is jejune). Instead, the characters are a conduit that assists return to our senses by insisting that to be free is to see cruelty face to face and to take up the challenge. And not relegating objectivity aside, so that we are able to simultaneously reflect on our creaturely condition even as we pass through life's purgatory. Maggie Nelson has summed up the spirit of the times when she says: "Given our inarguable complicity in all kinds of systemic forms of global injustice: is there any space left for *not* watching, *not* focusing, *not* keeping abreast of all events and atrocities unfolding in the world, as an ethically viable option?" (Nelson, 2011). The route Kane takes in order to give expression to such a world of acute affliction is not gratuitous violence—like the Soldier says to Ian: "Can't get tragic about your arse" (Kane, 2001).

What is it that feeds us violence and pain in Kane, which is neither about waxing therapeutic nor about being Stoic to its *actual* effects? In *Phaedra's Love* (1996), the cruel boredom and depressed inertia of Hippolytus is only matched by the plebeians in Scene Eight who are undecided whether Hippolytus must be killed for being an inbred royalty or for being profligate. Should he die, because he has broken the tribal codes of morality, or should he be made an example of, because he is a minor and nonchalant royalty? Meanwhile, two policemen are undecided whether Hippolytus is a 'poor bastard' or that his comeuppance has rightly arrived since they have little daughters to justify his crime. One wants to move Hippolytus' carcass while the other would rather let it rot. A similar case of impasse plays out within the gray intimacy of Phaedra and Hippolytus, gradually leading the two to the gates of an inevitable catastrophe. It is a ring in which the two play, test, bait, love, maim and annihilate each other. So, who is burning whom here? It is extremely difficult to pass any judgement on either side. It would be hasty to conclude that the play is a commentary on British royalty. In fact, justice is suspended in any social sense as fate and action combine to guide Hippolytus to the raging mob; his carcass the food for vultures.

Cruelty is the other side of craving tenderness in Kane, part of an almost elaborate masochistic ritual service, played out step by step in each dramatic work. Wilhelm Worringer has tried to explain the style of such expressive action as an outcome between a fundamental conflict: one that arises "between my natural striving for self activation (which feeds a feeling of liberty and pleasure) and the one that is demanded of me" (Worringer, 2014). The object of craving is itself formed by each creature, something that actually does not exist in any real sense. But by coming to contact with another creature, each one of us gets into a mode of apperception which Worringer calls empathy. This coordinate is organic and vital in the naturalistic tradition. Connected empathy, which comes as erotic love in Kane, is vital and pantheistic. It is like how Weil talks about love: not as consolation, but as light. But this connected happiness is queered by a cosmic dread of space. Along with a sense of temporal mutability and contingency. The world bewilders man—the feeling that he is unfathomably entangled, but lonely in the huge cosmos. The sheer fortuitousness of his existence in an alien and dreadful world is a terrifying prospect. Worringer names this second component of style as abstraction. The instinct to touch the *thing-in-itself* begins to confront the artist who is torn between empathy and abstraction. Forms turn tortuous, instead of geometric when the artist wishes to address confusion. The material manifestation of abstraction is always empathy—such as we see in the repeated exhortation to love and god in Kane—trying to latch on to longing in real and material terms. But the immediate withdrawal from such pantheistic excess owes to her accurate sense as an artist of expression who decreates as much as she creates. There is empathy and then a sudden withdrawal of it. Passion is repeatedly liquidated in ecstasy. The vigorous combative relationship between empathy and abstraction leads to a refusal to indulge in personal pathos (what Barker calls 'miserabilism') or in any straightforward liberty of wonder. The cosmic dread of the play of force on the creature cannot be occluded anymore. Violence thus begins to turn literal, direct and focused in gestures, voices and dialogues, instead of being mediated figuratively. Pain becomes two dimensional: actual and technical. For it cannot be mimetically demonstrated in geometric representations. The coupling of force and pain begin to appear like splashes on a canvas, ringing in and out of focus, rather than following any narrative linearity or some space-time symmetry. All relations turn clear in Kane's plays, for contradiction is creature's clarity. This is of course a way to seek deliverance through art. But is art able to transcend life? Are freedom and mercy compatible? This realization of art's inadequacy perhaps makes Kane's last two works—*Crave* (1998) and *4:48 Psychosis* (2000) turn even more distilled with a sense of dread about the caprice of things that lay strewn around her, dread that Worringer eloquently calls in another context to be a kind of *spiritual agrophobia.*

The form of moral promiscuity that Kane gradually pushes her art towards is indeed a technique, a testament of acute concentration to the act of living so that the artist in her can stay clear of any collectivist assimilation—those offered by harmony, kinship, public or ideology—formations that foment what the protagonist in *4:48 Psychosis* designates as the "malignant spirit of the moral majority" (Kane, 2001). As Barker says elsewhere about those invested in the creature's levelling with catastrophes: they mock self-preservation, the reigning passion of our lives. One terminus of such concentration is to divest the self altogether of its material manifestation for we are all anyway 'fragmented puppets and grotesque fools'. Suicide is an inevitable drive that arrives in the morning hours of 4:48 a.m. *4:48 Psychosis* beckons us to decreate our entire life in a flicker, so that all cruelty/pain receives closure in and through silence. So, at the moment of severance the actor says—"body and soul can never be married" (Kane, 2001). Journeying from *Cleansed* to *4:48 Psychosis* we move into the nerve centre and to the mind, already leaving aside the body. Therefore, this act of severance of body and soul is not a spiritual turn. Nor is the play a resource for any forensic diagnosis of Kane's biography. Soul is the name of the artist's attention to living ("a consolidated consciousness"), the product of the tension that takes place between empathy and abstraction. The severance of body and soul through the act of self immolation is an acknowledgement and rejection of the "sea of logic/the monstrous state of palsy" (Kane, 2001). It is the rejection of the sociable consultant-therapist—Kane's antichrist.

Quest and Freedom

"My love, my love, why have you forsaken me?" is the only question worth asking, as asked by the writer protagonist at the brink of suicide in *4:48 Psychosis*. Forsaking is a given—it happens without any dramatic build up. The manner in which the sociable man deals with 'forsaking' is—foremost, by erecting a ring of make-believe invincibility about him. And second, by developing and invoking conscience about the plights of others and thereby diverting pain into a factor of mitigation. Given this situation, how do Kane's characters deal with the inevitable contingency of forsaking, which must come with sociability?

It is a two stage process by which the characters appear, interact and develop through the rapid 'folding' of events: first, each of them are *immersed* in the process of living, by taking full cognizance of the fact of contingent accidents, especially in relation to the familiar and the intimate. This second stage pertains to a mode of *emergence*, a kind of a new beginning (which could also be the end to the frantic cornucopia of dissonance) and a genesis into new forms of expression. But the second stage is no miraculous restitution of order; it is itself contingent and may or may not arrive in any complete and finished dénouement. Emergence could rather come as a trace, a kind of flicker of creaturely equity made incandescent to the spectators. Such a form of sensibility and engagement is very close to the Baroque, a sensibility that has been defined by William Egginton in terms of arriving at a different kind of truth:

> the incorruptible truth of the world that underlies all ephemeral and deceptive appearances on center stage, making it the ultimate goal of all inquiry; in the same vein, however, the Baroque makes a theater out of truth, by incessantly demonstrating that truth can only ever be an effect of the appearances from which we seek to free it. (Egginton, 2010)

Following Gilles Deleuze, it is possible to read each movement in *Blasted*, for instance, as a fold, over which the succeeding turn of events crash, which in turn fold over the following movements. The folding operates at two levels: one, at the level of material and sensual progression, through coiling of fold upon fold: the apparent sedate opening with Ian and Cate being ushered into the hotel room, followed by the developing gestural and dialogic tension developing between the two, Cate's stammering and her bouts of fit, the visceral divergences in their food habits and in the social/racial sensibilities, the violent act of his raping her and her sudden biting of his penis, the soldier's arrival and his molesting and maiming Ian, the blasting of the hotel, Ian's subsequent abjection, Cate's prostituting herself and carrying the baby, their eventual sharing of food and Ian's death. It is a breathless journey, with each movement ceaselessly dividing itself into the following ones. The falling of each catastrophic coil over the next is sharper than the previous one until we reach a state of total abjection and annihilation. But the upper level hides another kind of folding—that of the souls, and which sometimes sheds 'vibrations or oscillations' through small apertures on to the coils of material folds of the events. For instance, there is a short exchange about death between Ian and Cate in Scene One. It shows his vulnerability. He is scared of his mortality just like he is scared of cars. Cate tries to describe death nonchalantly: "You fall asleep and then you wake up," to which Ian replies, "How do you know?" (Kane, 2001). Later, the topic returns when he says he was scared of her death. This was a shared moment of illumination. Therefore, she reads him tenderly as 'soft'. Cate's moments of fit are also deeply ecstatic when 'time slows down'. The soldier too detects easily that Ian is incapable of killing anyone—if he did, he would not portray bravado in the manner he did. But the tenderest moments come at the end—in Scene Five. Both face their abjectness and realize there are no fairies or Narnia. It could be a pure absurdist moment, with each trying to punish the other by making him/her live. But at that moment, Cate says that she believes in God and Ian, who seeks scientific explanation for divine existence, fails to shoot himself. Immediately, Cate puts the reason on fate, which she uses interchangeably with God. And here is a remarkable stage direction. The one who was stammering at the beginning of the play now bursts out laughing—"unnaturally, hysterically, uncontrollably" (Kane, 2001). And then exhorts Ian not to see bad things or go to bad places. A flicker of hope is imagined. By the time Cate returns with some bread, sausages and gin, however, Ian has already eaten the remains of the baby. And only at that point, Cate sits next to Ian's head and feeds him with the remaining food. Ian is grateful. Is this shedding of the vibrations of the soul force over the coiling of events real? Yes and no. Cate's gesture and their mutuality is at once a moment of emergence, but also a veil, a *trompe l'oeil*, for comfort is but skin deep. The eating of the baby has already taken us to the depths of hyperreality. And Cate makes sure that she eats first, on her own. And once Cate finishes feeding Ian, she "sits apart from him, huddled for warmth" (Kane, 2001). Love does not provide warmth. The bereft creature returns to itself, huddles within. The instant of immersion in the familiar is also the moment of dreaded alienation.

Similarly, the gladiatorial exchange between Phaedra and Hippolytus sets the stage for the encounter between the Priest and Hippolytus. Phaedra wants to reach love and own Hippolytus through erotic pleasure. The question of the immediacy of consummation is consistently offset with the idea of lovemaking itself as voided inflection. That love is something unexplainable and yet tangible is countered by Hippolytus' gestures of bored scepticism about love's efficacy in cementing relations. But Hippolytus' masculine scepticism is quickly undercut when another woman is mentioned. He begins to protest that no one burns him. It is evident that he burns within and soon will be burnt by the mob with the help of Theseus. Meanwhile, the idea of hatred is folded on to the being itself. Asked by Phaedra as to the reasons of Hippolytus' hating her, his reply is terse: "Because you hate yourself" (Kane, 2001).

The fact that the 'cut', which marks all sociable intimacy, is actually the result of the hatred of the self, is brought to an explosive fore through Hippolytus' exchange with the Priest in Scene Six. Perhaps in all of works, Kane is most explicit as a social commentator in this section of *Phaedra's Love*. Kane's tortured relationship with Christianity bursts forth. There is simultaneously a rigorous baroque ritualization of the relics of ecstasy, surely inspired by her Catholic past, and yet a complete voiding of the institution called organized religion. The whole idea of redemption that religion promises is mercilessly mocked. The Priest pronounces very clearly the nature of Hippolytus' crime: "Your sexual indiscretions are of no interest to anyone. But the stability of the nation's moral is. You are a guardian of those morals. You will answer to God for the collapse of the country you and your family lead" (Kane, 2001). The nature and the business of moral gate-keeping are apparent. The man is a social pimp. His role is to extract confession from people who wish to believe that they have a conscience, which they would use for the good of mankind. This is what Kane takes down. In an illumined moment of *parrhesia,* Hippolytus declares to the Priest that he has no intention of covering his arse and that he will not allow the Priest to sin, knowing that confession shall save the latter and make him socially acceptable. And behold, contrary to his business, the Priest is forced to admit: "There is a kind of purity in you" (Kane, 2001). But such a variety of purity that Hippolytus manifests shuns all rules of sociability and goodness. The Priest performing oral sex on Hippolytus completes the apparent unveiling of hypocrisy. But we must never forget that the unveiling clarity of this scene is merely an interlude in the inevitable machine of tragedy that Kane contemporizes. The Senecan spirit of 'the wreak' is re-enacted one more time. The settings are merely altered.

In such a scenario is it possible for grace/love to trickle down through the baroque apertures of the events and make a difference in the fateful creaturely drama of recurring annihilation of its own embodied self? In response to the question, in Kane, the possibility of the miracle is always an outpost, a certain amplitude—a virtual reality. The amplitude turns more acute in the last two plays. As M says in *Crave* "Absence sleeps between the buildings at night" (Kane, 2001). The play is a meditation on 'lying low and saying nothing.' It is about half-love when lovers do not know whether the other person exists. Effulgence and free fall play hide and seek in the play. Light, like love, is a motion away, not a motion towards. Kane's works testify to the fact that incompleteness is one singular tenet of all unfolding catastrophe.

Immersion as Emergence

The likes of Howard Barker and Richard Foreman have pointed out that the theatre of catastrophe/ontological-hysteric theatre rejects the solution of discovering the truth (Brecht) or the gift of renunciation (Chekhov). It also exorcises the spectre of absurdism as a paradigm, though in Kane's case some commentators have noticed the refinement of the spirit of Antonin Artaud and Edward Bond. In the final instance though, the repeated emphasizing of the mask behind the mask, the turning of ourselves into phenomenon makes Kane's plays undigestible.

The question of deliverance in the baroque handling of catastrophe is always the beckoning of a real beneath the miraculous. The *plethoric play* (to invoke Barker), full of cascading catastrophes, often assumes a veil of appearances and then sends signals to the possibility of a space (Deleuze's upper chamber of folds?) beyond the appearances where hope and truth reside. But that sense of depth is always illusory, just outside our reach. As William Egginton has emphasized, mediation of the reality through atonality and hallucinations, actually turn them into concrete reality. The stage itself becomes reality. Space becomes a factor of volume, not extent. In a Christian or hermeneutic set up, death and decay would be the sites of emergence and redemptive beauty. For instance, pure art for Jacques Maritain is a form of 'angelist suicide'—such art at once takes from and leaves behind the vestments of the material world. Art places signs and turns those into shining salvific universals. Art is made radiant through creative intuition of the artist and the beholder alike. Proximate matter of art ends up depicting remote truths, as Roman Ingarden would say. Art is in this sense is wondrous to the redemptive vision. The particular atmosphere that art fosters penetrates us and transfigures us with its light. Sarah Kane could have taken this route but chose not to. Instead, her plays acknowledge the twists and turns of an elusive and partial truth. The sacred canopy stands disintegrated. Her super-real erotic cruelty is more than religion. It teeters on emergence but returns to immersion in living, which emphatically includes death. Everything cracks up and breaks down. Every creature scrambles. Faith, if is there, is desperate. Her plays are therefore sites of lies that tell the truth, for truth is not of our making.

But Kane's absolute attention to the moving tableaux of life, the parrying of her characters with love and cruelty, takes us to unbidden areas. Such dogged attention provides her works with a rare shining power, away from all ethical immediacy. Kane represents the power of the forever ignorant, the one who refuses the delusion or clarity of simple humanism in order to traverse to a deeper and capacious cosmovision of the simpler creaturely. That is the reason Richard Foreman, in a similar spirit, has said that convincing the audience is no theatre. Such theatre imprisons and degrades the audience as the "theatrical production tries to convince of its mastery in that manipulation" (Foreman, 2013). Theatrical productions can at best 'frame and exhibit' the residues of failure. Therefore, in the spirit of *dissolving mastery*, each play in Kane's repertoire tells us, as it were, that it is through the clash of relentless violence and surpassing attachments, *we come to ourselves.* We begin to flow in unison with humiliation, soul damaging force and occasional miracles. It is this freedom to swim with force and affliction that makes adults out of her spectators; those who are able to at once take charge of their lives and yet read life's variegated gifts in lucid and lyrical terms.

Howard Barker has beautifully summed up the crux of the theatre of catastrophe in which, "transgression is the one we commit against ourselves, the transgression of leaving our conscience in the lurch and seeking a forgiveness we can never achieve and that, ultimately, is a crime against the body, of the secret knowledge of the relationship between beauty and cruelty, of a sacrificing solitude"

(Barker, 1989). The triumph of Sarah Kane lies in the fact that we begin to confront our own demons through her works; by keeping aside all baleful invocations of conscience. We see vividly how our wrong actions turn into pure moments of terrible beauty. It does not make theatre *effective*. It depicts. She shows that fate must be confronted with an iron hand. And with absolute lucidity. If there is any emergence, this is it.

References

Barker, Howard. 1989. *Arguments for a Theatre*. London: John Calder Publishers Ltd.

Deleuze, Gilles. 1993. *The Fold: Leibniz and the Baroque*. Translated by Tom Conley. London: The Athlone Press.

Egginton, William. 2010. *The Theatre of Truth: The Ideology of (Neo)Baroque Aesthetics*. Stanford: Stanford University Press.

Foreman, Richard. 2013. *The Manifestoes and Essays*. New York: Theatre Communication Group.

Halpern, Richard. 2017. *Eclipse of Action: Tragedy and Political Economy*. Chicago and London: University of Chicago Press.

Juhan, Deane. 2002. *Job's Body*. Barrytown, NY: Barrytown Ltd.

Kane, Sarah. 2001. *Complete Plays*. London, New York, Oxford, New Delhi, Sydney: Bloomsbury.

Ndalianis, Angela. 2004. *(Neo)Baroque Aesthetics and Contemporary Entertainment*. Cambridge, MA: The MIT Press.

Nelson, Maggie. 2011. *The Art of Cruelty: A Reckoning*. New York and London: W.W. Norton and Company.

Ranc, Gaelle. 2002. *The Notion of Cruelty in the Work of Sarah Kane*. http://www.iainfisher.com/kane/eng/sarah-kane-study-gr0.html. Accession date: 24 April 2021.

Singer, Annabelle. 2004. "Don't Want to Be This: The Elusive Sarah Kane." *TDR (1988)*.Vol. 48.2, Summer: 139–171.

Urban, Ken. 2001. "An Ethics of Catastrophe: The Theatre of Sarah Kane." *PAJ: A Journal of Performance and Art*. Vol. 23. 3, September: 36–46.

Wolfflin, Heinrich. 1984. *Renaissance and Baroque*. Translated by K. Simon. Cork: Collins.

Worringer, Wilhelm. 2014. *Abstraction and Empathy: A Contribution to the Psychology of Style*. Translated by Michael Bullock. CT: Martino Publishing House.

The Creature Aflutter

The Incantatory Kabir Suman

Harold Bloom had made it clear many times that his investment in the Greek literary critic Dionysius Longinus, writing in the 1st century AD, was a way to address and revisit the fundamental *encounter of the sublime* in our living. Commentators have noticed a remarkable 'agon' being played out in Bloom's career: between his idealizing enthusiasm in romantic-messianic visions and his equal investment in gnostic wisdom and stoic classicism. This *agon*, or contestation, was his way of addressing a certain space of the uncanny in dealing with art and literature, in contrast to the modernizers and tropologists who, he believed, rejected subjectivity itself as a fallacy. Not Bloom—who had always claimed that the 'strong critic' is a kind of poet. As he saw it, literary criticism is an ongoing tussle between the pathos of the heroic will and the 'literalizers' who deal in tropes and textual juggleries. But has he been successful in strictly distinguishing the analytic from the daemonic? Can the sensory and the figurative be elevated over the uncanny and surpassing?

Here is a singular song, penned and sung by Suman Chattopadhyay (now Kabir Suman) decades ago.

In an instant you returned
a simple glance, gazing.
Look, in your eyes
my fresh new verse, homing.
That verse, harmonized
kindles a song of two?
The naïve arithmetic of charm
in that simple glancing touch
you returned to my eyes.

I am grateful to Nishita Khattar, Annette James, Arnav Gogoi, Anibal Goth, Anugya and Mantra Mukim for long hours of discussions on sublimity and poetry through the past years.

Says age, "Here I grow."
And death, "So near I wait."
Life adds, "Life, you say?
Mere hide-and-seek I play."
Advises sense, "Grasp right now
the future that is a mirage."
In the pyre cools every bonfire -
Such is life! phew and phooey!
Yech and yuck, phew and phooey,
Time ekes away in this drudge
The wish to live free of vexation
is now an insignification!
This stormy whirlpool of desire
You seized from me strolling by
By the simple graze of a gaze
You returned the glance to my eye.

এক মুহূর্তে ফিরিয়ে দিলে
সহজ চোখে তাকিয়ে থাকা।
ওই তো তোমার চোখেই আমার
সদ্য লেখা পদ্য রাখা।
পদ্যটাতে সুর ছোঁয়ালে
গান হবে কি দুজন মিলে?
সহজ কৌতূহলের অঙ্ক
চোখের ছোঁওয়ায় মিলিয়ে দিলে।

বয়স বলে, "বাড়ছি দেখো !"
মৃত্যু বলে, "কাছেই আছি"।
জীবন বলে, "কোথায় জীবন?
খেলছি শুধু কানা মাছি !"
বুদ্ধি বলে, "গোছাও কিছু –
আখের মার্কা মরীচিকা"।
ফুরোবে সব চিতা'র কাঠে –
এই তো জীবন! দুত্তেরিকা !
ধ্যাত্তেরি আর দুত্তেরিকা
বলতে বলতে সময় কাটে
বিরক্তিহীন বাঁচতে চাওয়ার
ইচ্ছে এখন বেগার খাটে!

বেদম বেহাল ইচ্ছেটা কে
চলতে চলতে কুড়িয়ে নিলে।
সহজ চোখের ছোঁওয়ায় তুমি
আমার চোখে ফিরিয়ে দিলে।

The song (almost an incantation) pivots around nailing the temporal aspect of the arche emotion of the sublime experience [a combination of astonishment (*ekplêxis*) and wonder (*thaumasion*)] that Longinus had proposed long ago: where the point of origin for surpassing sublimity is a certain occasion, the right moment (*kairos*), which is always 'happily timely'. But that same moment is also uncanny and interruptive.

In an instant you returned
a simple glance, gazing.

A breathtaking gesture, this—I glance and beckon and someone takes heed, turns around and looks at me. Two moments coalesce in a single and unified knot. The first sub-moment is purely extempore in nature: without any prior notice someone decides to invoke me through a glance. This is a direct, simple and naïve gaze, a wondrous and silent call. And I respond without any overt intention of doing so. Something in me responds. *It* responds. The instant gaze interrupts my time and turns it around. This encounter was always about to happen *and it has happened now.* The moment and the initial gestures of the song take place in the gap between the call and reply. The initial glance *brings forth* the response and the simple arc gets completed. The singular swish of the completed and uncut moment unfolds.

The responder recognizes me by the simple and unconditional return-gaze. The unknown is admitted to my known world; a moment of miraculous reassurance. In the blink of an eye I stand exposed, and my exposure is responded to by a similar vulnerable gesture. In the gap, a certain closeness is being gestured at; but is the distance surpassed? The crucial question for the sublime lies here: is it a moment that flies up fatelessly, its success lies in the *kairotic* instant itself. Or does this moment transcend all the other significant motivations of our living and make life worth celebrating in terms of discovering eternity within the shell of this instant, which then can be kept alive as an afterlife through the rhythm of the art or reached through some contemplative mechanism?

But behold! It seems that emboldened by the return of the gaze, the initiator wishes to prolong the moment:

> Look, in your eyes
> my fresh new verse, homing.
> That verse, harmonized
> kindles a song of two?

The composed verse is of course the glance itself, which has concentrated within itself the intensity of all that versification can ever achieve. And yet, this is also a self-conscious acknowledgement that you are not just creating this moment collectively, but also that objectively you can detach yourself and see the moment unfolding. You further hope that this *instantiated moment* can now be given a future and chronological dimension. This projected futurity is also marked by a singular hierarchy: that between poetry and song. The magic of the lightest touch of the glance, and the poetic result that it has achieved, can be prolonged by you if music descends between the two-some, now that the arc of the sublime moment is completed. From the singular and localized ethereal instant of the reciprocity emerges the *not-yet*. Surely, the *not-yet* summons us towards prolonging and making the already versified instant into something more ethereal: hoping to make the fleeing instant a surpassing one, by injecting music into it. Making a song out of a verse where rhythm and tune conjoin. And yet this is just a hope, self-consciously enacted by the poet-beholder. The interrogation mark at the end of the sixth line shows the hope involved in this extension of the moment. This hope materializes since the participating beings are witnessing something in their own lives about which they have always heard. In one of the most beautiful utterances ever pronounced in the history of literary criticism, Longinus says: "It is our nature to be elevated and exalted by true sublimity [*hypsos*]. Filled with joy and pride, we come to believe we have created what we have only heard" (Longinus, 1965). This is at the heart of genuine and 'transporting' intersubjectivity fostered by the sublime moment: a fictive creation of joy and pride by believing in the reality of togetherness. Within such a transporting microcosm, no analytical access is allowed.

But the shimmering nature of the moment also makes this hope just that: a hope. Can the moment be really held and made into an incantation? The sensuousness of the reciprocal gazing is all that can be shored up, perhaps? Here is one of the enduring conundrums of the 'happy occasion' of reciprocal and sublime beholding—it *overwhelms us*, and by doing so breaks down our egotistic cores into utter and complete vulnerability (which is the classical-modern component); yet the same moment also *elevates us* into a fairy-tale world of boundless and surpassing joy (the idealistic/transcendent component). The first impulse takes us closer to frailty, incompleteness and hence, gradually closer to self-reflectivity. The second, towards accomplished fulfilment and elevation. Hit by the force of the encounter, the moment summons the fleeting and the fulfilled at the same time. The naïve arithmetic of charm is completed by the reciprocation. It is indeed the equation of 1+1=1, as the arc circles back into that moment. Perhaps, this is bliss. And yet, can that simple glancing touch hold eternity within? Is this epiphanic moment metaphysically harmonic and whole, or does it show us the power of the fleeting aesthetic reckonings of our contingent living through psychological and linguistic imaginings of a material being—a mode to reach the state of 'profane illumination'?

The long middle of the poem is conceptual and thoughtful. It gives us a tableau of other temporal moments that must eventually lead to nothingness. And our wants and desire for the essentialities of living must remain most abstract (as opposed to the image of the illuminated moment). Between the many enchantments of life, one feels the sense of time's fleetingness since all human flourishing, 'every bonfire' must eventually lead to the pyre. And that sense makes life banal and wasted. This is the manifestation of urban ennui, as has been enacted in art and literature in many different ways in the past two centuries. Chattopadhyay has used two remarkable unlyrical expressions here—ধ্যাত্তেরি and দুত্তেরিকা (yech and yuck, phew and phooey) in order to cement the notion of our everyday drudgery, and hence affirm our distance from the simple conjugation of a rare reciprocation. To live a life free of vexation is what we aspire for, which is at best a life of fastened anchorage. But the moment of illumination has now made life lyrical, by that 'graze of a gaze'. And so we hanker. But this hankering is a hope through which the creature wishes to turn more than itself, so that it can recompense the drudgery of reality and touch immortality.

The classical-modernist axis of the poem relies on several factors—the levelling simplicity of the fleeting gazes, the plucking of the gaze by the responder most unceremoniously (seized from me strolling by), the bravado of the hope of extending the moment, the restive nature of desire seeking anchorage, and the arguments marshaled in the middle for 'seizing the moment'—all depicting the poet's self-conscious capacity to recapitulate the encounter, reflexively gathering thoughts and images and performing the lyric through a fine structuration of first delineating and projecting the heightened moment, followed on by a conceptual list of four personified abstractions (age, death, life and sense), and then taking us back to the initial image: the gathered equation of the moment's respite. The profane/classical-modernist way of approaching instants of sublimity is through aesthesis/structures, which are always cultural products. Affect and style can be read, deciphered and accounted for in this manner. It is the transitory quality of life that makes life worth it: for genuine sublimity is always contingent. Only through contingency can such singular events, such as the one sung by the illumined minstrel here, gain universal validity. The very solidity of living lies in the astonishing surprise element of all that is fleeting and wondrous in this universe, in contrast to the drudgery involved in merely serving time. Is the sublime moment then a way of enacting a kind of *compensatory affirmation* of the self? Or is it that such affirmation must remain a heroic hope? Does the rhythm of life, in this case the *subtle knot* of the gaze, actually allow any assured recompense?

The metaphysical-idealistic axis resists this reading. It seeks a visionary and surpassing pattern within such lyrical instants. It seeks repeatability and harmony. It believes that that we cannot only hold sublimity within a cosmic frame but can extend it to eternity by various means—through summoning of mnemonic memory, beckoning and moulding imagination, submitting metaphysically to the aura of the sublime event and so on. In transporting and ecstatic moments, we are in thrall of the daemonic, from which there is no respite. It keeps beckoning us and we submit to its charm involuntarily. Enchantment is a one-way route to faith and repose. It is a meditative process, by which creatures are transformed and brought closer to the harmony that inheres in the cosmos. Sublimity thus turns into *a moment of integrity*, a subtle knot that cannot be severed.

In his most visionary moments, Harold Bloom affirms Ralph Waldo Emerson's observation from the essay on *Self Reliance:* "Power ceases in the instant of repose; it resides in the moment of transition from a past to a new state, in the shooting of a gulf, in the darting of an aim" (Emerson, 2016). But it is the same Bloom who plays the shaman and the analyst who meticulously culls out gestures and allegories within such surpassing moments that great art bequeaths us. Though beholden to Longinus, Bloom knows that we live by certain essential fictions, which make life incandescent. The messiah never arrives and yet we keep envisioning his arrival. Therefore, an essential wisdom, a certain stoic ennui vies with an incandescent vision in his critical output. Bloom gives this state a name: 'achieved anxiety'. Here, one elevates and deflates illumination at the same time. But what creature hopes to preserve blinding luminosity? The *erstwhile and evanescent* Suman Chattopadhyay, in his oracular moments of minstrelsy, must have experienced the pangs of similar agonistic journeys. But do the incantatory transfigurations bear fruit? Once transfigured, can elevated matter-form remain in that state?

The issue of fictionalization of shining moments, captured through the rhythm of life (musicality?), is actually at the heart of the Longinian aspiration: a reparative wish to gather the most lyrical of babbles, those which he knows to be ecstatic, and therefore, fleeting. The wistful desire to capture the supplement, the excess of ache in the sublime moment is a mad wish to keep experiencing and extending the rhythm of life. As the two lovers traverse beyond their selves, they also wish to immortalize the instance in and through an idealized notion of elevated temporal fixity. But the immediate threat of loss brings forth and weaves in the deepest form of lack in the very moment when all time stops. Longinus's way to tackle this conundrum is to take refuge in figures of speech. Longinus wishes that the lovers achieve sublimity and 'make it theirs' for keeps. But can language save the lyric, which is pure voice and absolute gesture?

This tenuous thread and threat is at the heart of the lyric sensibility. This is the flight that aesthetics promises to the fundamental miracle and lack in our living. But is rhetoric able to bring to light (clarify) the mystery that must remain hidden? Can it dare to exorcise the dread of loss limned at the moment of the uncanny union and reciprocation of the mutual gaze? For in the moment of sublimity, the past is played out in the present, which also adumbrates the future of the perennial loverly instance: the miracle of the caressing gaze. The shattering moment can be unconcealed, but the price and effects of shattering itself can hardly be retrieved or recuperated in any complete and unified newness. Nothing can be tidied up, least of all miracles. And yet miracles are not dreams, nor are they theatrical performances. The power of the moment, the event and the reciprocal gaze itself is felt like an electric shock to the two lovers that does indeed transfigure what we call reality. It makes for the exceptional within the everyday, by 'making' a parallel universe possible among the mundane. The preternatural sublime is thus at once present and absent, pure material force and an evanescent *trompe l'oeil*.

The gaze returns much later, as pure longing in another of Kabir Suman's mature lyrics, as the unhoused, eternal lovers reappear in various mythic-temporal avatars. Moments flicker past creatures, the mortals—in each encounter that life offers. And moments must return as absolute contingency. This return of contingency constitutes the illusion of necessity. The minstrel-poet, therefore, does not desire immortality (অমরত্বের প্রত্যাশা নেই), since he knows that the only reason to live this fleeting life is to desire the lover (এই নশ্বর জীবনের মানে শুধু তোমাকেই চাওয়া). That is the maximum *density of purpose* that one can achieve in our anxious, aching existence. No 'schematism of figures' shall be able to assist in recuperating and restoring the condition of vulnerability and loss. The aching fiction of desire is far too real. The lyric sensibility is, therefore, hardly about gathering wisdom. It is at once blessed and doomed to appear and reappear as the moment of the disintegrating miracle.

References

Bloom, Harold. 1983. *Agon: Towards a Theory of Revisionism*. Oxford: Oxford University Press.

———. 1989. *Ruin the Sacred Truths: Poetry and Belief from the Bible to the Present*. Cambridge, MA: Harvard University Press.

Bloom, Harold. 2015. *The Daemon Knows: Literary Greatness and the American Sublime*. Spiegel & Grau.

Carson, Anne. 2001. "Foam: (Essay with Rhapsody) On the Sublime in Longinus and Antonioni". *Conjunctions*: 96–104.

Culler, Jonathan. 2005. "The Hertzian Sublime." In *Comparative Literature Issue*. Vol. 120.5: 969–985.

Deguy, Michel, Philippe Lacoue-Labarthe, et al. 1993. *Of the Sublime: Presence in Question*. Albany: State University of New York.

Doran, Robert. 2007. "Literary History and the Sublime in Erich Auerbach's Mimesis." *New Literary History*. Vol. 38.2: 353–369.

Emerson, Ralph Waldo. 2016. *Compensation, Self-Reliance and Other Essays*. Edited by Mary A. Jordan. Sydney: Wentworth Press.

Ferguson, Frances. 1992. *Solitude and the Sublime: Romanticism and the Aesthetics of Individuation*. Routledge.

Friese, Heidrun (ed.). 2001. *The Moment: Time and Rupture in Modern Thought*. Liverpool: Liverpool University Press.

Hertz, Neil. 1985. *The End of the Line: Essays on Psychoanalysis and the Sublime*. New York: Columbia University Press.

Kant, Immanuel. 1951. *Critique of Judgment*. Translated by J.H. Bernard. London: Macmillan.

Longinus. 1965. "On the Sublime." In *Classical Literary Criticism*. Translated by T.S. Dorsch. Harmondsworth: Penguin. pp. 97–158.

Lyotard, Jean-François. 1994. *Lessons on the Analytic of the Sublime*. Trans. Elizabeth Rottenberg. Palo Alto: Stanford University Press.

Monk, Samuel H. 1935/1960. *The Sublime: A Study of Critical Theories in XVIII-Century England*. Ann Arbor: University of Michigan Press.

Quinney, Laura. 1995. *Literary Power and the Criteria of Truth*. Gainesville: University Press of Florida.

———. 1994. "Weiskel's Sublime and the Impasse of Knowledge." *Philosophy and Literature*. Vol. 18.2: 309–319.

Tsang, Lap Chuen. 1998. *The Sublime: Groundwork towards a Theory*. Rochester: University of Rochester Press.

Santayana, George. 1955. *The Sense of Beauty. Being the Outlines of Aesthetic Theory*. New York: Modern Library.

Thomas, Weiskel and Portia Williams Weiskel. 1976. *The Romantic Sublime*. Baltimore: Johns Hopkins University Press.

The Enchanted Creature

The Fragile Durations of Jean Starobinski

One can imagine a certain immobile time, a time of eternal present. In such a time, there are no battles or notions of property. No death, only easy sleep. There are free moments of song and dance, music rather than work. Men and beasts understand each other perfectly—in music and in melody. The eternal present extends and turns back on itself in sinuous folds of flowing arcs and circles. Becoming for each creature is a light movement in this present, a fluid élan. Only an interval is sometimes required in order to renew such moments of plenitude and felicity. But such a golden age is only the retrospective consolation of an unhappy humanity.

Jean Starobinski begins his remarkable *tour de force* on operatic synaesthesia by wondering whether human beings tried enacting such brief repose through their festivities right from the outset of community life. But will such a conclusion not be a mere echo, a ritualized commemoration, a souvenir of some fabulous origin? Or are there also moments of the body and the voice in such re-enactments which might help cross the threshold of the realm of the dead? Is the moment of performance also a moment to witness the abolishment of the mortal consequences of time? In other words, does performance release creatures to a realm of aesthetic freedom or is it the instance of the restless re-enactment of a mythical past?

Perhaps, the performance that reconquers a parcel of eternity also witnesses its own duration measured. Is it that the poet and the musician who have relived the atemporal plenitude of the origin only turn and fall back into time and death, creatures of fire and wind as they are? Surely, the creative spirits must at first hold onto the temporal space and build their fable. But they must also know how to close off such enactments, with a final cadence and a lifting of the masks—with a salute to the spectators, who witness divinity for a certain duration. The spectators applaud the enchantment that was, the very exploit of art. Was it all a distraction, a sublime phantasm?

The paradox in the operatic mode is twofold: first, representation in this form is part of our being enthralled with what Bernard Williams has called 'manifest artifice' (Williams, 2006). Aesthetic pleasure is derived at once from the heightened sense of passion and expression, but it "also occurs as a conscious enjoyment of the techniques used to engineer the representation" (Dammann, 2010). In melo-dramaturgy, absorption in the surplus of the sublime experience goes hand in hand with delight in the artifice of it. Has there been a sense of hyper-mediacy in the genre right from the inception? This condition is doubly emphasized through the fact that opera combines spoken drama through music, that is to say, speech is represented by a genre which is an excess of speech: song. The composer is the dramatist here (and not the librettist), as Joseph Kerman had observed long ago. Opera is Janus faced, an art practice in simultaneity. In fact, in its versatile malleability, opera stands higher than poetic drama. Ulrich Weisstein observes: "The operatic composer commands a variety of means of expression—from the conversational to the symphonic, from ordinary speech via *Sprechstimme*, melodrama, *recitativo secco* and *accompagnato* to full-fledged arias, ensembles, and purely instrumental music—that is unparalleled in regular drama" (Weisstein, 2006). Opera/music-drama is indeed a futuristic form of total art, what Wagner had designated as *Gesamtkunstwerk* in *The Artwork of the Future* around 1850—a multimedia form, where all the powers of the fine arts are united, the space in which the process of the marvellous is achieved in the theatre stage (Lindenberger, 2010).

How does Jean Starobinski address these paradoxes? Is this the way human beings wish to skirt their creaturely condition and are they able to steal and restore some reprieve? There is a still deeper question: if there is sometimes a lack of poise and equity between an emotion and the context in which the emotion is expressed within the drama of the opera, how does one come to terms with the messiness of the creaturely circumstance—say in death or in love? And if feeling is highlighted in such excessive terms, do some of the greatest operas that indulge in the *life of the feelings* give us no answers to our creaturely condition, as fate begins to take over the plans of the characters and the directions of the plot-lines? Perhaps, to give in to feeling means never to grasp the world of its excesses. Indeed, the question of the operatic form must simultaneously pass through the ceremonial expression and limits of the excessive. A captivating form, opera is also a form of captivity.

The Perishable Minute

Everything begins with enthrallment though—in and within the instantaneous. Ulysses had strapped himself to the mast of his ship to resist such an experience. What is so dangerous about this song, for the one who had succeeded in resisting the temptations of immortality? The Sirens, thrice perfect minstrels, companions of Persephone, would live as long as they could stop every passer-by, but as soon as one passed without stopping, the sirens would perish. The enchantment was so complete that the travellers would be bewitched, and forgetting their homelands, oblivious to food and drink, they would die of starvation:

> Come here, renowned Ulysses, honour to the Achaenean name, and listen to our two voices. No one ever sailed past us without staying to hear the enchanting sweetness of our song—and he who listens will go his way not only charmed, but wiser, for we know all the ills that the gods laid upon the Argives and Trojans before Troy, and can tell you everything that is going to happen over the whole world. (Homer/Lattimore, 1963)

If Ulysses had listened to the Sirens, he would have encountered the image of his own past transfigured by music. He would have believed that his life is forever saved from oblivion, and he would have forgotten to live—like all other travellers whose white bones litter the Sirens' shore. Here is a fascinating music that develops another relationship to time outside of the one that emanates from the golden age, a music linked to narrating speech that can only deploy itself within a succession of temporal events: *a happy fluidification*, in Starobinski's words. This is the music of becoming, a music that elevates to the perfection of song, to bloody entanglements and to heroic patience and endurance to suffering. Are lovers and heroes arche-creatures then, learning and displaying joyously the spirit of perdurance that can only arrive through agonizing travails and ordeals? Ditties and tales put an imprimatur to their impossible sagas.

We enter into a time that will be transmitted to future generations by enacting the glorious immortality of the hero who has gone through the test of time and whose existence is saved by the song. For having accepted death, the epic hero will live eternally in and through speech. But Ulysses is also bitter, since he is stripped and solitary. The pleading castaway and the hero in songs of the minstrel Demodocus are the same:

> His glorious song celebrates a past action, and the surviving hero, if he is to avoid demeaning himself, must take the place of the minstrel and become the narrator of his own miseries … and elevate them to the plane of musical immortality, just as the minstrel did for his military services. (Starobinski, 2008)

Here is a particular mode of deliverance, of spirit rendered in and through an immaterial sonorous condition. Time is simultaneously imagined as the age of heroes, subsisting in our past as sheer memory. And yet it destroys all our illusions by asserting its own dominance only through material life spent on the earth. There is an interior historicity to the operatic time. This is the most sensual and fragile of durations: *the vibration of the perishable minute.*

Indeed, *singing* and *seducing* are intimately related. What creature is unscathed from seduction? To seduce, etymologically, means to *lead aside.* What is the force that attracts one away from the straight and narrow? There emerges a fatal creature of shattering beauty, speaking in silken voice and offering unknown pleasures. You should have listened and avoided its glance. One step off the sure road leads to another, and suddenly you find yourself wandering in a state of perdition. At the end, a kind of dizziness sets in—a concoction arising out of ecstasy, enthusiasm and intoxication. When the hero travels by road, through the wilds or by sea, the enchantress watches for him by the side of the road or haunts him, lurking over the island when he comes ashore. One can also see that sometimes, the reverse happens and vulnerable heroines are seduced by wicked suitors. This has been the fate of the girls who listened to Don Juan's compliments or those who had accepted Faust's gifts. To be enchanted is to give in to a strange foreignness. But it would be erroneous to describe it through drives and beliefs and phobias. Nor are these moments' anxiety dreams. Such moments of foreignness of a legendary past are transformed into a present enchantment in the opera—as one sees action unfolding and hears the notes being sung. Destiny, as it were, breaks into the present. In the words of Starobinski, "In the most beautiful operatic productions, one observes the double energy of a memory that persists and an imagination that invents" (Starobinski, 2008). Can the concoction of memory and imagination free living creatures of their affliction? Or does the operatic is what it is: the sweetest of hallucinations?

The ancient alliance between speech and music is crucial for enchantment. Air and aria designate the body of the seduction, and extend it to the atmosphere, which breathes in anticipation. This relationship brings the remembered legend within the bounds of sensorial proximity. The action is a service to the ear: "Listen! Listen to the one you doubted and whom you have found again. Listen to the one who loves you and who never stopped loving you" (Starobinski, 2008). The opera, as it were, begins to shed more light on its already sacred destinies, commemorating a new art that would transform the epic, grand historical scenes and chivalric romances. The stage itself is both concrete and metaphorical, since it can represent a palace or an underworld. The show must keep the mind and the senses in an equal state of enchantment. Sometimes, enchantment could come to connote a certain regressive childishness or supernatural constraints, especially in old romances. But it is more often than not associated with the natural affect of feeling (love) or aesthetic success (the party). In the second sense, the illusion could be restrained. Does this bring creatures back to the real, even as they travel within the marvellous?

Marvellous Action

The admixture of ritual and novelty in opera represents for us: marvellous action. The opera produces its own myths, which are lavishly fantastic. Apart from the decoration, Rousseau for instance, insists on the amalgamation of the enchantment of the melody and the effect of the declamation in the operatic. But the musical marvel itself is another kind of seduction. Starobinski reminds us that music's job in an opera is to get rid of the celestial gods and demons and deploy its own powers that issue from the soul of the musician and resonate with the feeling of the audience. Though opera employs its own machinery, music cannot become mere interest. Artifices cannot *flatter* the ear. The challenge then is how to enchant with a primitive art through forms that are essentially modern—arias and songs, choruses and symphonies. And the musician must also serve the poetry without at all trying to shine separately. Synchronicity between the strain and the ditty is of pivotal importance.

Rousseau, we know, was the inventor of a new kind of spectacle in which declamatory speech and music alternate. This form often borrowed scenes from Goethe's *Egmont* and Schumann's *Manfred*, inspired by Byron. For Rousseau, the enchantress appears first as Madame de Warens: "What I saw was a face radiant with grace, blue eyes full of sweetness, a dazzling complexion, the curve of an enchanting bosom" (Rousseau, 2008). This sense of enchantment will be transferred in *Julie ou la Nouvelle* when Saint Prex discovers Italian music: "Some unknown voluptuous sensation imperceptively came over me. It was no longer an empty sequence of sounds, as in or recits. At each phrase some image entered my brain or some sentiment in my heart; the pleasure did not stop at the ear, but entered the soul" (Rousseau, 1997). This state is perhaps what E.T.A. Hoffmann called a penetration into the realm of the spirits (Hoffmann, 2004). The poet who composes the libretto in the opera, therefore, must also be familiar with the enchanted realm of the spirits. The interiority in an opera turns into images, which are delegates of a mythic consciousness. We turn into participants. But there is also a certain liberating weightlessness in the opera that Hoffmann notes. This sense of freedom Starobinski describes as "the irony that denounces the ridiculousness of the finite condition awards itself the prerogatives of infinity" (Starobinski, 2008). These counter-balancing forces are what the opera derives from the works of Ariosto and Tasso.

Nowhere is the power of enchantment and seduction felt stronger than in the Gnostic dualism of Wagner. Right from his youth, Wagner was attracted to themes of the betrayal of secrets (*Lohengrin*) and of redemption (*Erlosung*). He shall put terrible opposing forces of enchantment into confrontation in his *dramatic ballads*: nature, elements, gods, humans and tribes. Wagnarian heroes must submit to the law of fate, which imposes upon them the alternatives of destruction of deliverance. So, in *The Flying Dutchman*, we have Venus transformed into the evil enchantress Lileth, without taking away her radiant beauty. The opera shows how a gift of love or sacrifice can bring salvation. Later, both in *Parsifal* and in *Tannhauser*, one form of enchantment is juxtaposed against another—"perverse magic which obstructs the work of redemption, and the saving miracle that makes known the divine will" (Starobinski, 2008). The enchantresses—Kundry and Armide are on the receiving end in Wagner though. Enchantment remains a fleeting human mistake as the Christian knight leads to victory. Wagner tilts towards a communion of faith and the sorceresses, therefore, have to recede, having enacted their role. Such piety is what Nietzsche abhorred in Wagner (so did Adorno). He preferred Bizet's *Carmen* instead, because it *does not sweat*. The young man in *Carmen* is won over by the representation of "love as *fatum*, as fatality, cynical, innocent, cruel" (Starobinski, 2008). For Starobinski such an evaluation of *Carmen* implies that there could be a higher level of the marvellous to be obtained, by a renunciation of the ordinary. No magical panoplies there. No religious stakes. We witness a similar condition in *Salome* by Oscar Wilde/Strauss, when the tyrant Herod orders, "Kill the woman." Such a moment of enchantment, when an irrevocable and relentless passion takes over man, is what Nietzsche calls *inflexible necessity*.

It is instructive to note that unlike Nietzsche or Starobinski, Bernard Williams detects a realist Schopenhauerean version of pessimism in Wagner (especially in *The Ring*, which derives from *Siegfrieds Tod*). One central thread returns: "the kiss of love is the first intimation of death, the cessation of individuality" (Williams, 2006). Too decorative and athletic for his taste, Wagner's operas, he thought, *directly acts on nerves*. Any lyrical idea of redemption through love and wonder is put to rest in the quest for *limitlessness* in Wagner. Williams, who does not hide his hope for a moral claim for operatic enchantment, rues this stress by Wagner on the impossibility of innocence in art. Siegfried, who is close to nature courts disaster. William wistfully inquires: What role fantasy in a world of confusion and imperfection? It is tempting to respond that since Williams reads characters as beings who are buffeted by moral luck, he is unable to see the creaturely delight in giving in to the intimate coupling between love and death. He feels that pessimism and optimism are choices that agents are able to exercise freely. But fantasy and fate are inextricably bound. Like moths in flames, lovers and adventurers burn themselves off over the fantastic moment. Is that a choice they make or are they pulled towards the uncanny? It is this conundrum that powers such drama. Is Wagner trying to relate the heroic rebel with the alienated artist and the outcast outsider through such manoeuvres? Indeed, Linda and Michael Hutcheon have called such devout moments of consummation as exercises in the *art of dying*, an eroticization of death within the operatic canvas, when "death becomes invested with passionate sorrow" (Hutcheon and Hutcheon, 2004). They see such investment in death as redeeming, even transfiguring reality, rather than giving in to the real.

An Act of Initiation

The Lorenzo da Ponte-Mozart collaboration concerns a major portion of the book and Starobinski is at his masterful best in this section. The three operas under consideration are *The Marriage of Figaro* (1786), *Don Giovanni* (1787) and *Cosi fan Tutte* (1790). The coming together of an auspicious collaboration in opera is *an act of initiation*, as Hoffmann rightly notes: "the linked affinities of the poet and the composer are such that one could say they belong to the same church, because the mystery of language and sound is the same, and it is this which gives both of them access to the supreme initiation" (Starobinski, 2008). Mozart and Da Ponte chimed in unison. The poet-librettist's job is to arrange the scene in such a manner so that the spectator must visualize the subject matter vividly. The spectator is not particularly interested in hunting strict logic in an opera. He must rather form an idea of the plot from what he sees taking place. Da Ponte is able to do just that, by establishing a relay between the written words of earlier masters of poetry and the new music of Mozart. The three productions were seamless collaborations of musical exuberance and poetry leading to dramatized adventure. The singer, therefore, must first understand each line of poetry before rendering it.

Figaro is a sublime spectacle of a libertine engaged in substitution and yet returning to recognize faith in love (in Figaro and Susanna of course, but also witnessed in the diffused eroticism of Barbarina and Cherubino). Da Ponte wrote in his memoirs: "I set to work, accordingly, and as fast as I wrote the words, Mozart set them to music. In six weeks everything was in order" (Da Ponte, 2000). The conquering energy of the collaboration is palpable to the audience. One could feel that Mozart followed Diderot's dictum that musical composition was to be regulated by laws of successive departure and return, out and back. The tonalities of the different acts show exactly this distribution—in solo arias, duos, ensembles and the movement that would be accorded to the finales. As the bird catcher is tripped in a cage of his own making, order is restored. D major is both the shore and departure of return. Mozart goes into the heart of true lyricism and Da Ponte follows Mozart's intentions with speed and precision. We see a microcosm of human feeling in circulation. The polymorphic intonations of desire are expressed through gaiety, melancholy, cupidity, fear, malice, vanity, repentance, pardon and so forth. In the order of desire, all are equals and Da Ponte-Mozart refuses to give hereditary priority to the noble master. Enchantment, above all, reigns.

Circulation of Objects

Starobinski reminds us that the success of being seduced in an operatic production often depends on a certain *circulation of objects*. It is, as it were, that the movement of the passions required some material representation of conducting bodies. Feminine fetishes and gory objects of passion are at the centre of the spectacle: kerchiefs and ribbons, butterflies attracted by flowers, a spilled drop of blood, a localized pin-prick, and the sword as the counterpoint. Such a circulation of objects gives the opera its tactility, a certain tempo and an epidermal sensation. These are also currencies of exchange, vehicles of deception and passion, of illusion and attachment. Hence, Starobinski says: "There is a singular resemblance of form—the image of an unfolding—that links the ribbon and the staffs on which the music is jotted down" (Starobinski, 2008). The interior movements and the visual accessories of the show are intertwined.

Everything outside the straight and narrow is an indulgence of the *excess*. That is what seduction, and life, is all about. The registers of excess are captured in *Don Giovanni*. *Excessus vitae* is the exit from life, the access to 'another life'. It is a moment of trance where soul leaves its anchorage in order to visit a superior place. But it is also a name for death. Excess is poetic. It spreads. Trance is contagious. If it traverses beyond the limits of body and soul—it is deliverance. But excess is also disproportion and sickness—anything that compromises the networks of tensions inside the body. Libertinism is such elegance in Don Juan.

Excess is at once an overflow, an exit, a malady and a means by which an individual or a set of individuals exclude themselves from communal law and ethical obligation. What would a man be without grace? The theological answer was that he would remain mired in self-love, appetites and delinquency. But the excessive forces that *Don Giovanni* celebrates are pure transgression, inverting the very notion of ecstasy. Starobinski makes us aware that we do not see an ordinary libertine in Don Juan, but man in general, the universal human being, living magnanimously with the absolute ideal of voluptuousness. We can even detect a counter-religious spirituality in Juan, a religious dimension within the order of evil. Sin is perfidy. It is an internal abyss. The diabolical is the spectral obverse of the seductress.

Aromatic Atmosphere

If the excessive reigns at one end of seductive charm, the *aromatic atmosphere* is its other signpost. *Cosi fan Tutte* affirms the philosophy of universal and inevitable flux of emotions. To be unfaithful is all too human and both *tutte* (women) and *tutti* (men) mutually exchange their image of inconstancy. To be ridiculous and clumsy is being as truthful as it is to be emphatic. Hence, we cannot have an opera without modulations and paradoxical effects: experiments in separation, indignation, fawning, jealousy and weakness. And love above all, as a conquering agent, is the very soul of opera. Starobinski says this with reference to Fenelon's *Idomeneo*, something that holds good for the operatic mode in general:

> The man or a woman who consents to die in the place of the first designated victim is demanding nothing other than the power to rescue a beloved voluntarily—without any other condition ... the voluntary victim wants only to receive death and in exchange asks only for the survival of the one who should have died. The voluntary victim will never be able to possess what he or she obtains, or even knows if it has been obtained. (Starobinski, 2008)

This spiritual drive lies at the heart of the operatic. The encounter with the seductress makes the hero discover an internal force of which he was unaware and of which he now takes possession.

In a section called 'Usurpations and Revolts', in one final flourish, Starobinski takes us through the heart and soul of six indomitable seductresses in the history of the opera: *Poppea, Alcina, Juliet* (Bellini/ Romani production), *Manon*, *Ariene* and *Elektra*. Monteverdi's *Poppea* made seduction into a supreme art. Her desire "increases our discomfort", says Montaigne. Tacitus writes that she "was indifferent to her reputation, yet insensible to men's love, and herself unloving." She was decidedly a free woman. It seems she was also an expert on the subject of beauty treatments. She broke her mirror and wished to die when she discovered marks on her face. She was an anachronistic disguise herself. Starobinski describes her debauched camaraderie with Nero and Othon in great detail, summing it up with: "Poppea is the law of the world, the centre towards which everything moves ... in her one sees a solar myth of love joined to a solar myth of power" (Starobinski, 2008). In her conjoins enormous self-love with captivating sensuality. But not she, love is the true master and the universe must finally recognize this fact in the opera. As she makes her lover's dependence intolerable to himself, he proclaims to obey no master whatsoever. Handel's *Alcina* is the mistress of all that can be offered in an instant: palaces, gardens, amusements. Lutes and harps and lyres play in sweet harmony at Alcina's table, poets praise the joys and follies of love and two lovers speak freely of love: "Everything is luxury and fulfilled dream." She metamorphoses her lovers into trees, animals and rocks and it seems that they have received the immortality of the material. There are several pyrotechnics, as eventually her palace crumbles, the sea washes its ruins and liberated men emerge out of the waves into which they have been liquefied. She eventually shares the destiny of Dido, Medea and Cleopatra. But all of these comprised within a cosmic frame. Bellini's musical about the Capulets and the Montagues is taken from Giuseppe Maria Foppa. It is a spectacle of passion that seeks death. Love unto death. There is an intense sadomasochistic element in Bellini which Shakespeare had humanized. The baroque ingenuity is the soul of the opera and we see that the grave (after the lovers die) is strewn with torches, shadowy areas, statues, arches and niches. The mournful graveyard lends itself to a canticle of basses: "Against this background two voices (Juliet's soprano and Romeo's mezzo in thirds) rise, float, take wing and descend, sliding or palpitating" (Starobinski, 2008). The voices in unison transcend all pain. It is the moment when Bellini's musical instinct attains its highest power of seduction. All breathing stops and music evokes the moment.

The Sonorous Secret of the Infinite

Des Grieux, the hero in Massenet's *Manon,* wonders how seduction works. How and why does love turn into this insurmountable force? We hear this word—charm, which must be taken in its archaic sense. Charm is magical incantation, from Latin *carmen*, "the formula that witches knew how to pronounce to capture hearts and make the moon dance in a wooded clearing" (Starobinski, 2008). To set Manon to music is to translate her charms into a new language. The senses are all powerful in Manon. The hero is in disarray and Manon fluctuates. She is a rococo creation—discontinuous and capricious. Eroticism is diffused in the music and in the construction of the set. Charm is in the air—the indefinable light that belongs both to a face and to the imagination of the enthralled spectator. In *Manon Lescaut* (1893), Puccini will not hesitate to reuse the discovery of Manon as an enchantress supreme. Eventually, she distances from her own charm and announces her death. The melodic effusiveness of seduction is akin to the final moments of living: *I am no longer myself; it is no longer my voice.* Des Grieux, the lover renounces all and her tears and games represent an absolute order to him. These sacrifices again equal the demand of religion. This sacred character of passion is at the heart of Starobinski's exposition.The dazzling nothings that decide everything—seduction and death.

The story of *Ariane and Bluebeard* (1901) concludes an entire phase in Maeterlinck's theatre. It has been dominated by death and fatality. "Uncertain of themselves, inhabited by mystery, they called for loving compassion, and one saw the machinery of misfortune inexorably unfold" (Starobinski, 2008). Maeterlinck makes evident a lost connection in art: between synaesthesia (perceptional associations between sound and colour) and mysticism. He had translated the work of the theologian Jan van Ruusbroec:

> When you find yourself amid the blinding rays of the sun and you avoid looking at all colours and avoid particular attention to distinctions and objects illuminated by the sun, if then, you simply follow with your eyes the clarity and rays that flow from the sun, you will be guided into the very essence of sun.... (Starobinski, 2008)

Enchantment is such a light listened to. This light will shift into an equally powerful night that is held captive. The chiaroscuro of imagination is central to the operatic imagination. Finally, in discussing the Hofmannsthal/Strauss version of *Elektra*, Starobinski addresses the motif of animalness and saintliness in the seductress. She is a wild cat—spits, yells, casts poisonous looks and cannot stand anyone looking at her. And she sees animals about her—dogs, flies, vermin. This destructive rage is actually turned towards herself. But Hofmannsthal also deftly introduces Cassandra into Elektra and this amalgam makes love take a different shape in Agamemnon. Eventually, she prophetically senses that all her joys and ferocity will culminate in death: "So I die happier than I lived." She dances herself to death in the opera, submerged beneath the weight of happiness.

Enchantment always addresses itself to a plural, to an indeterminate 'you': *You who know what love is.* The romance is sung for it to travel to the ends of the earth. Each production that Starobinski tries to relate to seems to be produced by the vibrations of a sonorous body, a fundamental secret of the cosmos, from which follow the geometric proportions that regulate all the laws of nature, but set up in tangible time and space. To give in to enchantment is the very opposite of indulging in a "pharmacopeia of emotion" as Bernard Williams implies about composers who work in the Wagnerian vein (Williams, 2006). Traces of enchantment can only flicker. And disappear into eternity. This fundamental insight has been a lodestar in much of the recent aesthetic, literary and ethnomusicological takes on the operatic mode—for the issues of subjectivity, voice and desire, must recur as creaturely motifs in all scholarly reflections on the subject. The best of operas combine the lightness of a fairy tale with the solemnity of a religious service, through images, music and stage movements. Enchantment is unalloyed death: a willing captivity that evolves into liberation and light.

References

Adorno, Theodor W. 2004. *In Search of Wagner.* Translated by Rodney Livingstone. London: Verso.

Corse, Sandra. 2000. *Operatic Subjects: The Evolution of Self in Modern Opera.* Madison: Fairleigh Dickinson University Press; London: Associated University Press.

Da Ponte, Lorenzo. 2000. *Memoirs.* New York: New York Book Review.

Dammann, Guy. 2010. "Opera and the Limits of Philosophy: On Bernard Williams's Music Criticism." In *British Journal of Aesthetics.* Vol. 50.4, October: 469–479.

Hoffmann, E.T.A. 2004. *Musical Writings: Kreisleriana; the Poet and the Composer.* Translated by Marytn Clarke. Cambridge, UK: Cambridge University Press.

Homer. 1963. *The Odyssey of Homer.* Translated by Richard Lattimore. University of Chicago Press.

Hutcheon, Linda and Michael Hutcheon. 2000. *Bodily Charm: Living Opera.* Lincoln: University of Nebraska Press.

———. 2004. *Opera: The Art of Dying.* Cambridge: Harvard University Press.

Kerman, Joseph. 1955. *Opera as Drama.* Berkeley and London: University of California Press.

Kramer, Lawrence. 2004. *Opera and Modern Culture: Wagner and Strauss.* Berkeley: University of California Press.

Lindenberger, Herbert. 1984. *Opera: The Extravagant Art.* Ithaca: Cornell University Press.

———. 2010. *Situating Opera: Period, Genre, Reception.* Cambridge University Press.

Rousseau, Jean-Jacques. 2008. *Confessions.* Translated by Angela Scholar. Oxford and New York: Oxford University Press.

———. 1997. "Julie or the New Heloise." In *Collected Writings of Rousseau.* Translated by Philip Stewart and Jean Vache. Vol. 6. Hanover and London: Dartmouth College Press.

Starobinski, Jean. 2008. *Enchantment: The Seductress in Opera.* Translated by C. Jon Delogu. New York: Columbia University Press.

Treadwell, James. 2003. *Interpreting Wagner.* New Haven: Yale University Press.

Weisstein, Ulrich. 2006. *Selected Essays on Opera.* Amsterdam and New York: Rodopi.

Williams, Bernard. 2006. *On Opera.* New Haven, CT and London: Yale University Press.

Zizek, Slavoj and Mladen Dolar. 2002. *Opera's Second Death.* London: Routledge.

The Upright Creature

Expression, Wish-Landscape and the Riddle of Arrival in Ernst Bloch

In the final section of *Avicenna and the Aristotelian Left*, Ernst Bloch speculates on the question of 'labour of artistic design'. I say 'speculation' advisedly, for at its root, the word comes from *speculari,* to catch sight of/ look around/to keep a lookout. What does it mean to collectively look around us? Can we venture a leap—a real and a concrete one?

Art, Bloch feels, releases matter-form into existence. And matter is dispositional, and for that very reason, matter is also liberating. Here is Gotthold Ephraim Lessing, who recalls Avicenna and Aristotle, in suggesting that art must deal in plastic nature without the falling off of its inner disposition that time and material decay seem to make it unavoidable. While the resistant matter is of the material of 'what-is-considered-possible', the plastic matter-form, the sub-atomic differentials of matter, keeps wondering at its own image and eventually *conjectures into* 'what-may-become-possible'. Active matter actualizes its pleni-potentiality (*dynamei on*) in and through the medium and the conduit—which is the artist. Art, therefore, provides clarity to the already predisposed matter-form. Art is this drive towards completion and arrival. In Lessing's words, all art is *malleably impelled*. Bloch's term for predisposed matter is: form-pregnant-matter-Nature. In a different context but in a similar spirit, Bloch explores Marx's early dissertation on *The Difference between Democritean and Epicurean Philosophies of Nature*, especially the Epicurean "the doctrine of *a swerve in the fall of the atoms*, and the cosmogonic innovation therein" (Bloch, 2018). By exploring matter in the spirit of his own innovations, as instances of an *energizing principle*, Marx is able to oppose mechanism and fatalism. Form is the *fiery truth* of matter, as Avicenna and Marx understand the relationship, and Bloch iterates. Art realizes such forms in their *probability of arrival* in and through objective conditioning, not in any strict singularity of nature or through subjective pathos.

The Aristotelian Left

The question turns slightly textured when Bloch begins to draw a distinction between Schopenhauer and Hegel and their respective takes on art. Schopenhauer nurtures an intuitive belief in the artistic genius. For him, the genius, as it were, "understands nature's half-spoken words" (Bloch, 2019). Nature, with its latent form-in-matter can only stutter while the artist, by imprinting the form on marble, cloth or clay, gives clarity to nature's intentions. Once the art work is crafted, the artist turns to nature and enquires whether it had wished to express itself in such a form and manner? And the reply comes from the knowing connoisseur that indeed nature's intentions have been actualized in the new found form. Hegel, on the other hand, contrasts the animal from the human artist. He believes that the artistic transformation of nature is occasioned through conscious beings. He trusts the created artistic object itself. In such a view, the spirit and the inner soul of the art-form develop into art. We move from darkness to light. There is a direction and *telos* in Hegel that does not enthuse Schopenhauer. The force of the artistic artefact could be liberating as it could be perfecting.

In a 1968 interview to Michael Landmann, Bloch makes the following comment:

> Aesthetics should not be confused with contemplation or considered disinterested. Often, certainly, the true, the good, or the beautiful, or rather what is proclaimed as such, has nothing to do with daily life and so serves the purpose of deception, as an opiate of the people.... Stage and story can be either a protective park or a laboratory; sometimes they console or appease, sometimes they incite; they can be a flight from or a prefiguring of the future. (Bloch, 1988)

The sharply contrasted notions of protective park and the experimentation-driven, risk-taking laboratory is the distinction that only a revolutionary would make in order to define aesthetics. All flights happen as a distancing act from consolation or appeasement. All flights reveal form as art and thus anticipate futurity.

This bringing-forth of art is what Julius Scaliger would call *typical-real*, Bloch informs us. The artist as Prometheus is a humanist-romantic idea whereby art emerges via the active intervention of the artist.

For Bloch though, the artist is not a self-standing individual. He is someone who gives shape to "the indicated perfection of the norms and dimensions of matter-nature" (Bloch, 2019). Art ought not to depict or imitate, but develop further whatever is already immanent in matter. In this sense, all embellishment is artificial since art chisels whatever is already latent and created as an ideal. The matter-form concept, when transferred to art, then implies both *latency* and *tendency*.

In this context, one would recall Bloch's passionate debate with Georg Lukács on the efficacy and nature of modernist art practice, especially Expressionism. Lukács would uncharitably describe Expressionist art practice as "forlorn perplexity of the petty-bourgeois" (Bloch et al., 1977). Bloch, on the other hand, attests to the "the revolutionary element their cries contained, even if that was undisciplined and uncontrolled and dissipated a considerable amount of the classical heritage" (Bloch et al., 1977). Modernism could not be abandoned as the byproduct of decay under capitalism, lock stock and barrel. That would be a mechanical and an undialectical evaluation of the relationship between latent matter-form and its emergence.

Can authentic reality be also discontinuity, as opposed to the coherency and totality of Lukács' objectivist concept? This is the crucial question that engages Bloch as he begins to reflect upon the Expressionist impulse. Demolition may not always mean decadence. It could prove to be a shock therapy, deployed to break out of our reified conditions. Art could be an intimate estranging mechanism rather. Therefore, one must delve into the question: what might be the dialectical links between growth and decay? Bloch feels that Expressionism considers the genuine fissures within the behavioural level of interrelations. It tries to methodically discover the new from within the crevices of such fissures. Bloch specifically highlights the romantic disruptive elements in Expressionist art. Such art converts the baroque, the impulses of storm and stress and forms of primitivism into stark and elongated artefacts. The mentally sick, the ordinary, the folk, the prisoners are the staples of such art: plebs and neglected souls all. Bloch welcomes the 'organic-psychic' style of such art, which he feels, sharply hits the aristocratic ethos at its root. In Expressionist tapestries and 'linear ornamentation' one detects a Nordic style but without the beastly features that is often branded to castigate its politics.

Bloch clearly discerns the dynamism within such art forms. This he calls the *temperament of art*. Art-works with no temperament, by contrast, are those that are distilled and abstracted. Such cold formalism ought to be the foremost antagonist of all transformative art-practice. In fact, chaos and crudeness bring Expressionism closer to the people and hence, closer to creaturely dynamism. It has little to do with mindless decadence. The artistic equivalent of natural law seems vapid to Bloch; an approach that takes art away from the 'typical-real'. Besides, genuine Expressionist art is also the obverse of garishness, the latter arising out of the display cabinets of bourgeois kitschy existence.

Lukács' line of argumentation, Bloch feels, is riddled with two kinds of omissions: "the observer possesses neither the intuitive grasp typical of people, undeformed by education, nor the open-mindedness which is indispensable for the appreciation of any new art" (Bloch et al., 1977). This essentially means Lukács was in a no man's land—neither organically connected to the people nor able to accept genuinely new and transformative modes of expression, which has the ability to convert matter-form to expressed form. In fact, Bloch has never hid his differences with Lukács on these very grounds. This is what he has to say to Michael Lowy in an interview in March 1974, in *New German Critique*:

> As you remember, in *The Soul and the Forms*, he (Lukács) compared Paul Ernst to Sophocles. How was that possible? It was his neo-classicism. And, you see, this neo-classicism of the young Lukács (which I didn't go along with) was later called 'orthodox Marxism'—also composed only of order, straight lines, the adoration of Greek beauty, and Stalin's kitsch constructions in Moscow, etc. There's a transition here, a point of contact between the two, in the bias of his passion for order-which also manifests itself in the way he uses Nikolai Hartmann because he is so classical, so orderly. Later, during the 1930s, these differences of opinion between us developed further in our discussion on expressionism. You're familiar with this debate, I imagine? (Bloch et al., 1973)

For Lukács, art is the reflection of social reality, which in turn, arises out of human consciousness. Political art and aesthetic autonomy would thus productively collide in his world. He castigates Expressionism *tout court*: "What then of the Expressionists? They were Ideologues. They stood between leaders and masses. For the most part, their convictions were sincerely held, though they were also mostly very immature and confused. They were deeply affected by the same uncertainties to which the immature revolutionary masses were also subject" (Bloch et al., 1977). Chaos of reality as actually expressed does not impress Lukács. Since emergence of consciousness is social rather than natural for Lukács, art must be wary of nature-as-such. To reveal nature-as-such is merely expressing decomposition and not the essences of things for Lukács. It is another matter than Bloch never professes revealing nature as such through art.

Through an interesting detour, Cat Moir recounts the relative differences between the two thinkers that pertain to the very process of transformation in art (Moir, 2019, pp. 85–87). The subject is landscape painting and Lukács thinks a 'pernicious chasm' gets opened up between the subject and object in undertaking such an exercise. With industrialization, the idea of landscape becomes methodized as humans stand outside of nature and begin to fetishize it by romanticizing terrain in this manner. Consequently, landscape painting at the same time hides and highlights human alienation in postindustrial societies. Modern bourgeois imagination and consciousness is trapped in such abstract necessities. We lose the sensuality of the species-being that Marx so valued. Going through this loss of self-consciousness and creating a pure universality in its own essence was a new form of consciousness to Hegel. This reflectivity takes us to modernity, a higher form of consciousness. Lukács turns this on its head and feels the reflectivity is deeply alienating. Within art practice, indulging in landscape painting is a perfect instance that depicts the chasm which alienates man from his historical-social consciousness. For Bloch however, man's interest in landscaping and landscape art reveals the obverse: his alienation from matter-form. The dead artwork is a testimony that man stands outside of nature. Human consciousness is thus detached from the possibility of engaging with and in the dynamism of form that ought to unite all art with a transformative consciousness. Bloch takes such a turn, since he does not wish to keep the non-human world of enchanted matter to be used by mechanical philosophers crudely. And more importantly for Bloch, conscious life is as much natural as it is social. It cannot be deduced from a mechanistic perspective. Nature to him ought not to be mechanized, nor spiritualized, but seen as a dynamic, ever transforming principle. The poverty of landscape imagination misses the self-moving and self-altering power of matter and makes nature static.

From such a perspective, the question of Expressionism is directly connected to a form of messianic redemption: it pertains to the seeking of the 'the form of the inconstruable question', to which only art can provide some answers with. Here is Zipes:

> Life is going on all around us and does not know where it is going. We ourselves are still the lever and motor. The external and especially the revealed sense of life is faltering. But the new ideas have finally broken out, into the full adventures, into the open, unfinished, dreaming world, into Satan's rubbles and darknesses, providing the cutting off itself. Life also goes around girded with despair, with our spiteful presentiment, with the tremendous power of our human voice, to name God and not to rest until the innermost shadows are expelled, until the world is doused with that fire that is behind the world or shall be ignited by it. (Zipes, 'Introduction', *The Utopian Function of Art and Literature,* 1988)

Satan's bargains and methods must be invoked, so that we can get rid of all torpor and inertia. Such methods provide the 'cutting off' from our static and inert selves. Expressionism is such a technique of moulding and purification; deployed eventually to take us into the *socialist open.* Art performs an alchemical job so that our innermost shadows are expelled. But can pain be doused and stupefaction transformed through art's cleansing fire?

Viceroy of an Articulate Utterance

What has not happened shall transform everything once that happens. This idea of transforming matter-events is central to Bloch's invocations to music as well. Music is the ideal ground to test the notion of *Vor-Schein,* or anticipatory illumination. Almost half of *The Spirit of Utopia* is an elaboration and exploration on music. Bloch essentially takes up Expressionism again by converting its fascistic possibilities into forms of left-utopianism or into what he has elsewhere designated as the Aristotelian/Avicennaean left. He does this primarily by means of critiquing modern forms of reified existence. He also hopes for unanticipated positions of arrival. Music operates at the threshold of corporeality. It deals in time rather than in space. The expressive nature of music is simultaneously primal and prophetic. It could take creatures more clearly towards freedom from the domain of necessity but without negating the necessity of latent matter-form in the first place:

> Musical expression … is the viceroy for an articulate utterance which goes much further than is currently understood…. Should visionary hearing of that kind be attained … then all music we already know will later sound and give forth other expressive contents besides those it has had so far, then the musical expression perceived up to now could seem like a child's stammering toy by comparison…. Nobody has yet heard Mozart, Beethoven or Bach as they are really calling … this will happen only much later. (Bloch, 1984)

What is child's stammering and is only partially revealed shall in some future moment find full and grand expression. Such an expression can only be hoped for. But the expression that is about to arrive is already inhered within 'Mozart, Beethoven or Bach as they are really calling.' The calling, the real calling in music, as it were, lies boxed within matter-form. Prefigured, it awaits liberation. None has, as of now, truly heard such material and transformative music. For that to happen, the listener too has to prepare herself, for that would be a visionary hearing. This particular essay, *The Exceeding of Limits*, from which the above lines are taken, argues for a music to come that is *sui generis*. Bloch insists that music cannot be the 'mere illustration of literary imaginative devices'. Music itself is the expression: "That is to say, the sum total of its meaning, signification and representation and of that which it represents so mistily and yet, in both senses of the word, so grippingly" (Bloch, 1984). It is remarkable to see how Bloch juxtaposes the two attributes of reception, that of listening—'mistily' and 'grippingly.' The music to arrive shall hold you in its full materiality and yet such an arrival will not be complete. Music is its own *poiesis*.

It is fitting to recount Moir's observation about a tale that Novalis had narrated:

> Novalis' fragmentary novel *Heinrich von Ofterdingen* tells the story of a medieval Minnesänger seeking absolute knowledge in the form of a mystical union with divine nature. In the second half of the book, the pilgrim meets a mysterious girl who responds to his questions with cryptic answers, and leads him away from his path. When he asks, 'Where are we going?', she simply replies 'Always homeward [*Immer nach Hause*],' the word 'always' expressing the ultimate impossibility of reaching the intended destination. (Moir, 2019)

But the generative tension in Bloch, his acute attention to the utterances of Schelling and Novalis is constantly counterbalanced by Hegelian impulses of sense and perfectibility. So, in the same essay he writes: "In the last analysis, then, musical expression as a whole *is the viceroy for an articulate utterance which goes much farther than is currently understood*" (Bloch, 1984). The grand phrase 'viceroy of an articulate utterance' shows that articulation is still a hope, and musical representation of the absolute is possible. It can go much further than the current state of being shackled by an inner ear-muff.

By contrast, the hour of eloquence is revelatory and yet deeply material in nature. "What Isolde hears as a fountain, in the nocturnal silence, still sounds like a fanfare of horns to Brangáne" (Bloch, 1984). Visionary listening shall transform such false hiatus that now develops between the artist, the art and the receptor. The key element in music is its lyrical nature, stemming from within matter-form. This is the utopian art of music: "sung word to both its undertone and overtones" (Bloch, 1984). The music to arrive shall be transformative since we shall be fully aware of its halftones and atones alike, its silences and excesses. This he calls music's 'rhythmic melodic summons'. The summons of tonality to Bloch is a material concern, spread across the universe. Bloch's attention and belief in the material cognition of art is paramount, an attribute forever cloaked in the abstract tones and appearances in the capitalist society.

But there is even a greater element in music, something that can only perhaps be rivalled by lyric poetry: "But music is also subjective in a significantly different sense, in that its *expression* not only mirrors the *affective looking-glass* reflecting *a given society and the world as it occurs* in *affective correlates*. Music also comes close to the subject-based *hearth and driving force* of events, as a subject-based exterior" (Bloch, 1984).

Bloch was particularly insistent on the indeterminacy of the receptor as well as that of musical expression, experienced during the moments of musical encounter. There is a peculiar ferment in music, where the relationship between the musical expression and the listener has not yet taken shape in any objectively stated form. It is a mutating condition. The objective indeterminacy of the musical ambience is what makes it deeply material in its potentiality. It can provide a truly transformative direction to the creaturely predicament. Therefore he goes on to say that "Accordingly it is the art of pre-semblance [*des Vor-Scheins*] which is related to the flowing existential core (instant) of that-which-is-in-beíng most intensively, and to the horizon of the latter most expansively. *Cantus essentiam fontis vocat*—music names the essence of the fountainhead" (Bloch 1984).

His emphasis on expression in art is of paramount significance—both in music and in other forms of art like painting. And expression is never mirroring. This is where he fundamentally differs from Lukács. Subjectivity is not bourgeois interiority to Bloch, nor is it any transcendental turn away from matter-form. The emphasis on organicity is evident as he refers to *hearth*—a place where things marinate, slow-cook and then erupt as eloquence. That is music's revolutionary potential. This state of ferment is essential for art to emerge. The hearth is the subjective materialization of such artistic events to arrive. The hearth bypasses 'dissonance' and 'cadence'—relatively new and artificial ways of defining music in the civilized world, ways which merely produce "strict, immobile rows" (Bloch 1984). The 'pre-semblance' is the form that inheres and ferments musicality. Music has the ability to name all that we feel manifestly—both vertically as intensive flow and horizontally as its vastness and expanse. These twin dimensions shall *grab* the yet-to-arrive listener simultaneously.

Bloch rejects the debate between form and emotion, between naivety and sentimentality, in musicality. On one side is the music of pure mood, unformed and spectral. On the other: mastery in combination and calm skill in achieving equanimity. The first one romantic, unrepresentable—what he calls "shapeless rushing or a warm bank of mist" (Bloch 1984); the other: classical formalist, one that follows almost a mathematical and astronomical logic in its progression. He finds the debate academic, though his vote surely goes towards expression rather than form. Here is a fundamental tension between his idealist impulses and his left Aristotelian groundedness. That is the reason he was also worried with Lukács' investment in classical and sedentary forms of art. The issue with Keplerian formal scientificity, when transposed to painting and music, is the following: "The problem raised is not only *melos* without expression but deriving *from the self-sufficient canon's ideal and image of perfection—melos* without an 'I', music dictated by rules" (Bloch 1984). Such an approach to art testifies the reproduction of cosmic fixity. Imperfection and daring, on the other hand, comprise the essence of all transformative art. Music is the very existence in this latter case, not a matter of reification through theory and the rules of the harmonic-contrapuntal. Matter-of-factness can never be self-transcending. The revolutionary-romantic elements in Bloch come to the fore time and again as he reflects on art practice. All kinds of aural form-fetishes are therefore the very obverse of actualizing matter-form in art.

Indeed, as a Marxist, Bloch castigates music that celebrates mere animality or indistinctiveness. And yet music re-deifies all social barricades and hollow distractions of the capitalist universe. And it harks to the future in its *manifold pastorale*:

> Hence even when, precisely when, music constitutes a reveling in the rules of composition, it is transmitting the prophetic language of that which fills the human and man-related bosom of all existence and which, in consequence, belongs extensively to the *iñsistent disquiet and dawning possibility which are lodged in reality*. (Bloch, 1984)

The dawning possibilities are real and the prophetic language of music feels the throbbing human, and not the beautiful beast of the fascistic imagination. If there is any harmony of forms, that must first be broken in order to reconstitute it for an arriving futurity. All disintegration is a preparation for some eventual utopian artistic revelation "becoming the *source-sound of self-shapings still unachieved in the world*" (Bloch, 1984).

In this context, Gary Zabel recounts that reworking of the Pan-Syrinx legend of Ovid in *The Spirit of Utopia*:

> In the story, Pan is chasing a group of nymphs, and ambushes one of them, Syrinx the dryad. She flees from his erotic advances, but her escape is cut off by the river. In response, she implores her sisters

> the waves to alter her appearance, and when the god attempts to seize her, he finds him-self with only a reed in his hands. While Pan is lamenting the loss of his beloved, the wind produces notes in the reed-bank. Gripped by the beauty of the melody, he binds together several reeds of varying lengths with wax and plays them by blowing into them. Pan's invention allows him the consolation of union with the nymph, who is missing and yet remains present in the sound of the flute. For Bloch, the virtue of Ovid's story is that it explains both the need for music in the experience of lack, and the origin of music as a well-ordered series of notes, a genuinely expressive medium. It shows the way in which the subjective and utopian dimensions of music are intimately connected. The power that allows subjectivity to articulate its innermost depths is also the vehicle of a utopian refusal of deprivation. (Zabel, 1990)

It is in this manner that the source sound is matter-form and the shapings are the release of those forms into a still unarrived destination and event. Bloch would sometimes call this process: *revolutionary-gnosis.*

Wish Landscapes and Promised Lands

Jack Zipes tells us that in his early days, Bloch's "home was characterized by what he called 'mush', dreariness, and lack of love, understanding, and stimulation. He filled the void as he could with daydreams, voracious reading, music, theater, letter-writing to eminent philosophers, rebellion against traditional schooling, and concern for social democratic politics" (Bloch, 1988). Bourgeois space and time creates and fosters emptiness. Home (*heimat*) is this filling of the void with an infinite and revitalized aesthetics and practising of an *upright gait.* This state of filling can be achieved only by generating a certain *staunen*—startlement and wonder—in oneself as well as among one's interlocutors and readers. Passing through the state of wonderment, one could arrive at some kind of self-authentication.

The surplus of art (what he called *Uberschuss* or overshot), which it would release in an anticipated future, makes Bloch pursue its many dimensions. Surplus can only be imagined by an artist when he realizes what we are missing in life and living. Art is thus, also a process of self-discovery. For this self-discovery to happen, Bloch begins to define sublimity in an ingenious fashion in his seminal theoretical essay on art: *The Wish-Landscape Perspective in Aesthetics, The Order of Art Materials According to the Dimension of Their Profundity and Hope.* Sublimity in old aesthetics is all about deriving impartial pleasure and terror/dread. But the element of dread can be converted dialectically into an uplifting state away from religious and spiritual terror. That would mean tapping the material profundity of sublimity itself. Bloch invokes Goethe to tell that trembling (*Schaudern*) is the best part of humankind. Sublimity leaves a mark as an objective condition as well as "the presentiment of our future freedom" (Bloch, 1988). The revealing of the subjective in objective conditions means that abstract appearance of art is untenable. Therefore, Goethe distinguished such intervention among the objects that produced a poetic effect. He never emphasized any of the closed abstract illusions. Rather, he focused on those that were representative or symbolical insofar as they converged upon a *material profundity that they held in common,* just so long as this profundity with its unity and comprehensiveness (*Allheit*) in the poetical effect defines itself and makes a demand upon itself (Bloch, 1988).

Goethe's observation is in keeping with the Blochian formulation of anticipatory illumination: "a real possible wish-fulfillment landscape; this landscape lies in the windows of art" (Bloch, 1988). All genuine art holds up a possibility of such an immanent anticipation in an 'activating way'.

In this context, one recalls Bloch's fondness for the term *colportage.* Colportage refers "to the cheap materials sold by the colporteur or traveling bookseller of the seventeenth through nineteenth centuries. The colporteur carried bibles, chapbooks, cookbooks, primers, medical books, calendars, manuals, prayerbooks, romances, fairy tales, and adventure books" (Bloch, 1988). By the end of 19th century, the colporteur turned into the dream merchant, fulfilling the wishes of the lower classes which sought freedom in the fantasy world of such fares. Such books shattered the routine drabness of the lower classes by providing them with imagination and an alternative realm to operate. Colportage gave direction to daydreaming and distraction. As a utopian

Marxist, the point for Bloch was to recreate such alternative ways of engaging with such cultural artefacts by shunning inertia, sadism and militaristic and marketing ideologies that such wares might also foster among common people.

Bloch's abiding interest in fairy tales must be placed within this larger context of wish-landscape—tremulous, dreadful and liberating. On the one hand, we have petty bourgeois dreams: "The lightning of gold radiates upon them in a fairy-tale-like way. The sun shines upon them from commanding heights. The name of the fairy-tale world is publicity (even if it is only for a day). The fairy-tale princess is Greta Garbo" (Bloch, 1988). But once divested off this bourgeois apparel, great fairy tales of longing can be modernized. And if done in the right spirit, such transformed works would contain the eternal within their belly. He cites Cocteau's and Molnar's plays and films as new fairy tales that carry with them the matter-form of dream and disillusionment alike: "scenes in which the lover seeks to appear as a triumphant general, as brilliant diplomat, as famous artist, or also just as a humble servant who is gradually humiliated because of his broken heart and obliged to carry out the commands of his mistress" (Bloch, 1988). He finds similar impulses in Jules Verne's imaginative universe. These are not *mere fairy tales* anymore but eternal forms in magical incarnations. One day the eternally new shall become the technological-magical utopia. This Bloch writes in 1930. Almost 30 years later, in 1959, in an essay titled *Better Castles in the Sky at the Country Fair and Circus, in Fairy Tales and Colportage*, Bloch further elaborates the point as he gives a radical futuristic definition of the fundamental hailing addressing mechanism of the fairy tale: "Once upon a time: this means in fairy-tale manner not only the past but a more colorful or easier somewhere else" (Bloch, 1988). Little heroes and poor people win in such times and tales. And the hero is courageous and cunning: the lion and the fox fuse together. Essentially, Bloch gives fairy tales a leftward turn:

> as Lenin says, always the existing revolutionary elements that tie the given strings of the story together here. While the peasantry was still bound by serfdom, the poor protagonist of the fairy tale conquered the daughter of the king. While educated Christians trembled in fear of witches and devils, the soldier of the fairy tale deceived witches and

> devils from beginning to end—it is only the fairy tale that highlights the 'dumb devil'. The golden age is sought and mirrored, and from there one can see far into paradise. (Bloch, 1988)

What nature refuses to grant the real world, the fairy tale does allow: play, magic and wish fulfilment in the temporal space of 'once upon a time'. Sometimes, such tales take us away from wish fulfilment though, when imagination does not match the power of action, as in the tale of Don Quixote. Some tales also end up in hunger and fatigue. Some tales are even comical. For all its magical and despairing possibilities we can say: *real like in fairy tales.*

The simple and uncorrupted identify with the side shows of the fair and the magic of the circus. The magic of such locales are foreign and yet ordinary. Nature is dealt out in such an extravagant way that it turns hopeful: "And, in addition to the abnormal faraway realm, the fairy-tale realm reappears continually and also that of the horror story: the oriental labyrinth, the jaws of hell, the haunted castle. That is the fair, a colorful, peasant fantasy" (Bloch, 1988). The circus is an open place for mirth and joy to mingle. Magicians and stable-masters, gypsies and trapeze artists work in this open space with two dialectically intertwined possibilities: 'eccentricities and precise ease.' Everything is contrived here and yet the impeding expressionist horror in such places is palpable and real. Levity and seriousness collide in the fairground and in the circus: "Such a style can be traced up through surrealism, and it is connected to the ambivalent, two-headed completely allegorical genre" (Bloch, 1988).

All these take us to the neglected world of the colportage, where crude, forgotten creatures laugh and joke, die and resurrect once again. And finally, there is material hope beyond the neglect: "The dream of colportage is: never again to be trapped by the routine of daily life. And at the end there is: happiness, love, victory" (Bloch, 1988). It is a dream, but a real one, precisely because such fantasies and spaces are a distraction, a liberating release of matter-form in our mundane world. It is in this context that Bloch makes the comment about the necessity to daydream in his short but powerful work, *On Karl Marx*:

> A daydream about a perfect life that is objectively mediated, and therefore can be retained, thereby overcomes its predisposition to be duped as well as any tendency to dreamlessness itself. The latter,

> which is associated with standing still or with a realism which only appears to be such, even in a state of resignation, is actually the ruling state of mind of many thinking though unperceptive people without perspectives. (Bloch, 2018)

Eyes are averted in the condition of dreamlessness and there is fear, not hope. The risk is that the condition of dreamlessness can be turned into destiny, an inward *eschaton*. Bloch is almost suggesting that dynamic and objective idealism is better than drab and static realism.

The whole Blochian universe is kind of a giant detective expedition; with clues and escapades, 'knitting and knotting', metamorphoses, hiding and rescuing—darkness and intrigue everywhere, but finally a hopeful and revolutionary resolution, once the masks drop off. The threefold stage in a detective novel is guessing, unmasking and discovering. For this process to complete, we return once again to the notion of speculation—looking about and around us. It is exactly the intersection that constitutes the artistic side of the speculative terrain—the triangular relationship among expressionism, colportage/wish-landscape and real utopia—that Bloch unfurls in his essay titled *A Philosophical View of the Detective Novel*, originally written in 1965. The detective novel is an extension of the baroque to begin with, the suspense derived from the uncanny and the distorted. The uncanny starts with a pre-narrative, even before the storyline unfolds: a crime precedes the beginning—which Bloch calls 'the dim focal point' of all colportage wares, in a manner of speaking: "The problem of the omitted beginning affects the entire detective genre, gives it its form: the form of a picture puzzle, the hidden part of which predates the picture and only gradually enters into it" (Bloch, 1988). Suspense, act of discovery, evidence gathering, micrological issues and digressions follow. The central factor pertains to an inauthentic atmosphere and a general mistrust in human affairs. But the discovery happens about something that has occurred *ante rem*.

This darkness which hovers around—the pre-given matter-form of the uncanny works as the Expressionist form in certain eternal works of art—like the Oedipus narrative—"the unknowing murderer of his father, unknowing husband of his mother. One recalls the resulting plague inflicted upon Thebes and the interpretation of the misdeed after it occurred by the Oracle at Delphi" (Bloch, 1988). But for Bloch, following Hegel, "the landscape of hope, even in the image of horror, is much more the aesthetic omega" (Bloch, 1988). The truth unfolds as particular dimensions of the universal is brought about through a process of detection. Hegel calls such a state—eternity in mortality. We detect the matter-form in new guise, an attribute that was always present, prior to when the uncanny narrative unfolded in front of our eyes. The detective theme begins to relate the wondrous, the dark and the ordinary and transfers these into the future. All great art is, therefore, revolutionary to the extent that each follows through the repercussions of our expressive decisions in living. Speculation about matter-form is such a process of detective uncovering. But this primordial event, the monstrous crime, must be renewed in newness and passed through the revolutionary fervour.

All self-revelation is this play between law and the eruptions of lawlessness that lurk at the foundations of our interactions. Art gives shape to this ancient battle, in ever new ways. Could this search and transformation also lead to healing and cathartic realizations for the creature? Will that be the real breakthrough, liberation of form from within matter iterated as renewal? Who can tell! But it is instructive to note that in the final instant, Bloch discovers his revolutionary hero in Prometheus rather than in Oedipus. The Promethean form is able to confront contingency, what Bloch calls "hazard or objective non-warrantablity" (Bloch, 2018). This form is at once luminously alienated and militant—in Prometheus, man depicts his *upright carriage,* Bloch's favourite expression gleaned from Marx. Able to mediate hope, the form lies at the cusp of yearning and fulfilment, latency and tendency. This Promethean form is for the same reason also the thing of the future, that of anticipatory illumination: for "non-warrantablity … *sets hope squarely at the front*" (Bloch, 2018). In his *novum* of a dialectical utopian materialism—terror, daydreaming and hope reside side by side. Here gestates the riddle for art's arrival.

References

Bloch, Ernst. 1968/2018. *On Karl Marx.* Translated by John Maxwell. New York: Penguin Random House.

Bloch, Ernst. 1988. *The Utopian Function of Art and Literature*. Translated by Jack Zipes and Frank Mecklenburg. Cambridge, MA and London: The MIT Press.

———. 1984. *Essays on the Philosophy of Music*. Translated by Peter Palmer. Cambridge and New York: Cambridge University Press.

———. 1963/2019. *Avicenna and the Aristotelian Left*. Translated by Loren Goldman and Peter Thompson. New York: Columbia University Press.

Bloch, Ernst, Georg Lukács, Berolt Brecht and Walter Benjamin, Theodore Adorno. 1977. *Aesthetics and Politics*. London: Verso.

Bloch, Ernst, Michael Lowy and Vicki Williams Hill. 1973. "Interview with Ernst Bloch." In *New German Critique*. No. 9, Autumn: 35–45.

Boldyrev, Ivan. 2014. *Ernst Bloch and His Contemporaries: Locating Utopian Messianism*. London: Bloomsbury.

Landmann, Michael. 1975. "Talking with Ernst Bloch: Korcula, 1968." In *Telos, Critical Theory of the Contemporary*. No. 25: 165–185.

Lilienfeld, Robert. 1987. "Music and Society in the 20th Century: Georg Lukács, Ernst Bloch, and Theodor Adorno." In *International Journal of Politics, Culture, and Society*. Vol. 1: 120–146.

Moir, Cat. 2019. *Ernst Bloch's Speculative Materialism*. Leiden and London: Brill.

———. 2020. "The Archimedean Point: Consciousness, Praxis, and the Present in Lukács and Bloch." *Thesis Eleven*. Vol. 157.1, April: 3–23.

Zabel, Gary. 1990. "Ernst Bloch and the Utopian Dimension in Music." In *The Musical Times*. Vol. 131.1764, February: 82–84.

BOOK IV

Decreature

Affliction and Attention in Simone Weil

An Honest Letter

An exceptional testament about the nature of violence in times of civil war appears in the form of a letter: the one sent by Simone Weil to the novelist Georges Bernanos around 1938, being moved by his novel, *A Diary of My Times.* In his work, Bernanos, a devoted monarchist and a visionary, candidly describes the ferocity and casualness of violence on the part of the nationalists and church dignitaries as it unfolds at Majorca during the Spanish Civil War. Weil had participated in the war on the Republican side. In her first encounter of the Civil War in 1936, nearsighted as she was, Weil stepped in a pot of boiling oil and completely burnt her lower left leg and instep. She found enough courage to return to combat. Should there be any confusion about the sides the two chose, she tells Bernanos early on in the letter that her native inclination has always been to side with the 'despised strata of social hierarchy'. This was the left radical Simone Weil, who in her many teaching assignments and the gruelling factory work among unskilled female labourers in the early 1930s realized and conveyed to everyone that 'the organization of labour is the deepest root of oppression'—something that produced humiliation, which in turn, produced fatigue. But that confession of being with the oppressed strata is qualified immediately in the letter by a simple yet momentous addition: that the same associations were of a nature that proved instrumental in 'discouraging all sympathies' for her.

What had happened that had led to such a fundamental perceptual hardening in a person who is exceptionally dedicated and driven in her acts, politics and thoughts? What did dehumanization look like at the front? The letter is actually a dialogue and an inner battle with her selfhood and its alterations as it passes through such extraordinary violent times. Writing the letter to her ideological antagonist, who is equally alive to little acts of fiendish bestiality and its effects during extraordinary violent times seemed an obligation to Weil. It was a levelling with what actually happens behind the lines during violent outbursts that takes humans to the brink of the purgatorial state of nature. In such circumstances, what does it mean to participate emotionally in a war, and at what price such first-hand knowledge?

In the letter we come to witness, Weil is addressing a fundamental truth about nodes of intensity among the combatants: that grandeur and vice sometimes find a simultaneous natural outlet, so that all idealistic, righteous ventures are always sieved and purified at a point through the realist-determinist lens. But when the volunteer who joins the battle of resisting and fighting fascistic forces comes to square up with the realities of actual warfare, she often begins to weigh in the returns of her idealist immersion in the first place. On the one hand, the realist lens refracts back to sacrificial ideals as she ruminates upon the large catholicity of the anarchists. They did allow everyone to join their ranks. But what happens when idealists begin to waste themselves in a rut that begins to take a life of its own? Were the genuine radicals outnumbered by those who were impelled to political action by baser forms of violence? On the other hand, it is evident to those who live such a bloody war that love, an ambiance of brotherhood and, the demand for dignity among the humiliated are more than recompensed by a mix of immorality, cynicism and cruelty among those who profess equity and human dignity. In Bernanos, Weil found a kindred soul, who breathed the same odour of blood and terror as her, albeit the two nurtured diametrically opposite views about the political temperament of their times.

In the rambling, confessional middle of the letter, Weil recounts several tales, which depict the unleashing of actual anarchist terror, which is always offhand and banal: her almost witnessing the execution of a priest, a boy killed and his father instantly going mad, and a young prisoner given 24 hours to join the anarchist camp and having refused that option, shot dead in cold blood when he refuses. In a different instance, the radicals, having discovered some haggard souls in the caves, shoot them to death lest they join the fascists. The reasoning for the mass murder is the key point: since the poor souls had not joined them and awaited the fascists, they were considered to be fascists themselves. It is not possible to hold on to any middle ground to those caught in the crossfire of civil war. And there are always justifications for such brutality: as some others were spared, the anarchists considered their acts as humane and just.

The final story concerns the manner in which an anarchist leader narrated the following incident to Weil: two priests were apprehended by the anarchists. Having shot one, the other was asked to leave. At 20 paces, he was shot down too. Weil concludes the tale by pointing out the surprise on the face of the leader when he noticed that she was not laughing at his retelling of the incident. Such punitive and murderous expeditions were rife in Barcelona at that time. But the vital point is not about the number of people murdered. It has more to do with the attitude of those who committed those crimes in the name of transformation and equity. Weil emphasizes that she never saw among the intellectuals any remorse or disgust for the pointless killings. Rather, the obverse was more forthcoming: 'a brotherly smile' whenever the killing of the priests/fascists was recounted to others. Civil war converts human beings to automatons. Fear is offset by a strange kind of courage among the partisans which inure them to all human loss and tragedy. After a point, you go with the tides and perform the motions. Shall we call this courage? Perhaps, every act of courage has an underside. Perhaps there is no use in giving names to such doings.

It was there. It is here.

At this juncture in the letter, Weil comes up with an extraordinary insight about our creaturely predicament:

> I acquired the feeling that, whenever the temporal and spiritual authorities have placed a category of human beings outside of those whose life has a value, there is nothing more natural to a man than to kill. When one knows it is possible to kill without risking either punishment or blame, one kills; or at least one surrounds those who kill with encouraging smiles. If perchance one feels a little disgust, one keeps quiet about it, and before long one extinguishes it, for fear of seeming to lack manliness. One is swept up. (Bernanos, 1971)

The attestation that the tendency of being 'swept up', is an instinctive human condition is not idle speculation on Weil's part. She has already given actual evidence of casual lynching perpetrated by a group of which she was a part. More importantly, she dwells upon the curious connection between valueless drifting and bizarre workings of the restive, crooked human mind. Indeed, she has given us ample grounds to ponder as to why a group of renegades and exiled people are likely to flee from all rationalizations of human behaviour—may those well be modes of communicative reason or appeals to higher values of human interaction and respect for forms of life. Perfectly normal people kill and maim with a brotherly smile. Others encourage such acts by being fellow travellers or by remaining passive and silent, so as to not disturb the settled codes of group dynamics. There is yet a third group, vile and canny, the members of which "bathed in this atmosphere soaking in blood with visible pleasure." Weil reserves her greatest revulsion for such a category of opportunists. In the letter, Weil calls such turns as intoxication, impossible to resist without some exceptional strength of soul, which she was yet to encounter in the battlefront. Henceforth, one coordinate of Weil's philosophy would be to seek and define the nature of such an exceptional strength of soul in the face of spiralling downward force—what she calls *gravity*.

She concludes the letter by affirming that such an ambiance immediately negates the very goal of struggle. There is a twofold disjunction among those who are apparently on the same side—one that develops between the revolutionary intellectuals and the militia and the second between the militia and the common people. As Weil puts it—"an abyss separated the armed men from the unarmed population," like the one that separates the rich from the poor. The first group is nonchalant and condescending while the second is submissive and panicky. This temporal condition, where creatures and classes would be at once separated and connected, is what Weil would call *metaxu*, a term borrowed from the Platonic vocabulary. What kind of equity and transformation are we talking about with such an inbuilt wall that distributes and redistributes power among those who are supposed to fight a common war? Who acts the saviour and under what people's mandate? And there is no question of any regard for the enemy. The whole tenor and thrust of the letter come from a realization that the ideals of sacrifice that drive the volunteers to join a radical Republican movement in the first place, turns eventually into partaking of a cruel and casual war of the mercenaries. And it is in this bedrock realization: war is the repugnant business of humiliating one's enemy—that Weil finds herself infinitely close to Bernanos, her ideological foe, instead of her fellow militiamen of Aragon. It was the innermost camaraderie of two souls who have experienced wanton brutality of the basest order and the 'elastic reciprocity' of violence that impelled Weil to pen the letter.

No Comforting Fiction

In a crucial section in *Gravity and Grace*, Weil delves into the root cause of war as well as the delusion that follows:

> there is in every man and in every group of men a feeling that they have a just and legitimate claim to be masters of the universe—to possess it. But this possession is not rightly understood because they do not know that each one has access to it (in so far as this is possible for man on this earth) through his own body. Alexander is to a peasant proprietor what Don Juan is to a happily married husband. (Weil, 1999)

Possession is a richly created *trompe l'oeil*. For war, like eros, is an ever-receding pursuit. It is impossible to be the master of the universe for the simple reason that all possession is partial and piecemeal, relative to the creatures. Every being possesses a part of the earth by means of its very embodiment. Our views are also partial. To Alexander, possession means owning and maintaining large swathes of several continents, whereas for the peasant his holdings are his lifeline—all that is worth possessing. The very idea of possession accrues differently from differing vantage points.

In a couple of years' time, in the December 1940–January 1941 issue of the monthly *Cahiers du Sud*. Weil published her long, magisterial essay—*The Iliad, or the Poem of Force*. She took an acrostic pseudonym—Emile Navis to write the piece. The celebrated opening lines are worth quoting one more time:

> The true hero, the true subject, the center of the Iliad is force. Force employed by man, force that enslaves man, force before which man's flesh shrinks away. In this work, at all times, the human spirit is shown as modified by its relations with force, as swept away, blinded, by the very force it imagined it could handle, as deformed by the weight of the force it submits to. (Weil, 1956)

Only those acute souls who realize the intensity and might of force shall appreciate the power of that 'purest and the loveliest of mirrors,' which is the *Iliad*. One of the running threads in the essay concerns the truth that the pitilessness of force shrouds the perpetrator and the sufferer alike. To the perpetrator, force is an intoxicating weapon; to the victim—a crushing, blind machine. But neither possesses it truly. In the *Iliad,* almost everyone has to encounter the blinding power of force at one time or another. Nor is any hero—Achilles, Ajax or Hector, spared from confronting fear, an otherwise unheroic emotion. Victory is much less about valour and more about destiny. But destiny is not blind. It is wryly just in the sense it apportions misfortunes equally among all participants. There is parity in misery. Weil goes back to the Gospels in order to make her point: "Ares is just, and kills those who kill" (Weil, 1956).

The fundamental and nagging disquiet about violence, experienced in close contact during the Spanish Civil War that Weil had spelled out in the letter to Bernanos reappears as *force* in the essay, as she confronts the epic in a totally unsentimental and direct manner, but with an enormous understanding of creaturely contacts and conflicts. We shall do well to remember that during 1938, after spending the Holy Week in Solesmes, a great illumination descended upon her: "Christ came down and took possession of me" (Allen, 1985) she says. Clearly it is a different kind of possession; the only possible one according to Weil's perceptions. She left Paris around 1941, once it was declared an open city, and as anti-Jewish strictures began to take a toll upon her daily routine. She soon reached Marseilles and wanted to share work with agricultural labourers. This was not an idle wish, but a well thought out, long term plan. Later, in the Fall of 1941, she would work full 8 hours in a grape harvest in the Ardeche region. She would assiduously carry Plato's *Symposium* with her to the vineyards and try to teach and discuss the work with her fellow labourers during recess. It is in the middle of such a context that she began thinking afresh about the *Iliad.*

The first trait of force is that it converts anybody who is subject to it literally into a *thing.* The *Iliad* shows us that the creature called human being with all its vaulting ambitions and desires is turned into complete inert matter in quicksilver time: "*Somebody was here, and the next minute there is nobody here at all,*" in the words of Weil (Weil, 1956). The empty chariots rattle about in the battlegrounds but the noble charioteers lie defiled and lifeless on the ground, pure carrion—closer to the birds of prey than their loved ones. As the soul flies away to Hades, all pride of youth and valour comes to naught. And Weil is equally unsparing: "*The bitterness of such a spectacle is offered us absolutely undiluted. No comforting fiction intervenes; no consoling prospect of immortality; and on the hero's head no washed out halo of patriotism descends*" (Weil, 1956).

The force that annihilates is unswerving and plain. But there is an even greater and more poignant variety of force: to be unpersoned. It can kill but will not. It suspends the final move by always tending to kill. Such a force also turns creatures into inert bodies: living dead, by exercising the power to halt body movements and by repressing flights and fancies of the soul. The energy and power of the soul of the creature is folded and pleated in such a suspended state. The weapon pointed at him is focused and the man, who is aimed at, still breathes but "*he is simply matter; still thinking, he can think no longer*" (Weil, 1956). In the epic, suppliants often lose the right to even twitch their nerves and muscles—like Priam standing in front of Achilles, killer of so many of his sons. Everyone can see the suffering creature but none can see it. There is no overt sentence issued against him. Yet he is forgotten. This is *affliction* (*le malheur*) proper. And as Weil reminds us: a human being "crushed by *malheur* is hideous as life in its nakedness always is, like the amputed stump, like the swarming of insects" (Zaretsky, 2021).

The instinct of the afflicted to seek survival, to latch on to any and every support, constitutes a permanent state of torpor. For support is the name of an ever receding mirage. What seems to provide support, in fact, returns as a clandestine and even more devastating crushing force. Even if in some future moment there is a chance to resurrect, the inert beings refuse to believe in any form of human cordiality, for there are none when creatures scar and maim each other intimately: "*Pushed, they fall. Fallen, they lie where they are, unless chance gives somebody the idea of raising them up again. But supposing that at long last they have been picked up, honored with cordial remarks, they still do not venture to take this resurrection seriously; they dare not express a wish lest an irritated voice returns them forever to silence*" (Weil, 1956). Life congeals to matter. So, such creatures tremble and acquiesce, a cross between a man and a corpse. Curses, complaints and weeping are a privilege to others—not for someone with no right to plea or show emotion. Not for a slave or an exiled one. The slave loses his inner life. Weil compares the tyranny and relentlessness of force with nature and extreme hunger—those having the power of life and death. It even silences the grief of the mother or the suppliant's ability to communicate in a coherent manner. Slaves keep silent or blabber in *sotto voce*. Bereaved mothers live on—

> But the thought of eating came to her, when she was tired of tears.

The one who exerts force seems to be shielded by some strange element that does not allow anything to come between the instinct and the act. Most of all there is no reflection in the one who wields the scimitar. Reflection is a later development and shall forever remain an ideal. Rather, in such moments man relishes his apparent capacity to humiliate, numb or maim other beings at will. There is no greater delight than making the other man silent, trembling in some unknown fear. But what rout lasts indefinitely? Does not misery and confusion, which he thought was the lot of the Greeks, haunt Achilles and become the reason for his own death? Weil reminds us that the enforcer often forgets that force is given to him only on loan. It is not a free pass. He forgets that his relation with other humans is a kind of balance between unequal amounts of force. Therefore, he exceeds the limits of enforcing his will upon other kindred creatures—composed of sinews and bones, blood and pus, enthusiasm and reflection. But the wheel of fortune must turn. And at some point, there lies no armour between him and the tormented ones. As Weil puts it: retribution has a geometrical rigour to its workings. Nemesis is the soul of Greek literature. The nature of man and the universe turns radiant through its workings. No limits, no measures of equilibrium can dare put an end to its unerring, periodic rumblings.

A Tilting Board

But the ebb and flow of fortune is a continual see-saw. So is a war, especially the one that relies on attrition. All victory is transitory. Perhaps the victor will be there tomorrow to rejoice? Perhaps not.

Both Hector and Agamemnon make the same mistake—nurturing a sense of invincibility. They have to, therefore, stand alone when fortune strikes. Each must stand alone to face his death, trying to steady the soul. As Weil memorably puts it: "*But the auditors of the Iliad knew that the death of Hector would be but a brief joy to Achilles, and the death of Achilles but a brief joy to the Trojans, and the destruction of Troy but a brief joy to the Achaeans*" (Weil, 1956).

Violence must exterminate all who come within its purview. Moderation is not a virtue in the epic though we sometimes hear the voice of reason. But an all-pervading sense of indifference in the enforcer is the fatal temptation to which man hurtles. It is a contagion that engulfs others too. Whose doing—these our giving in to excesses? Fate's dicta? Or opportunities that we grab now and resent later? Are we condemned to such cycles?

At certain conjunctures, those who feel that force is on their side, simply *embark*. Embarking is an instinct and a temptation. As if it is a game. The other side has still not shown its presence or its fangs. The war still seems an abstraction. Heroism turns performative to one group as it begins to destroy life, like children breaking toys. In an epic, this sense of invincibility is doubly reinforced if it is sensed by the heroes that some divine machinery shall intervene on their behalf. To win becomes an inevitable gamble: "*Then war is easy and basely, coarsely loved*" (Weil, 1956).

But soon war takes its own life. The participants begin to smell death. They start to lose comrades and raw fear hovers about their existence. Death becomes an unendurable prospect, lurking at close quarters. Indeed, for the warrior, death is not a limit to the future, but *the future itself*. He wakes up to its presence every dawn. Is this the appointed day? The soul is then "*strung to a pitch it can stand only for a short time; but each new dawn reintroduces the same necessity*" (Weil, 1956). The soul begins to shear off all aspirations. Bit by bit it castrates itself. The whole purpose of the war itself turns blurry. What was the original aim of the bloody conflict? Such deathly conflicts cannot stand any moderate end. To be outside of the spiralling bloodiness seems unthinkable to the combatants, for the price would be too steep to pay. To be inside it is to be unable to fathom its end. The sufferers are not given any straw to extricate themselves. A dead-end is reached. War of such dimension staggers and meanders. The only deliverance is death. And thus violence finds its own gravity.

Any moderate form of a solution is unthinkable that cannot be held up—even as memory. Terror and humiliation, grief and exhaustion, deaths and lynching of comrades—the drowning power of force—continually devours the soul: "*The idea that an unlimited effort should bring in only a limited profit or no profit at all is terribly painful*" (Weil, 1956). How can one master such terrible memory? One wishes to die then and there as the loved ones are maimed and destroyed. And on the other hand, the soul wishes to destroy the enemy. When such a dual need for death consumes the whole of the being of a man, he becomes part of a different race from the race of the living: "*To respect life in somebody else when you have had to castrate yourself of all yearning for it demands a truly heartbreaking exertion of the powers of generosity*" (Weil, 1956).

Homer rarely gives us such generous characters (except for Patroclus?). The conquering Homeric hero constantly dodges the spear thrust of his antagonist and awaits the opportunity to repay the debt. He is possessed—in every sense of the term. The hero and the slave are finally one and the same matter. Inert thing. Pure momentum. That is the reason heroes in the *Iliad* are often described as fire, wind, or wild beasts or as trees and frightened creatures—all set in motion by force. The true object of such deathly conflict is the transmutation of the soul of the characters that cross each other's path. Once admitted in the realm of force, our souls must petrify. Force purifies all ambiguities by burning them in pure luminosity. Rarely do miracles take place in the epic. There are only few moments of hospitality, courage and love (often condemned to sorrow, which is when love basks in absolute purity), in which man rediscovers his self. Inner deliberations are even rarer. The greatest miracles happen when mortal enemies turn to friendship. Those are the moments of pure grace.

At the conclusion of the essay, Weil touches upon a unique theme: "bitterness that proceeds from tenderness and that spreads over the whole human race, impartial as sunlight" (Weil, 1956). Bitterness never degrades into lamentation in the epic, and yet everyone's unhappiness is laid bare. The equity of misery is universal, the common fate of humanity. Caprice and malice of the Gods bear fruit."*Neither victors nor vanquished are admired, scorned, or hated*" (Weil, 1956).

There is only that single regret: that man is capable of such transformations. Each spirit bears the subjection of force differently according to his or her virtue, but the apportioning is equitable. Is subjection to force, our common lot? Are we to love only sorrowfully, for the dominion of force lurks about us? But the affliction must be attended to—the one in which "the shame of the coerced spirit is neither disguised, nor enveloped in facile pity, nor held up to scorn; here more than one spirit bruised and degraded by misfortune is offered for our admiration" (Weil, 1956). It is in the simultaneous laying bare of our divinity and our bestiality that we rise above the common muck. Misery is the absolute precondition for love. And a sense of shifting fortune marks all human traffic and transaction.

"*Only he who has measured the dominion of force, and knows how not to respect it, is capable of love and justice*" (Weil, 1956). This is the lucidity and simplicity that Weil brings into all her works, acts and silences. To pass through the flames of the force—to undergo suffering and death joyfully—is also for her the greatest Christian and communist act. This is the message she has also gleaned from *Bhagawad Gita*. The forces of *gravity*, which pulls us down, and *grace*, which gives us flight—are inextricably intertwined. One bears one's anguish in perfect love—lets it pass through the eye of the heart. And in order to face the misery that force must inflict upon us and to rise above it, Weil proposes an illuminative technique that she would call *decreation*.

The Quartering of the Self

A human body that has surrendered to gravity, and therefore, has experienced free fall, is a strange creature—at once a corpse and a throbbing entity. Her will, desire, or outcome is irrelevant once the inevitable routine for the fall is initiated. The significant aspect for the creature in the clutches of force is that even with some kind of a harness, *gravity* does not go away. Its presence lurks about. A body under *gravity* realizes that it is subject to forces that are beyond its mastery. The universe, as it were, enters into the body in pain. How do we become mindful of such primal vulnerability without immediately seeking protection that refuses to arrive? Can we sustain corporeal integrity by resisting free fall? Isn't such falling as natural as the falling of ripe fruits, water or a meteor? And then, the final act of gravity: to be pulverized into utter oblivion.

Gravity is an edict.

As a response to this conundrum about force, an astounding claim has been made by Weil scholar J. Heath Atchley: "If one could learn to live with the body rather than in it—if one were body through and through rather than a kind of ghost occupying an empty shell—would not that change things, somehow?" (Atchley, 2010). Or, in Weil's own words: "*One does not consent to [affliction] with abandon, but with a violence exerted on the entire soul by the entire soul*" (Weil, 1970). This is the sense we get when Weil refers to the soul-killing lacerating force that is manual labour. There is no explanation as to why the labourer was selected for such crushing alienation in thus eking out her life. As a manual worker, Weil herself was left

> in pieces, soul and body … the affliction of others entered into my flesh and my soul.… There [in the factory] I received forever the mark of a slave, like the branding of the red-hot iron the Romans put on the foreheads of their most despised slaves. Since then I have always regarded myself as a slave. (Weil, 1978)

We flinch at the very sight of true affliction—such is its overwhelming force. We can only look at it by considering affliction at a distance (Zaretsky, 2021). Henceforth, to be marked to lead a life of the afflicted suffuses all her thoughts and pronouncements about love, fairness and justice in a world that is at once callously ruthless and also fated to affliction. Beings are at once perpetrators and sufferers.

Fated affliction is one of the faces of the divine. The other face is love. But there is a process of labour through which one might touch such grace. Weil gives it the name of *attention*. How might attention look like? Here is a clue how Weil thinks about the subject—

> Attention consists of suspending our thought, leaving it detached, empty and ready to be penetrated by the object. It means holding in

> our minds, within reach of this thought, but on a lower level and not in contact with it, the diverse knowledge we have acquired which we are forced to make use of. Our thought should be in relation to all particular and already formulated thoughts as a man on a mountain who, as he looks forward, sees also below him, without actually looking at them, a great many forests and plains. Above all our thought should be empty, waiting, not seeking anything, but ready to receive in its naked truth the object which is to penetrate it. (Weil, 1951)

One can detect in the passage the playing out of two movements. The attentive being awaits the object of its attention to penetrate its body and soul. The being itself does not have any agency by which it can *petition* the object of attention so that it could be granted grace *gratis*. Instead, grace, if it ever appears, must surprise the beseecher. The other factor is even more crucial: the seeker does not actively seek, but her mind is *receptive to waiting*. Waiting is the emptying of the self, a manner of 'spiritual quartering.' For naked truth to shine forth, grace must penetrate the soul of the receptor, but the receptor herself must remain passive. Using knowledge for understanding has nothing to do with attention. The key is to suspend all thought. Readiness to receive grace means cultivating a kind of severe lateral vision like the man atop the mountain—simultaneously looking forward and below.

Such passivity is required in order to counter our self-centeredness, which hopes to protect itself from the privations of body and soul. In such a state, one begins to see things only as one wants to see them or give in to a condition of fear and insecurity. Weil says:

> The principal claim we think we have on the universe is that our personality should continue. This claim implies all the others. The instinct of self-preservation makes us feel this continuation to be a necessity, and we believe that a necessity is a right. We are like the beggar who said to Talleyrand: "Sir, I must live," and to whom Talleyrand replied, "I do not see the necessity for that." (Weil, 1951)

I live by constantly inserting my personality in the world of relevance. To the world that is of little significance. Is there a way to reverse this process and speak *incidentally of myself*? Attention is this process by which we turn outside, away from our selves. It requires us to alter the direction of our heed and awareness. Attention makes us *face* the world on an altered gradient. What might we direct our visages to?

The act of love is the highest form of attention. In love, the creature is gratuitous and generous to the point of being disinterested, oblivious to the presence of the infinite. Is attention that aspect of one's being which is not tied anymore to the vagaries of necessity for it has already tasted its severity? And what is the proper object of attention? That infinite object is certainly God. But Weil is not a believer. She refused to be baptized. In fact, she makes an untimely differentiation: "*the Gospel contains a conception of human life, not a theology*." This is a negative way of reaching the infinite. Susan Anima Taubes has drawn our attention to an agonizing paradox, where "God, however negatively conceived, explains the world, explains the nothingness of God in the world" (Taubes, 1955). As a heterodox thinker, Weil shuns all dogma as exclusionary and resistant to individual mystical practice. She calls herself—*anathema sit*, one who is not allowed to enter the Church. She has decided to stay outside of dogma since she believes that there is much to appreciate outside of any settled creed, which is also a world full of things that God loves: the heresies of true brotherhood, practices of other cultures, the spirit of humanism.

Is the infinite object a form of Goodness then? Again, Weil does not wish to skirt tormenting forms of Evil in order to prematurely touch the Good. There is nothing like an absolute and ultimate Good, but there are contingent forms of Goodness that abounds around us. One cannot take a leap unto the Good by espousing some kind of penitent, frugal living, or by forcing oneself to conduct good acts. Is attention then a kind of frame of mind and body, a temper that helps us transcend the immediate by being intensely mired within the tableaux of the fleeting forms of the immediate? Is it a realization that all things that are brought about are not through purpose but through necessity? Impersonal causes of an inflexible order reign in the cosmos. And like a pendulum, the infinite oscillates between *gravity* and *grace*.

But if the infinite is the object that does not correspond to the reality of existence, how does one come to fix attention on to it, howsoever passive that might be? Here is the paradox about the infinite object: *through absence it manifests itself.* Humans speak to and can hear

God, the Good or the infinite grace of Love only by waiting limitlessly. In the temporal realm of destitution, where crushing gravity rules, man begins to communicate with the infinite as two prisoners signal each other by knocking on either side of the wall. The wall separates them but also allows them to converse with each other. The absent presence of the infinite displays man's true vocation. But it is only through the crushing force of gravity that we are able to glimpse the infinite; not by being overtly pietistic. Attention is not a project. It is consent to nothing, which is another name for acute concentration. It involves the painstaking process of relentless digging at one's soul so that one is able to come closer to apprehending totality, the world as a whole.

Every separation is a link.

Attention is a calling. It brings us within the ambit of *our necessary connections* and throws aside all extraneous forms of distraction. And there is an essential porosity between the unconditioned object of attention and one who is in quest. Such is the intensity of attachment in the quester-perceptor that she is released from the object of attention altogether. She is released as soon as she has put herself in the tracks of attention. But giving in to attention is hardly a benign or neutral process. Sharon Cameron, the Weil scholar, has most incisively examined the nature of a certain clinical and uncompromising violence done to one's own self when it is led through the stages of attention. It is only a severe and lucid commitment to attention that allowed Weil the ability to resist suicide at different points in her life. The difficulty lies in the fact that such a depth perception through which the ego reduces its heft is so alien to the mental processing capacity that we flinch from meeting it in Weilian terms, even as we acknowledge her honesty and clarity of vision.

Renouncing What Never Existed

Being attentive is the first step towards *decreation*. To Weil, attention is foremost a practice (which has little to do with fastings or keeping vigils), to be cultivated for fulfilment. And the cultivation of attention is a naturalistic process. But how can cultivation be natural? The process involves a productive contradiction. From the side of the afflicted, the first step towards being attentive is to train oneself to turn irrelevant by gradually annihilating excesses of the self. The second step is to wait: so that one is ready to receive the grace of infinity and with it, a sense of total order. Denuding of the self is a meditative process. Cameron makes a subtle point not just about the process of *decreation*, but about the proper attitude towards relinquishing self-hood: "Weil is constantly dramatizing the relation between these two nonequivalent positions—preserving an I that is nothing at all, renouncing an I that never existed" (Cameron, 2003). What does it entail when she refers to the turning of our visage to the infinite? One way to think about the subtraction of the ego is to pledge to correct an error because all that exists is actually non-being. This will be a mode of gathering and preserving the self—a position that is not attentive to the godhead or goodness. Such a mode is rather about following one's personal thoughts, which is a mechanical way to address mere grievance. Grievance has nothing to do with affliction. The other way to consider the issue is to realize that the question of the self does not even arise if one is to renounce selfhood that never ever existed in the first place. Attention always penetrates the limits of personal thoughts. In such a state, the afflicted body, battered by *force*, simply waits. Grace may or may not arrive. That is all. The process of *decreation* begins here.

The other half of denuding pertains to the infinite and its responsibility to the beseecher. That is the reason we cannot pin-point its existence since the infinite cannot be restricted nor can its advent be predicted. But the infinite gets progressively reduced to nothingness, much like the self on the other side. The facelessness of the infinite not only makes its arrival absolutely contingent; it also means that the denuded self cannot expect any consolation for affliction from such a reduced entity. The attention of the quester-perceptor has to be that much more naturally unfocussed so that it can prepare itself for such a power to arrive. That is the reason Weil insisted that complete attention is like unconsciousness: "it is a state that does not entail a particular action or stance, but instead suggests a form of reception, open and non-judgmental, of the world" (Zaretsky, 2021). Such receptivity fortifies the power to take in contingent storms. To experience free fall is to be 'like a fly against a pane'. Affliction is compelling but it does not have any explanatory form so that there could be any possibility of easing. The relationship between the decreated and the afflicted selves are now in a suspended state. But the divided selves continue to converse with each other like the prisoners in two adjacent cells. The dull sting of affliction persists even as the self alters its facing. In the eloquent words of Cameron: "we are up against what harms, without grasping the harm and also without escaping it" (Cameron, 2003).

The idea of well-being is alien to Weil. Well-being cannot address a hallucinatory I. Rather, in order to meet the torment head-on, Weil recalls the words of Paul Valery—"*A difficulty is a light. An insuperable difficulty is a sun*" (Weil, 1956).

To look directly at the source of insuperable difficulty is the only possibility to emerge from its tentacles. Only by tearing out all energy is one washed with light. Like the sun, force irradiates us with naked light and ferries us to a concentrated state of attention. We cannot circumvent its righteous glare. As the afflicted faces its torment, her orientation changes forever. As she considers her own change of fortune and its relationship with other lives, she begins to stand outside of perspectives and viewpoints. Weil calls such a state *turning anonymous*. This is also a foundational state—one of discovery.

Rudiments of Attention

Weil provides a few fine and rudimentary examples for cultivating such a state. One such might be deduced from the following passage:

> A little child who sees something bright is so totally absorbed in his love for the shiny object that his whole body leans towards it and he quite forgets it is beyond his reach.... A child does not will to obtain the bright object or the milk, he makes no plans forgetting them; he simply desires, and cries. (Weil, 1970)

Absorption is here reflected in the form of pure bodily inclination. Attention is a tendency, an alteration of posture. The leaning happens not owing to any will or plan on the part of the child. She simply desires the object. And her attention is so focused that she forgets that the bright object or the milk is beyond her reach. Hence, she begins to cry. But this is not a wail that manifests any hurt. Crying is the child's prayer, a gesture of complete concentration for her object of desire. In order to attain the object, she has even forgotten the reach and limits of her little muscles. She must only learn to wait until the shiny object comes to her eventually.

The second example pertains to school studies like geometry problems or Latin lessons—initiatory. but demanding forms of mental exercise. In order to achieve the goal of mastering such problems, the pupil must be absolutely concentrated in her attention, be like someone in meditative prayer. Such anatomy of training does not depend on the outcome. The very effort is rewarding in the sense that such a form of elementary concentration shows us the value of unalloyed attention that we might give to our object of study. We begin to develop an intrinsic interest in matters that occupy us. Weil specifically says that such a form of attention goes beyond will power. It has nothing to do with the 'stiffening of the muscles' that makes us exert over success. We have to *learn to wait* until the solution to the geometry problem flashes before our mind's eye. Is such school exercising a form of the sacrament? Cameron has named this mode a kind of *negative effort*, something that keeps us away from tiredness or suffering. This is what guardians actually mean when they ask young ones to be 'attentive in class'. It connotes submersion in the *force of the problem* that is at hand by keeping aside our instrumental selves for the time being. This is the starting point of effacing all peripheral concerns and getting rid of the pangs of primary narcissism.

The other instance of attention pertains to our behaviour with the neighbour. Weil feels that one should be impelled towards one's neighbour by the infinite. "*The love of our neighbour in all its fullness simply means being able to say: What are you going through?*" (Weil, 1978).

Weil and her brother Andre were greatly moved by the suffering of the soldiers in the First World War. At the age of five, she stopped eating sugar since the soldiers did not have access to such luxury. The siblings would send letters, chocolate treats, and Easter eggs to the soldiers—their adopted godchildren. At this time both decided not to wear knee-socks any more even at the coldest of months. This attention towards our neighbours, in quietly asking what they are going through is at the heart of all revolutions and transformations. This is how one tries to reach the source of the affliction of the persecuted, the scavenger, the migrant, the mutilated warrior, all who are daily humiliated—by placing soul upon the soul. We change the relationship with the world as we approach our neighbour in the way a workman-apprentice changes his relationship with his tools. Loving one's neighbour does not mean there is equal love for everyone. It rather implies that we initiate and nurture a relationship with the neighbour the way we do with the seasons and the stars. An attentive relationship with my neighbour is an exchange of vital matter in which both sides bathe. Neighbourliness affirms the rhythm of life.

Weil is, however, alive to the fact that to be captivated by the object of our attention (geometry, the neighbour, beloved) does not mean a captivation of it. Denuding of the self is not the submission of self to the object of attention. Waiting for the infinite is not a state of enslavement. The process is two way: the master also waits for the beseecher. Attention is not bondage—though Weil sometimes comes close to it ("he will have become different, after being eaten and digested by God"—Weil, 1978). Nor is it an ensnarement. This crucial question is how affliction or the working of force on our body and soul can be converted into attention. Is the very separation from the object of attention also a possibility that can lead to inseparability: *every separation is a link*. Affliction is thus inextricably bound to love. But the link is not constitutive of each other. I have no choice in being stunned and rendered immobile by the casual cruelty of the beloved-tormentor. But I have every choice to give myself to the love of my tormentor. Betrayals and devastations cannot transcend the afflicted as long as she is attentive to the creaturely condition as such. It is only that one must pass through such extreme points of devastation in order to gain clarity. Therefore, Weil—

> When the attention fixed upon something has revealed the contradiction in it … a sort of unsticking process takes *place.… Each* thing that we desire is in contradiction with the conditions or the consequences attaching to that thing.… Contradiction is our wretchedness, and the feeling of our wretchedness is the feeling of reality. For our wretchedness is not something that we concoct. It is something truly real. That is why we must love it. All the rest is imaginary. (Weil, 1956)

The Green Emerald

When a contradiction cannot be resolved except by resorting to a lie, we are truly in front of a door, Weil says. The excruciating contradiction cannot be solved. But solving is merely an imaginary dispelling of a paralyzing condition. Attention is not interested in understanding a problem—like in geometry. To be attentive, we recall, is to be decrepit—to be able to remain in a state of immersion within the contradictory and the infinite. One comes to the infinite in spite of oneself, not voluntarily. In many ways, Weil tries to impress upon us that only after privation and disorientation can endurance arrive. And eventually: fusion with the object of our attention which is also, paradoxically, sometimes the source of our affliction. The conditions of the real—wretchedness—cannot be transcended by an imaginary I, by means of skirting affliction. One must rather convert one's inevitable bondage to force into freedom. And yet in that freedom one is left out and excommunicated—*anathema sit.*

Difficulty lies in the relation between "being insensible to every kind of grief and joy" and being "sensible to all the nuances of grief and joy" (Cameron, 2003).

Weil does not give us the exact contours of decreation. She provides us certain oracular utterances through her aphoristic and denuded writings. Like when she says. "*I am God's abdication. The more I exist, the more God abdicates. So if I take God's side rather than my own I ought to regard my existence as a diminution, a decrease*" (Weil, 1970). One is reminded how she took to George Herbert's poem *Love* (1633) and would recite that again and again at various points in her life, devoting all her attention to the tender phrases of the poem. Herbert's poems taught her the value of abdicating and submitting "*to the presence of a love, like that which one can read in the smile on a beloved face*" (Weil, 1978). Abdication is a relational obligation. One consents to abdicate so that others *can be.* The uncreated part of our existence is not autonomous. It belongs to the infinite. The rest is the created weight of the being. Decreation is the conversion of the created part of our being to the uncreated. We begin to shear off the weight of our care and prepare ourselves for the great gift to arrive as we face the truth. Those who have already faced truth either joyously by means of love or have been brought to bear terrible forms of truth by confronting and enduring force, have begun the journey of decreation. Weil describes decreation as consent to stay anonymous and die—to submit wholeheartedly to fortune and necessity. The infinite presents us with two faces: love and necessity, Weil would say many times. Decreation is our orientation to these faces, an acknowledgement of the relationships that exist independently of us. It is not about accepting our utter vulnerability when facing love or destruction, but the acknowledgement that there is something, someone more important than us. In the process, all traces of the self are gradually obliterated. Grace means to be able to live with neighbours as one wakes to the sun and the birds every morning. Decreation is the consent to being a creature.

> God loves, not as I love, but as an emerald is green.... And I too, if I were in the state of perfection, would love as an emerald is green. (Weil, 1970)

To be able to say, "What are you going through?" means to love as an emerald is green.

References

Allen, Diogenes. 1985. "George Herbert and Simone Weil." In *Religion & Literature*. Vol. 17.2, Summer: 17–34.

Atchley, J. Heath. 2010. "Attention, Affirmation, and the Spiritual Law of Gravity." In *The Pluralist*. Vol. 5.3: 63–72.

Bernanos, Georges. 1938. *A Diary of My Times*. New York: Macmillan [London: The Bodley Head, 1945].

———. 1971. *Correspondance inédite 1934–1948: Combat pour la liberté* (Plon). https://www.madbeppo.com/text/lettre-a-georges-bernanos/. Accession date: 10 May 2021.

Cameron, Sharon. 2003. "The Practice of Attention: Simone Weil's Performance of Impersonality." In *Critical Inquiry*. Vol. 29.2: 216–252.

Cha, Yoon Sook. 2017. *Decreation and the Ethical Bind*. New York: Fordham University Press, 2017.

Doering, E. Jane. 2010. *Simone Weil and the Specter of Self-Perpetuating Force*. Notre Dame: University of Notre Dame Press.

Finch, Henry Leroy. 2001. *Simone Weil and the Intellect of Grace*. Edited by Martin Andic. New York: Continuum.

McLellan, David. 1990. *Utopian Pessimist: The Life and Thought of Simone Weil*. New York: Poseidon Press.

Pick, Anat. 2011.*Creaturely Poetics: Animality and Vulnerability in Literature and Film*. New York: Columbia University Press.

Reed, Robert Charles. 2013. "Decreation as Substitution: Reading Simone Weil through Levinas." In *The Journal of Religion*. Vol. 93.1: 25–40.

Rozelle-Stone, Rebecca and Lucian Stone. 2013. *Simone Weil and Theology*. London: Bloomsbury.

Taubes, Susan Anima. 1955. "The Absent God." In *The Journal of Religion*. Vol. 35, No. 1: 6–16.

———.2007. *Impersonality: Seven Essays*. Chicago: University of Chicago Press.

Weil, Simone. 1978. *Waiting on God*. Translated by E. Craufurd. Glasgow: Collins.

———.1999. *Gravity and Grace*. Translated by Emma Crawford and Mario van der Ruhr. New York: Routledge.

———. 1956. *Iliad, or the Poem of Force*. Translated by Mary McCarthy. Wallingford, PA: Pendle Hill Pamphlet.

———.1970. *First and Last Notebooks*. Translated by Richard Rees. London.

———.1956. *The Notebooks of Simone Weil*. Translated by Arthur Wills, 2 vols. New York.

———. 1951. "Concerning the Our Father." *Waiting for God*. Translated by Emma Craufurd. New York: G.P. Putnam's Sons.

Willox, Ashlee Cunsolo. 2008. "The Cross, the Flesh, and the Absent God: Finding Justice through Love and Affliction in Simone Weil's Writings." In *The Journal of Religion*. Vol. 88.1: 53–74.

Zaretsky, Robert. 2021. *The Subversive Simone Weil: A Life in Five Ideas*. Chicago: University of Chicago Press.

Index

About the Author

Prasanta Chakravarty teaches English at the University of Delhi. His works include *Time, Doubt and Wonder in the Humanities* (Bloomsbury, 2019), *The Opulence of Existence* (2018) and *Like Parchment in the Fire: Literature and Radicalism in the English Civil War* (2006). He is the editor of the anthology *Shrapnel Minima: Essays from Humanities Underground* (2016) and *Populism and Its Limits: After Articulation* (Bloomsbury, 2020). With Sukanta Chaudhuri, he is currently engaged in editing *Machiavelli Then and Now: History, Politics, Literature* (forthcoming).